4-75

D1794138

WITHDRAWN

Gift book donated by
Lysle Meyer, PhD
Minnesota State
University Moorhead

LAWRENCE G. GREEN (*Photo by Terence McNally*)

THE BEST OF LAWRENCE GREEN

EDITED AND COMPILED BY
SCOTT HAIGH

Who is the happy Warrior? Who is he
That every man in arms should wish to be?
– It is the generous Spirit, who, when brought
Among the tasks of real life, hath wrought
Upon the plan that pleased his boyish thought:
Whose high endeavours are an inward light
That makes the path before him always bright:
(WILLIAM WORDSWORTH)

HOWARD TIMMINS

CAPE TOWN

1973

This book is copyright under the Berne Convention. No portion may be reproduced by any process without written permission. Inquiries should be made to the Publisher.

ISBN 0 86978 046 8

Printed by Citadel Press, Lansdowne, Cape

CONTENTS

FOREWORD	7
I. THE SPRINGBOK MIGRATIONS	11
II. LORDS OF THE DESERT LAND	27
III. FIRE-WALKERS OF AFRICA	49
IV. CAPE TOWN CHARACTERS	59
V. UNDERWORLD OF CAPE TOWN	73
VI. THE LONELY RIVER	85
VII. IN THE WHEAT BELT	111
VIII. COUNTRY HOSPITALITY	125
IX. LEIPOLDT THE CHEF	137
X. EIGHTH WONDER OF THE WORLD	147
XI. RUSSIAN ARMADA OFF THE CAPE	165
XII. UNDER SAIL	175
XIII. EPIC OF THE KARATARA	185
XIV. EVERY BEACHCOMBER'S DREAM	199
XV. WOODSMOKE AND WINE	213
XVI. THE PEOPLE AND THE TREES	229
XVII. SALISBURY CAMEO	243
XVIII. A VISIONARY RIDES BY	255
INDEX	267

FOREWORD

I have not attempted to bring up-to-date the chapters I have chosen from the prolific works of Lawrence G. Green. Interminable footnotes and ponderous currency conversions can only irritate and distract the reader. Pounds in money parlance remain pounds. Lawrence Green, I know, thought and wrote in terms of miles not kilometres. Thus I have not dared to tamper in any way with his immaculate prose. Nor have I even been tempted to do so. Each chapter is reproduced exactly as it was written. Nothing has been altered, not even Lawrence Green's preferences in nomenclature as they changed in the course of the years.

Yet readers need not fear chronological confusion. In the introductions to the chapters I have indicated the time and period in South Africa's tale when these chapters first appeared.

To compile this anthology I read over 30 of Lawrence G. Green's books. I read them all in a mood of sadness tinged and even assuaged by gratitude. I sorrowed to reflect that there could be no more from his brilliant pen. My heart lightened with my gratitude for the privilege of his friendship and a wider gratitude for his enduring contribution to South African history, literature and for the warm companionship his works gave and still give to so many anonymous people who journeyed with him back into time and on so many delightful adventures.

There can never be another Lawrence G. Green. He was incomparable. In presenting this anthology I would like to quote from a magnificent tribute to him from Mr J. M. Sterban, of Pretoria, which appeared in The Star, Johannesburg, shortly after Lawrence Green's death:

"Now that he is dead, who will bring alive the past with such skill? He was an adventurer and traveller and his books although similar in theme, never failed to fascinate and delight me. He was a man of the Cape and no matter how far he journeyed the spirit of the Cape is there in all his works.

"Although he has died, there are many of his volumes in print so it will always be possible, one grey day, to open one and hear again the clatter of the high-wheeled fish carts coming up from False Bay through the suburbs with the strident bleat of the fish horn riding triumphantly on the South Easter.

"Close your eyes and you will hear the quiet ticking of a clock in the darkened voorkamer of a high-ceilinged Stellenbosch home, shuttered against the heat of a Boland summer Sunday...

"... Well, now the journey *is* over and we can only feel gratitude for the fine work that Lawrence Green has done for South Africa: a gratitude tinged with sadness that a man who could describe with such touching simplicity a tranquil scene, such as the dipping and darting of swallows over a farm dam with the Hottentots Holland peaks in the background brushed with the pink of a summer sunset, is no more."

SCOTT HAIGH
Rondebosch, 1973.

Spirit of the Karoo

THE vast enigmatic Karoo in all its moods and grandeurs has attracted the pens of many poets and writers. Olive Schreiner and Pauline Smith too responded to its allure but their reactions were sombre, gloomy and sometimes frankly depressing. But I believe that Lawrence G. Green more than any other writer has captured the true spirit of the Karoo. In *Karoo*, published in 1955, there are several magnificent evocative chapters. Many admirers believe *Karoo* is the best of all Green's books and I am not scornful of that view. Understandably many authors wilt before the challenge of the mighty, enigmatic Karoo and brood, meditate and moralise to the tedium of their readers. Lawrence Green, however, brings the Great Karoo and the Little Karoo to vivid life; old patriarchs and other great characters living in solitude are depicted movingly. Vast irrigation schemes and tarmac speedways may in a decade or two change the character of the Karoo. But for the genius of Lawrence Green's reporting, the Karoo of today and yesterday, the ways of its lonely people and the valour of the stubborn men and women wringing a living from its often harsh soil might soon vanish from memory forever.

I believe that the third chapter from *Karoo* deserves pride of first place in this anthology. In it Lawrence Green tells the dramatic story of the vast Springbok migrations which devastated parts of the Karoo up to the end of last century. This is majestic reporting, simple in its tension and power of description. Listen . . . "At last came a faint drumming. No doubt the Bushman had sensed this drumming hours before, with his ear to the ground. Only now could Gert hear it . . ."

To tell in full the story of what he himself described "as the most dramatic scenes in the whole world of mammals" Green travelled miles to warm the memories of gnarled men with personal tales to narrate of these amazing Springbok migrations.

This chapter too recreates the simple philosophy of men and women to whom the Karoo, the vanishing Karoo of yesterday, is still their only world.

Thousands of South Africans reading this gripping tale for the first time will find Lawrence Green's narrative unforgettable.

CHAPTER I

THE SPRINGBOK MIGRATIONS

*The countless springboks are my flock
Spread o'er the unbounded plain*
—Thomas Pringle

THOSE vast springbok migrations which devasted the karoo districts of South Africa almost up to the end of last century must have formed the most dramatic scenes in the whole world of mammals.

One cannot see everything, but I am sorry these cavalcades of fur and flesh occurred before my time. There was a *trekboer* once, a natural artist as a story teller, whose tale gave me the human side of it; one of those tales which carried the ring of personal experience in every vivid detail.

This man had left the Transvaal with his family in the eighteen-seventies as a boy of ten. They were members of the first "Thirstland trek", a group of people impelled by real or imaginary grievances, and certainly by a restless spirit, to seek a new country. Many died in the desert. Some reached Angola. But this family of Van der Merwes broke away from the ill-fated wagons and headed south. They spent their lives trekking with their sheep and cattle in search of grass. When the old people died, the son Gert went on living the only life he knew; sometimes in Bechuanaland, in the Kalahari and often in the North West Cape. By the time he was twenty-one he had a wife and three children, two coloured shepherds and a Bushman *touleier* to lead the oxen and find the way from one water-hole or vlei to the next.

One morning Gert van der Merwe's wagon was plodding along the dry, hard bed of the Molopo river where it forms the southern border of the Bechuanaland Protectorate. Gert noticed that the Bushman seemed worried about something. In the middle of the morning the Bushman left his oxen suddenly and ran off into the bush on the high northern bank of the river. At noon Gert stopped for the usual outspan and meal. His wife had just settled down to the cooking when the Bushman raced into camp and urged the party to inspan and follow him immediately. "The *trekbokke* are coming," the Bushman declared. "It will be death to stay in the river-bed."

Gert packed up, wondering whether the alarm was justified, but remembering that he had his family with him. The Bushman led the wagon out of the river-bed, up the north bank to a hill. Van der Merwe drove the wagon up the hill as far as the oxen would pull it. Then they went to the summit of the hill and the Bushman pointed.

At first Gert could see nothing unusual, but later he observed a faint cloud of dust along the horizon. It was miles away and did not suggest any great danger to him. However, the Bushman persuaded him to cut and pile thorn bushes as a barrier round the wagon and cattle. The Bushman explained that if the running springbok came over the hill instead of round it they would trample every living thing in their path to death. However, he hoped the thorn bush and the wagon would make them swerve.

After protecting his wagon and stock, Gert climbed the hill again. By now the dust was only a few miles away, rising high in the air and spread over a wide front. Gert's hill appeared to be in the centre of the oncoming game. Now, for the first time, he felt a little nervous, for he realised that anything could happen if such a stampede passed through the camp. So he ordered his wife and children into the wagon and made the dogs fast under the wagon tent. With the aid of the two coloured men and the Bushman he gathered heaps of dry wood and placed them in front of the wagon. By throwing green stuff on top of each pile he hoped to send up enough smoke to startle the buck and cause them to swing aside.

Gert waited on the hill summit. The buck were still hidden in their dust screen, but hares and jackals and other small animals were racing past the hill and taking no notice of the human beings. Snakes were out in the open, too, moving fast and seeking cover under the rocks on the hill. Gert and his men threw stones at the snakes that came too close, but the snakes seemed to be dominated by a greater fear. Meerkat families and field mice also appeared in large numbers.

At last came a faint drumming. No doubt the Bushman had sensed this drumming hours before, with his ear to the ground. Only now could Gert hear it. The cloud of dust was dense and enormous, and the front rank of the springbok, running faster than galloping horses, could be seen. They were in such numbers that Gert found the sight frightening. He could see a front line of buck at least three miles long, but he could not estimate the depth. Ahead of the main body were swift *voorlopers*, moving along as though they were leading the army.

When the buck came within a mile of the hill the Bushman ran to the wagon and climbed in despite the growling of the dogs. He was taking no chances. Gert and the coloured men then moved back, pausing only to light the fires. They remained with the cattle, which had sensed the danger and were milling round and lowing nervously. Gert's wife wanted him inside the wagon; but he was gripped by the vast spectacle and climbed on to the hood for a better view.

The first solid groups of buck swept past on both sides of the hill. After that the streams of springbok were continuous, making for the river and the open country beyond. Then the pressure increased, the buck became more crowded. No longer was it possible for them to swerve aside when they reached the fires and the wagon. Gert said he could have flicked the horde with his whip from where he sat on the wagon tent. Some crashed into the wagon and were jammed in the wheels, injured and trampled upon. The wagon became the centre of a mass of dead and dying buck; and Gert saw more biltong than he could have secured in a year's expensive shooting. But the thorn barrier had broken, and the buck were among the cattle. Before long the terrified, bellowing cattle stampeded and vanished into the dust in the direction of the river. Gert had to let them go. There was only death for anyone who ventured after them among the horns and hooves of the buck.

At the height of the rush, said Gert, the noise was overwhelming. Countless hooves powdered the surface to fine dust, and everyone found it hard to breathe. Gert's wife, who had been watching the rush with frightened interest, had to draw the blankets over herself and the children. The dust had almost smothered them. Everything in the wagon was an inch deep in pale yellow dust, and the coloured men had also turned yellow.

Within an hour the main body of springbok had passed, but that was not the end of the spectacle. Until long after sunset, hundreds upon hundreds of stragglers followed the great herd. Some were exhausted, some crippled, some bleeding. Gert wondered what had happened to the hares and jackals, and the snakes which had not taken cover in time. Next day he found the answer.

All night lone buck passed the wagon. The air cleared, but dust rose again when there was any movement in the camp. At daybreak Gert climbed the hill to see whether he could find his cattle. He had food, and there was a water-hole not far away in the dry river-bed; but without the oxen he was stranded.

The morning air was so clear, the day so bright, that Gert felt for a moment as though the events of the previous day had a nightmare quality. Then he saw that the landscape, which had been covered with trees of fair sizes, green with food for his cattle, were gaunt stumps and bare branches. The buck had brushed off all herbage in their passing, and splintered the young trees so that they would never grow again.

Far in the distance Gert thought he could see a few of his oxen. After breakfast he set off with his men to recover them. Every donga leading into the river, every little gully was filled with buck. It seemed that the first buck had paused on the brink, considering the prospects of leaping across. Before they could decide, the ruthless mass was upon them. Buck after buck was pushed into the donga, until the hollow was filled and the irresistible horde went on over the bodies.

Other sights reminded Gert of the fate he and his family had escaped by accepting the Bushman's warning. Small animals were lying dead everywhere – tortoises crushed almost to pulp, fragments of fur that had been hares. A tree, pointing in the direction of the advancing buck, had become a deadly spike on which two springbok were impaled.

For a fortnight Gert camped on that hill beside the Molopo, searching for his cattle. He found half of them. The fate of the others remained a mystery. They might have been borne along by the impetus of the stampede until they fell and were trampled to death; or they might have escaped from the living trap far away from the wagon. Gert inspanned the survivors thankfully and the wagon rolled on, away from the scene of destruction. When he told the tale, it was clear that he regarded it as the most memorable episode in a life which he regarded as the finest on earth. "*Ons lewe lekker. Dit is vir ons heeltemal goed genoeg,*" declared Gert at the end of his story. "We live well. It is absolutely good enough for us."

Such was the experience which came unbidden to farmers and their families, usually in lonely places, though nowadays it is hard to find anyone who watched the stampede. There are legends which men heard from their fathers and grandfathers. I am never satisfied with a legend when I can find the living memory, so I sought more survivors, men in their seventies and eighties. Two of them were over ninety, and they had seen a lot; but they spoke to me in wonder of the *trekbokke*.

I know that the mighty elephants set out on slow migrations, sometimes in large herds. The great treks of the North American bison, the caribou moving northwards, were marvellous sights. The little lemmings of Norway, descending from their mountain homes in millions to lay waste the countryside, have been studied and discussed for hundreds of years. But the springbok also moved resolutely over wide areas in millions. They, too, were drowned in thousands when they came to rivers or the sea.

I once met a man who kept a store on the banks of the Orange River late last century. He saw the springbok form a living bridge over the river as they raced towards the Kalahari – "to reach better pastures," so he said. Many perished so that the main body might cross with dry hooves on their backs.

Then there was an ex-trooper of the old Cape Police named Cochran who had to patrol the south bank of the Orange River in 1897, along a fence put up in the hope of keeping the rinderpest out of the Cape Colony. Cochran saw the migrating springbok charge the fence along a front of five hundred yards and bring it down. The leading springbok fell and were trampled and crushed; and the strench was so revolting that a gang of Hottentots had to be employed digging trenches and burying the buck. "I collected two pairs of enormous springbok horns from the dead at the fence," Cochran told me. "They were so large that everyone wanted to buy them. Some of the young troopers with me flogged their souvenirs in the Upington bars for a few bottles of lager. I got six pounds for mine, but I should have taken them to England and given them to a museum. They were record horns."

That year, too, Cochran watched thousands of springbok trekking through Kenhardt village. Everyone in the place seemed to be shooting from his stoep. It was probably the most devastating migration within living memory. Police gave the alarm and distributed ammunition to farmers at half-price. The damage was tremendous, but it might have been worse. For the invasion ceased suddenly. The springbok horde turned and raced back to the Kalahari. It was said that rain had fallen behind them, and the north wind had brought them, over hundreds of miles, the irresistible smell of damp earth and young grass.

A farmer in the Calvinia district pointed out to me a plateau which rose gradually from the plain but ended in a precipice. Long ago, he said, the Bushmen saw thousands of springbok feeding there during a migration. They drove them cleverly towards the precipice, and then shot an arrow at one buck near the edge. As they expected, the panic-stricken wounded buck jumped over the precipice, and the herd instinct impelled thousands of buck to follow. Thus the Bushmen secured the greatest feast of last century. They sent word far and wide to the clans, they gorged and they danced. For years the bones of the springbok lay in deep depressions at the foot of the precipice.

Trained naturalists seem to have missed the springbok migrations. Thus the scientific picture can be built up only from hearsay and the scanty records left by farmers, hunters and travellers. John Millais painted the buck, but very few cameras were turned on the massed herds. Descriptions are vivid enough and tally extremely well until you come to the point where the observers try to explain the migrations.

The migratory springbok belonged mainly to the old Cape Colony. They were common in the Orange Free State and Transvaal, but the enormous herds were found in the Kalahari and the Karoo. Van Riebeeck and his men never saw a springbok. It was less than two centuries ago that the English gardener, Francis Masson of Kew, gave the earliest description of this antelope. Masson accompanied Dr. Thunberg into a country called "Kou Bocke Veld" or "cold country of antelopes, so named from a species called springbock." Masson declared: "This animal when hunted, instead of running, avails itself of surprising springs or leaps."

During a later journey, Masson reported that since the Cold Bokkeveld had been settled by white people the springbok were no longer so plentiful. Once in seven or eight years, however, the springbok came in flocks of many hundreds of thousands from the interior, spreading over the whole country and not leaving a blade of grass or a shrub. Peasants were obliged to guard their cornfields night and day, or the springbok would cause a famine wherever they passed.

Masson remarked that the migrating springbok were always followed by lions. "It is observed, where a lion is, there is a large open space," he wrote. (A later observer declared that a lion borne onward by the avalanche of buck was crushed to death, though it left much evidence of its wrath.) Masson himself admitted that he never saw more than twenty springbok in a herd; but he met a party of Dutchmen who had been pursuing Bushmen, and they informed him that they had seen great flocks of springbok to the north.

Then comes the first of many theories. Masson thought the springbok were forced southwards by dry seasons. When rain fell they returned to the interior.

Thomas Pringle the poet formed the same opinion about half a century later, when he saw the face of the country near the Little Fish River specked with springbok as far as the eye could reach. "We calculated we had sometimes within view not less than twenty thousand of these beautiful animals," Pringle recorded. "They were probably part of one of the great migratory swarms which, after long-continued droughts, sometimes inundate the colony from the northern wastes."

Landdrost (afterwards Sir Andries) Stockenstroom of Graaff-Reinet wrote to the Colonial Secretary about the springbok in 1821, a great drought year. "They have come from the parched desert in such droves that all numerical description must appear exaggerated," he reported. "An eye witness can only believe the fact that farms have been left on account of the exhausted state to which they have been reduced by these animals, which rendered the support of cattle on the same farms impossible."

Stockenstroom also wrote to Pringle on the subject. "It is scarcely possible for a person admiring the springbok thinly scattered over the plains to figure to himself that these ornaments of the desert can often become as destructive as locusts," he wrote. "The incredible numbers which sometimes pour in from the north during protracted droughts, distress the farmer inconceivably."

When the springbok approached (said Stockenstroom) the farmers surrounded their fields with heaps of dry manure, the fuel of the Sneeuberg, and set fire to it in the hope that the hordes would turn aside from the smoke. This seldom proved effective. Often the buck carried flocks of sheep along with them in the mad stampede, and the owners never saw them again.

Stockenstroom gave much thought to the mystery and stated boldly that although the farmers were baffled, he had solved the migration problem. The springbok, he pointed out, multiplied in the deserts to the south of the Orange River. There the herds were undisturbed save by an occasional Bushman hunter. Finally the desert swarmed with buck. Then a drought would leave the water-holes empty and the soil parched. Thirst drove the springbok out of the desert, and they returned only when rain had fallen on their secluded plains.

That was Stockenstroom's view. Not long afterwards the hunter, Major Cornwallis Harris, saw the Griqualand West area "literally white with springbucks, myriads of which covered the plains." He summed up: "On the failure during drought of the stagnant pools on which the springbucks rely, they pour down like the devastating curse of Egypt from their native plains in the interior."

Sir John Fraser, whose father was the Dutch Reformed Church minister at Beaufort West in 1849, left a memorable impression of the springbok invasion of the village in that year. A *smous* drove into the village one day looking bewildered, and told the people that countless buck were on the way, leaving the veld bare. This report was not taken seriously. Soon afterwards the people of Beaufort West were awoken one morning by the trampling of all kinds of game. Springbok filled the streets and gardens, and they were accompanied by wildebeest, blesbok, quagga and eland. For three full days the *trekbokke* passed the village, and they left the veld looking as though it had been consumed by fire.

Some observers have stated that a migration usually started with small herds of springbok becoming restless and seeking their own kind. They gathered in larger and larger herds, moving as inevitably as the tides. Sometimes the *trekbokke* sauntered along their instinctive paths. The kids travelled in a sort of migrating nursery on one side of the main body of buck; and at intervals the ewes would visit them and suckle their young. Suddenly huge groups of buck would take fright and begin "pronking", with backs arched, in twenty-foot leaps. Then came the stampede, all dashing along faster than horses and even more gracefully. They grazed hungrily but hastily and passed on leaving only torn earth. On the farms they broke through any wire fencing they encountered; though it was only towards the end of last century that they met this obstruction. Fearlessly they surged between homesteads and outbuildings. They filled the dams and trampled their drowning and their dead ruthlessly in the mud.

David Livingstone watched a small migration in 1875, and formed his own opinion. He discovered that the springbok often left their northern areas at a time when grass and water were plentiful. "The cause of the migration seems to be their preference for places where they can watch the approach of a foe," suggested Livingstone. "Oxen are often terrified in high grass. The springbok possesses this feeling in an intense degree and becomes uneasy as the Kalahari grass grows tall. Vegetation being scantier in the more arid south, the herds turn in that direction. As they advance and increase in numbers the pasturage gets so scarce that they are obliged to cross the Orange and become a pest of the sheep farmer in a country which contains little of their favourite food."

I found confirmation of Livingstone's theory in the more recent observations of G. W. Penrice, a naturalist who studied the springbok herds in the coastal belt of Angola. "At certain seasons they congregate in one vast herd and trek to some other veld where they again disperse into smaller troops," Penrice wrote. "One never finds springbok in country where there is high grass; they seem to like to be able to see all round. During one year of exceptionally heavy rain on the coast the grass grew very long, which resulted in all the buck trekking farther south to a more sandy veld."

The author and poet, William Charles Scully, was magistrate of Springbokfontein in Namaqualand when the last springbok migrations came that way. He, too, had a theory. He said that although the motive seemed to have puzzled hunters and naturalists from time immemorial, the explanation was really simple and obvious. Rain fell in Bushmanland in summer, but the winter was rainless. Bushmanland was bounded on the west by granite mountains rising from the sandy plain. "Here no summer rains fall, but in early winter the south-west wind brings soaking showers, and the sandy plains lying among the mountains become clothed for a few weeks with rich, succulent vegetation," Scully went on. "This occurs at the season when the springbuck fawns are born, and when, consequently, the does require green food. Hence the westward 'trek', which is, I believe, of hoar-ancient origin."

Scully described the most sensational of all recorded springbok migrations (in 1892) which ended in the South Atlantic. "The springbucks as a rule live without drinking," he pointed out. "Sometimes, however – perhaps once in ten years – they develop a raging thirst and rush madly forward until they find water. It is not many years ago since millions of them crossed the mountain range and made for the sea. They dashed into the waves, drank the salt water, and died. Their bodies lay in one continuous pile along the shore for over thirty miles, and the stench drove the trekboers who were camped near the coast far inland."

Some farmers in the track of the *trekbokke* believed that the movement was due to disease, such as *brandsiekte* (scab) or rinderpest. There is evidence that the rinderpest years of 1896-97 left the springbok untouched, though *brandsiekte* was certainly present in some of those shot. But the theory of illness is complicated by clear evidence that while the *trekbokke* looked emaciated in certain years, during other treks they were obviously sleek and healthy.

Mr. S. C. Cronwright-Schreiner (Olive Schreiner's husband) made a determined attempt to solve the mystery during the 1896 migration, the last of the great cavalcades of *trekbokke* ever seen. Travelling by Cape cart in the wake of the migration, he found every homestead festooned with biltong. It was estimated that hundreds of thousands of buck had been shot in the Prieska district alone that year, and nearly as many wounded. Motherless springbok kids were dying by the thousand. Yet the migration went on – in millions.

It baffled Cronwright-Schreiner. He studied the works of Darwin and Lloyd Morgan on migration, investigated all the South African opinions on the subject, and finally declared: "I do not think they afford sufficient evidence to justify any hard-and-fast conclusion. It is a fact that there are not sufficient, carefully collected, intelligently considered and rigorously tested facts to enable us to come to any definite conclusion as to the whole 'mentality' of these treks. Shall we now ever obtain such facts?"

No one plotted the springbok migration routes accurately, so that significant evidence on that point has been lost. It is believed that they never went back on their tracks, but travelled a huge square or oval. No one knows how long a trek lasted, though it has been stated that the *trekbokke* were always back in their original haunts within six months to a year. The speed of a migrating horde varied considerably. One hundred miles may have been an ordinary day's trek. The buck were capable of covering much greater distances.

Karoo farmers last century firmly believed in two varieties of springbok – the lean *trekbok* and the fatter *houbok* (about fifteen pounds heavier), which remained in one area. Such a reliable observer as Scully mentioned shooting a *houbok* in the Richtersveld which was nearly twice as large as the springbok of the desert. The adult springbok ram weighs from seventy to eighty pounds and seldom more than ninety. Only one species of springbok is found in South Africa, known to scientists as *Antidorcas marsupialis marsupialis;* and it has been established that differences in weight are simply due to age and condition.

In South West Africa, however, the springbok is of a heavier sub-species.

While farmers and trekboers did not always welcome the springbok invasions, they were able to profit or at least balance their losses by taking heavy toll of the herds. Convoys of wagons carrying whole families, intercepted the *trekbokke*, muzzle-loaders went into action, and one bullet often killed more than one buck.

This was hunting on a gigantic scale, and nowhere else in the world has such slaughter been known. Each group of hunters would form an old-fashioned laager with the Cape carts and wagons outspanned in the shape of a large horse-shoe. Men and boys would ride out to prey on the fringe of the migration. The women would help with the skinning and cutting of the biltong.

For decades last century each springbok skin fetched sixpence at the store. (The thin leather was used for bookbinding.) Biltong was threepence a pound, and it was a lean springbok indeed which did not provide eight pounds of dried biltong. Backhouse, in 1839, recorded that in the market at Cradock fresh springbok fetched thirteen pence apiece. There were long periods when a fat springbok could be bought in the karoo villages for one shilling and sixpence.

Were there really millions of buck in these migrations? Some naturalists have doubted whether the springbok could ever have existed in the numbers which staggered the early travellers. Descriptions of the *trekbokke*, however, are at least unanimous on this point. One of the finest accounts was given a century ago by that picturesque hunter Gordon Cumming, old Etonian, cavalry officer, red-bearded and kilted Scot. He travelled by oxwagon and shot mercilessly for five years, at a time when South Africa was indeed a hunter's paradise and no one seemed to realise that some of the animals would one day be exterminated. His bag was far larger than those of later, and more selective hunters such as Selous.

One night Gordon Cumming lay awake in his wagon for two hours before the dawn, listening to the springbok grunting and realising that a large herd was feeding near the camp. When he rose, he found that it was no mere herd, but a dense, living mass of springbok marching slowly and steadily.

They were coming through a gap in the western hills, pouring through like a flood, and disappearing over a ridge. "I stood upon the fore-chest of my wagon for nearly two hours, lost in wonder at the scene," recorded Gordon Cumming. "I had some difficulty in convincing myself that it was reality which I beheld, and not the wild picture of a hunter's dream. During this time the vast legions continued streaming through the neck in the hills in one unbroken compact phalanx.

"At length I saddled up and riding into the middle of them with my rifle and after-riders, fired into their ranks until fourteen had fallen, when I cried 'Enough'. We then retraced our steps to secure from the ever voracious vultures the venison which lay strewed along my track."

Gordon Cumming confessed that he could form no idea of the number of antelopes he beheld that day; but he has no hesitation in saying that "some hundreds of thousands were within the compass of my vision."

One of the boers in the area told Gordon Cumming: "You this morning beheld only one flat covered with springboks, but I have ridden a long day's journey over a succession of flats covered with them as far as I could see, and as thick as sheep in a fold."

Scully was lost when it came to counting the springbok he saw in the 1892 migration. "In dealing with myriads, numbers cease to have any significance," he declared. "One might as well endeavour to describe the mass of a mile-long sand dune by expressing the sum of its grains in cyphers as to attempt to give the numbers of antelope forming the living wave that surged across the desert and broke like foam against the western granite ridge."

Mr. T. B. Davie of Prieska recorded his impressions of four great springbok migrations between 1887 and 1896. "The whole country seemed to move, not in any hurry or rush, but a steady, plodding march, just like *voetganger* locusts," he declared. Mr Davie saw the springbok in one continuous stream from Prieska to Draghoender (forty-seven miles), plodding on, and just moving aside far enough to avoid the wheels of his cart.

A family on the farm Witvlei had to sit round the well – their last water supply after the springbok had filled the dam – keeping the buck off with bullets and stones. In the end the thirsty springbok beat down the defence, and soon the well was packed with dead and dying buck.

That year the springbok poured through the main street of Prieska, and the magistrate sat on the steps of his courthouse and picked off a few good specimens with his rifle. Prieska was always in the path of the migration.

During the 1888 trek, Mr. Davie and his friend Dr. Gibbons made a deliberate attempt to estimate the numbers of *trekbokke*. They were on the farm Nels Poortje in the Prieska district when the sea of antelopes overwhelmed the district. In front of them was a kraal which, the farmer told them, held fifteen hundred sheep.

"Well," said Dr. Gibbons, "if fifteen hundred can stand there, then about ten thousand can stand on an acre, and I can see in front of me ten thousand acres covered with buck. That means at least one hundred million buck. Then what about the miles upon miles around on all sides as far as the eye can reach covered with them."

They gave it up. No wonder men spoke of myriads of buck.

During the 1896 trek, Cronwright-Schreiner and two other farmers (all accustomed to counting small stock) surveyed the springbok on a vast, open plain and tried to form an accurate estimate with the aid of field glasses. They counted section after section, and agreed that there were half a million springbok in sight at that moment. But the whole trek covered an area of one hundred and forty miles by fifteen miles. "When one says they were in millions, it is the literal truth," declared Cronwright-Schreiner.

Millais, in his life of Selous, dealt with the wholesale destruction of game after the breech-loading rifle arrived in South Africa in the eighteen-seventies. He met a trader who kept accurate records of the skins he handled; and between 1878 and 1880 this man exported nearly two million skins, mainly springbok.

Yes, there were millions of springbok on the move, millions of buck followed by lions and leopards, hyenas and jackals, and vultures to pick out the eyes of those that fell. When the *trekbokke* raced through a narrow poort, it meant death for any human being in their path. At the time of the Great Trek a frontier farmer found his three young sons and his Hottentot shepherd trampled to death on the veld after the buck had passed.

Nearly seventy years ago there was a Kalahari trader named Albert Jackson. He was still living in Port Elizabeth in recent years, and he told me one personal experience of the springbok migration which helped to bring the scene to life for me.

"I slept on the veld during the 1896 migration," Jackson recalled. "Often I put my ear to the ground, and even at night, when the buck were resting, it felt like an earth tremor."

No longer is the springbok seen in millions. Yet the national emblem of South Africa, the only gazelle in the country, is in no danger of extinction. As recently as May 1954 large herds of springbok, possibly fifteen thousand buck, streamed out of the Kalahari and into the Gordonia district like the migratory swarms of last century. Farmers complained urgently that their fences were being broken and their grazing destroyed. The magistrate and a police officer flew over the invasion area and decided that there was no need to lift the ban on all hunting in force for three years in that district. Farmers would be allowed to fire their rifles to frighten the buck away – but only under police supervision.

Venison has a market value. In districts where shooting is allowed, farmers preserve their springbok herds carefully, and the guest who disobeys the rules at a springbok shoot will never be asked again. Only the rams and the old ewes are killed.

Seldom now will you see fifty springbok shot on one farm in a day; yet in the 'nineties of last century one hunting party would bring in a thousand, twelve hundred buck between dawn and sunset. The migrations and the massacres have ended but the mystery remains.

Land of Man's Ancestors

For Lawrence G. Green the story and the people of South West Africa held a strange spell. This brilliant chapter on the ever-fascinating Bushmen of South West Africa is taken from *Lords of the Last Frontier* published in 1952. In the preface Green described South West Africa as "a country which has always inspired me". Some of his earlier works included descriptions of his wanderings into the far corners of a remote land which since he wrote *Lords of the Last Frontier* has become a football of contention in the strident arenas of international politics. Long after the dialectical din over the destiny of the territory has died away Lawrence G. Green's masterpiece on South West Africa will remain alive, vivid, and instructive. "Instructive" is a word from which adult readers with classroom memories of didactical schoolmasters may be inclined to shrink. They need harbour no such fear about the chapter I have selected. Green's charm as a writer has always been that he informs, captivates but never lectures or harangues. He says in the preface, too: "At last I have been able to tell the whole story of South West Africa – the life, the people of all races, the towns and the villages, the farms, the lonely places and the desert and above all the adventure that still lingers on the last frontiers under the Union flag... I like South West Africa all the more each time I walk down the old Kaiserstrasse in Windhoek on the brink of another journey".

Green believed that South West Africa under South African rule had nothing shameful to hide from the world. His discoveries about quaint aspects of the German occupation and about the country in this generation contain messages more powerful than political polemics. Most chapters in *Lords of the Last Frontier* merit inclusion in this anthology.

Lords of the Desert Land wins selection because I am sure it will endure in an ephemeral world as a compelling study of those little people whom Green perceptively described as "man's ancestors".

CHAPTER II

LORDS OF THE DESERT LAND

*Thus I am lord of the desert land
And I will not leave my bounds
To crouch beneath the Christian's hand
And kennel with his hounds.*

Pringle

SOUTH WEST AFRICA is the last great home of the Bushmen, the little people who once roamed Africa from end to end. Now it is only in South West Africa that they can hope to survive.

Until recently scientists regarded the Bushmen as a doomed race. Along the Kalahari frontier of the Cape Province the Khomani and Auni clans of Bushmen have shrunk to a few individuals, and their end is near. In the whole Bechuanaland Protectorate there are not a thousand Bushmen left. Angola has three thousand Bushmen, which sounds impressive until you realize how fast an isolated group can dwindle or lose their identity by mixing with other races. For many years the Bushman population of South West Africa was estimated at five thousand, not a hopeful figure. Fortunately the latest rough census has revealed from ten to twelve thousand Bushmen in the territory. Given freedom in reserves of their own, these ancient hunters may flourish and recover their strength as the aborigines of Australia have done.

I have always looked upon the Bushmen as the most fascinating native race, the most romantic survival, in all Africa. This view is shared, I think, by nearly all who have come into contact with them. Farmers who have lost cattle, policemen who have heard the singing of poisoned arrows past their ears, cannot feel the same affection for the "lords of the desert land".

It is true that a magistrate, several policemen and a number of natives have been killed by Bushmen since the Union occupied South West Africa nearly forty years ago. (I met a police sergeant who was recovering from a poisoned arrow wound in the arm. One of his trackers, also a Bushman, had saved his life by sucking out the poison immediately after the attack.) Clashes between Bushmen, Hereros or Ovambos still occur, with loss of life on both sides. Yet it cannot be said that the Bushman clans as a whole are a serious menace to law and order. Within living memory they were outlaws, hunted like wild beasts and shot at sight. Now many of them are losing their extreme shyness. Sympathetic white officials and a number of farmers have gained their confidence at last.

Bushmen are among the smallest people in the world; not dwarfs, but perfect miniatures The slender limbs are capable of feats of strength. Hands and feet are beautifully shaped. Skull measurements show that the Bushman brain is the smallest in any living type of mankind. For this reason the Bushman has been placed at the bottom of the human ladder; but the belief is growing among scientists that the Bushman is not such a simpleton after all. Primitive he may be, still following the Cave Man's way of life, yet this is not always a matter of sheer necessity. When given a choice, such as work on a farm, the Bushman usually reverts to the bush. He is happier in the bush, and it is a sensible thing to do. His brain capacity is in proportion to his size. Within that tiny brain is stored a mass of knowledge which scientists are now learning to respect.

No other native race in Africa can compete with the Bushman's knowledge of nature. As hunters and artists, as students of snakes and insects and plants, as heirs to a rich folklore the Bushmen are unsurpassed. They are Africa's supreme dancers and mimics and tellers of tales. An old Kung Bushman was asked his age. With the help of a Hottentot-Bushman crossbreed interpreter, the old fellow gave his reply: "I am as young as the most beautiful wish in my heart, and as old as all the unfulfilled longings in my life."

Their sayings prove that the little skulls contain a wealth of imagination. "Food only tastes good when you have to use your brain and skill to get it," they declare. And no one will deny the descriptive power of this remark: "News is like the wind. It comes over mountains and valleys and brings with it the fragrance of flowers and also the bad odours of things."

South West Africa's main Bushman population is found in the bush country to the south of the Okavango river. It is a land where grazing is poor and there is no running water. Farmers do not covet this north-east corner of the territory, and for that reason the Bushmen have remained undisturbed. Dr. P. J. Schoeman, a qualified anthropologist who holds the post of "Protector of Bushmen", told me that his estimate of eight thousand Kung Bushmen in that area was not far out.

Kung Bushmen are about the purest members of the race to be found at the present time. They have the true yellow skin tinge, and they are the smallest of the small. (The Bushmen people of Angola, already mentioned, are similar to the Kung Bushmen and speak the same language; but they call themselves the "forest people" and they have mixed to some extent with Bantu tribes.) South of the Kung, in the Gobabis district along the Kalahari frontier, you find the Naron Bushmen in encouraging numbers. They are famous for their skill in making ceremonial dress of ostrich eggshell beadwork. In habits and appearance they do not differ greatly from the Kung people.

Up in the north, however, you will encounter tall Bushmen who lack the true Bushman's physical and other characteristics. These are the Heikum, often seen by visitors to the Etosha Pan. Dr. Schoeman carried out an almost exact census, and found twelve hundred Heikum men, women and children. He classes them as Bushmen, for they follow the Bushman way of life. It appears that the Heikum are the descendants of an extinct Bushman tribe which was conquered by Hottentots, mingled with them and lost many of their customs. Most of them also lost their language, and adopted the Nama dialect of the victors. The late Miss Dorothea Bleek, greatest authority of her day on Bushmen languages, discovered some remote Heikum people still speaking the Bushman tongue of their ancestors, similar to the Kung language. This discovery went a long way towards clearing up the origin of the only tall Bushmen in South West Africa.

Professor Raymond Dart, the anatomist, has traced similarities between the Bushman's semi-erect posture, his spinal column and feet, and the skeletons of the Neanderthal race which occupied southern Europe twenty-five thousand years ago. The Bushmen are living fossils. But the problem of their origin becomes more complicated when you examine the eyelids, which have the true Asiatic fold. The narrow, puckered, humorous eyes have been shaped by centuries of sun glare.

Peppercorn hair in patches is typical of the pure Bushman. Their bodies are almost hairless, though some men have faint moustaches and chin tufts. Faces are childlike and piquant, even in old age. Skin colour varies from yellow to chocolate. Dr. Schoeman discovered a Bushman clan entirely new to science in the western Caprivi Zipfel not long ago. They were small black Bushmen with long hair, speaking a click language of their own.

Dr. Siegfried Passarge, a German scientist who studied the Bushmen towards the end of last century, met one old man who claimed to understand the language of the baboons. Bushman dialects are more advanced than baboon talk, but they are the dialects of the dawn world and cannot be placed in any language group. The clicks defeat almost every European who attempts to speak the Bushman language, and only a small handful of white people have ever mastered it.

Once there were Bushmen clans scattered along the whole Namib coast of South West Africa from the Kunene river to the Orange. You have heard of those stragglers of the Kaokoveld, the Sandlopers. Further south, the Bushman has probably disappeared completely. As recently as 1931, however, Sergeant J. W. van Zyl of the South West Africa Police came upon a Bushman clan living in the Aurus mountains in the forbidden diamond area south of Luderitz. There were seventeen men, women and children at a remote, unmapped water-hole, living on game, ostrich eggs, honey and roots. They had lived there all their lives without any white people becoming aware of their presence. Thus it is impossible to say with certainty that all the coastal Bushmen have vanished.

In his natural surroundings the Bushman is the toughest specimen of humanity that doctors are ever likely to encounter. Though it is difficult to fix a Bushman's age exactly, there is no doubt that the percentage of centenarians is high – once you have allowed for the hazards of life in the wilds. I knew a Bushman, proved to be over a hundred years old, who had all his own teeth. And their strength is out of all proportion to their size. A young "tame" Bushman working on a farm in the Gobabis district learnt to ride a horse. He used the horse to pursue gemsbok; and having come up with his quarry he would leap from the horse at full gallop and strangle the powerful antelope with a riem.

The women give birth so easily that when a clan is on the march the mother simply drops out for a couple of hours and then hastens after the others with her baby. Children are not weaned until the next one is due, which may be three or four years later. A diet of meat, berries and roots would never do, and the Bushmen have never owned cows or goats.

Bushmen make light of serious injuries. A number of wounded Bushmen were brought into Grootfontein after a fight with the police. One young man had lost an arm, shot off during the fight. He went on firing his arrows, drawing the bow-string with his teeth. The police thought he would die from shock and loss of blood, but he recovered. Other members of the clan talked happily as the surgeon treated their bullet wounds.

Mr. Cecil van der Spuy, a magistrate in South West Africa for seven years, placed on record an accident in which a buck-wagon with a load of nine tons passed over a Bushman's head. The Bushman merely complained of a headache. I once met a Bushman whose lower jaw and palate had been pierced by a gemsbok horn. This did not inconvenience him except when he talked, and then he had to push a rag into the cavity so that he could express himself fluently. Professor E. H. L. Schwarz told the ghastly story of a Kung boy who was caught by the leg in a steel game trap. Having failed to open the jaws, he cut off his leg to free himself. He knew that a leopard would find him if he remained in the trap.

Kung Bushman and other clans living in remote places seem to escape the epidemics of civilization. The "Spanish influenza" epidemic of 1918, for example, left them almost untouched. Malaria is their most deadly enemy. Some of them have been persuaded to submit to smallpox vaccination in recent years. They have their own herbal remedies, of course, and the explorer Chapman often found relief in the Bushman treatment for headache – a root, heated in the fire and applied to the forehead.

Dr. Schoeman noted a high mortality rate among the Kung Bushman babies. In a wide area he was able to trace only three couples who had succeeded in raising five children; but there were many couples with two or three children. Survivors have acquired a high resistance both to disease and to periods of semi-starvation.

When there is meat, the Bushman's appetite is a wonder to behold. He can eat a fat-tailed sheep weighing thirty pounds at a sitting, though the meal will last somewhat longer than a civic banquet. If he did not possess this power he might die, for the game he shoots soon goes bad and there is no knowing when the next buck will come within range of his arrows. Nature has come to the aid of the Bushmen in this life of feast and famine. All the older people have wrinkled stomachs, capable of expanding like concertinas when food is plentiful. And the women, of course, have developed enormous buttocks and thighs, a condition known to scientists as steatopygy. While meat is the only food the Bushman really loves, he has often to satisfy his hunger with such trifles as locust porridge, "Bushman's rice" (a variety of termite), snakes and frogs. No other race could support life in the deserts where the Bushmen flourish. Even the children on their mother's backs can swallow water like camels. They, too, know that it is a long way between water-holes.

South West Africa has some of the finest and oldest Bushman paintings in the whole continent. They bear a strong resemblance to the cave paintings of the glacial period found in Spain – realistic pictures in which the artists relied more on composition than colour.

Only in recent years, through the enterprise of Dr. Ernst Schertz of Windhoek, have many of the remarkable Bushman paintings and engravings in South West Africa become known to the world. Dr. Schertz and his wife have photographed and listed six hundred examples of Bushman art in different parts of the territory. They have also conducted many parties of scientists, artists and others to the caves and shelters where the most noteworthy pictures are to be seen.

It has taken a long time to uncover these wonders of the rocks, for the really significant pictures are all in remote places. Explorers and early hunters either missed them completely or did not think them worth mentioning. I believe the first report of a Bushman painting in South West Africa was made in 1870 by Dr. Theophilus Hahn, the trader (not the missionary). Dr. Hahn saw a painting in black, yellow, red and white on a rock near the Khoichab river. The most important point about Hahn's discovery was that *he found an old Bushman in that area still painting*.

There are some who would rob the little Bushmen of the credit for these primitive works of art. The modern Bushman does not paint and can throw little or no light on the pictures left by his ancestors. Thus it has been argued that some other race adorned the caves. However, there is sufficient evidence to prove that the Bushman was still painting almost within living memory. Professor Sollas, authority on the ancient hunters, recorded a fight between farmers and Bushmen after which one of the fallen Bushmen was found to be wearing a leather belt with twelve little horns strung to it, each horn containing a different pigment.

Pastor C. G. Büttner, who made many treaties with the natives on behalf of the German Government in the eighties of last century, was the discoverer of the celebrated Ameib paintings. Ameib is a farm on the edge of the Erongo mountains to the north of Karibib; and in a cave there (now known as the "Philipps Cave" after the farm owner) the missionary Büttner came upon some wonderful animal paintings. The Abbé Breuil, the French archeologist, examined them recently and declared they were among the most impressive he had seen. He estimated the age of an elephant painting in the cave at five thousand years. The climate has changed greatly since then. There were flowing rivers in the Namib, and one of the paintings is of a crocodile. Human figures, men and women, are also found in this great cave – a mysterious composition, full of symbolism, a riddle which will not be solved easily. One feels the need for a "Rosetta Stone", key to the Egyptian hieroglyphics, when studying some of the South West African paintings. As it is, the theories of modern investigators are based largely on guesswork, and some have been proved to be ludicrously wrong.

In the Erongo area are other memorable paintings. The Etemba cave, five miles from Otjamapaue farmhouse, reveals a giraffe on the granite, groups of hunters and fabulous figures. Nearer the coast the Gross Spitzkop and Klein Spitzkop peaks and boulders rise from the sandy plain. Rhino Grotto at Great Spitzkop has a magnificent red rhino, hunters and also those enigmatic figures with human heads and the bodies and legs of animals. Not far away is the Paradise cave, a dizzy and difficult climb for the novice. Decades ago in the German time a party of hunters entered this treasure house of Bushman art and used some of the paintings as targets. Later visitors, more appreciative yet even more destructive, tried to remove a slab of rock and damaged the paintings. This cave holds the most lifelike buffalo paintings known to science. You do not find buffalo in the Namib today. Klein Spitzkop shelters the Ghost Cave, with its mysterious figures from Bushman mythology, and the Giraffe Cave where red and white giraffes reveal the old artists at the peak of their skill.

Within sight of the Spitzkop group, but eighty miles away, rises the mountain which has been rightly described as "a veritable museum of Bushman art". This is the Brandberg, granite on basalt. The southern aspects are sheer precipices, but climbers entering from the north and east find the island mountain mass rent by wild gorges.

To this wonderland, unknown and unmapped in 1907, came a German police officer, Lieut. Jochmann, with instructions to survey the mountain. Toiling up the Tsisab gorge ("the leopard's gorge"), he discovered a cave decorated with snakes with ears and other fabulous animals and dancing figures. This is now known as Jochmann's Cave. All round him were signs of Bushman occupation; but Jochmann was no archeologist, and he contented himself with putting the Brandberg on the map.

Next on the scene was Reinhard Maack, a professional surveyor. A prisoner-of-war in World War I, he escaped and took to the desert. For months he wandered undetected. Maack was a clever artist, and he copied Bushman paintings to pass the time. At the end of the campaign in South West Africa he gave himself up, but was released. By this time the lonely desert had fascinated him, and he decided to explore the Brandberg with one companion, Alfred Hoffmann. During three months in the wilds they made the most valuable series of discoveries of Bushman sites up to that time.

In the Brandberg they met no human beings, and the great silence was broken only by the hollow echoes of the south-west wind in the ravines. Yet there were footprints in the sand, and when they ran short of water they followed the tracks to a spring. The water was hidden under plaited grass, covered with sand. No one appeared. Even the animals seemed to be in hiding, though the desert round the Brandberg was alive with zebra, springbok and ostriches.

Such was the eerie atmosphere of the Brandberg when Maack and Hoffmann entered a cave that Jochmann had missed. It contained a number of vivid frescoes depicting large black human figures, buck and birds, fine studies of rhino, wildebeest, ostrich, cheetah and other animals. (One early painting appeared to represent a seal, a rare subject.) There was also a man with the head of an antelope. But the cavalcade which held Maack and Hoffmann spellbound, and all who have followed them, included animals, human beings and creatures from the spirit world. It was not the work of one artist; in fact, Bushman artists appeared to have been repainting and adding to the weird scene for centuries. Eland, gemsbok, springbok and hartebeest all found places in the procession. There were antelopes with human limbs, a man with the head of a crocodile and a half-man, half-baboon. Musicians and hunters were there, and finally a figure which has aroused the most violent controversy in the whole world of Bushman art.

Maack copied this figure and many other paintings. He sent them to Germany, to Hugo Obermaier, a recognized authority on Bushman art. Obermaier collaborated with Herbert Kühn, an artist, in editing a massive volume, *Bushman Art – Rock Paintings of South West Africa*, based on Maack's work on the spot. It is noteworthy that Kühn described the controversial figure as "the ornamented man with bow and arrow and flower".

Some years later Dr. Scherz photographed the procession. General Smuts studied the pictures, realized the importance of the discovery, and arranged for the Abbé Breuil to visit the cave. The Abbé identified the "ornamented man" as a white woman holding either a cup or a white flower in the right hand and a bow and arrow in the left. He described the body as "rosy-white from waist to feet", and regarded the white face as delicate, with nothing native about it. The Abbé went so far as to suggest that this was a Cretan woman of warrior breed, resembling the women bull-fighters of the island. He suggested that a ship from the Mediterranean had been wrecked near Cape Cross (seventy miles from the Brandberg), and that the ship's company had sought refuge in the mountains and left this painting.

The interpretation of rock paintings is a matter for experts. I went to the late Miss Dorothea Bleek, greatest South African authority of her day, with this problem. She declared firmly that all she saw in the painting was a Bushman woman with face and limbs smeared with pink clay. So much for the world-famous "White Lady of the Brandberg". Nevertheless, it is a cave to remember, with themes far more intricate than the lumbering elephants and lively buck of other Bushman shelters. Wisely the authorities have barred the "White Lady" cave against vandals and only approved visitors are given the key.

Elsewhere in this ravine is the Rain Cave with red rain streaming out of a cloud; though the painter may have intended to depict jets of blood spurting from a wounded animal. Here, too, is the Skeleton Cave, discovered by Jochmann, filled with symbols of death. One painting shows a man holding limbs of human beings in his arms, and he is being followed by a skeleton. An unusual subject in another cave close by is a painting of a kokerboom, the tree from which the Bushmen took bark for their quivers. For some reason the Bushmen never painted landscapes and seldom included landscape details. Plants were rarely depicted. A circle might represent a pool, but that was about the limit of the Bushman's ambition in that direction.

On the side of the ravine opposite the "White Lady" cave is a painting which the Abbé Breuil named the "Girls' School". It reveals a procession of ornamented Bushman girls with beads in their hair, led by an old hag of a teacher. This work gives the impression of a caricature, for the noses of the old woman and the girls are of various shapes.

Kühn selected two antelopes in the Tsisab gorge as the most beautiful subjects in the whole array. One is a profile with the head turned towards the front; the other is a front view. These paintings convey a strong sense of rhythm.

Other groups of the Brandberg have not yet received the same expert attention. The Abbé Breuil spent most of his time in the "White Lady" cave, sleeping at her feet for ten nights, and having all his meals sent in to him. Fine paintings exist in other parts of the range, however, especially in the Amis gorge on the west front.

Dr. Scherz discovered a number of rock engravings about a hundred miles north of the Brandberg a few years ago. One remarkable effort was a snake, six feet in length, with the head of a zebra. Along the Aub water-hole series twenty miles to the north-west of Franzfontein are fine open rock etchings of elephant, giraffe and rhino. Most of Dr. Scherz's work has been done in the north. Some authorities have ventured the opinion that Bushman paintings peter out as you travel south. I am sure, however, that a careful examination of shelters in the Orange River mountains would reveal a wealth of unknown art. A police sergeant who rode east from Sendeling's Drift told me that he found a cave on the north bank of the Orange River, fifteen miles from the drift, containing human figures. Probably this painting has been admired only by police and prospectors, for it does not appear in any of the scientific works. There must be many more.

With only a slab of sheltered rock to work upon, the little Bushman artist was often cramped for space. So, as time passed and ancient paintings grew dim, he superimposed his "modern art" on the masterpieces of his ancestors. But while a great Bushman painter lived – so Professor Sollas thought – or while the memory of the man lasted, his pictures remained untouched. Even the cave men recognized the colours and the drawings of true genius.

If you are still doubtful about the intelligence of the Bushman, then consider his poisons, antidotes and medicines. In this field he still baffles modern science. As a poisoner he is far more cunning than the Borgias. Chemists believe that only after centuries of research by trial and error did the Bushman discover the complex poisons he uses today.

Arrow poisons, of course, provided medical science with some of the most valuable drugs now used in tiny quantities in the treatment of heart disease. It is probable that the Bushman's pharmacopoeia contains other items of first-class importance; and if the race dies out these secrets will be lost.

Dr. Hans Schinz, one of the early medical men in the territory and a great botanical investigator, described an experiment he made on a Bushman who claimed immunity to snake and scorpion poison. Schinz selected twelve scorpions and placed them on various parts (including the most sensitive parts) of the Bushman's naked body. The scorpions whipped their tails over and used their poison sacs, some of them more than once. Not a sign of pain did the Bushman show. Schinz watched for symptoms, but no swellings appeared. The Bushman explained that he had protected himself by swallowing small doses of scorpion poison, and said that he could protect himself in the same way against snakebite. Schinz summed up in favour of the Bushman's claim.

Chapman, the explorer, found the Bushmen using a creeper, which he unfortunately failed to identify, as a cure for snakebite. They called it "eokam". First they incised the wound; then the medicine man chewed the "eokam" root, kept the pulp in his mouth and sucked the area of the bite. After that the patient was given a decoction of "eokam" seeds to swallow, which acted as an emetic. "Bushmen having a bit of this root on their necks laugh at snakebite," wrote Chapman.

Snake venom on an arrow tip is a more sinister affair, and few escape death once this poison has entered the bloodstream. Every clan has its own poison compounds, of course, according to the substances found on their hunting grounds. Puff adder and cobra venoms are the great stand-bys; but the trapdoor-spider also yields a strong poison. Kung Bushmen use a caterpillar with such deadly effect that even a lion bites the ground in agony after receiving an arrow. A black substance found on the walls of caves (possibly containing arsenic) has been noted. As a rule, the poisons are mixed with plant juices which may or may not be poisonous in themselves. Vegetable poisons do not act rapidly enough to serve all purposes, but they serve as fixatives.

Branches of the euphorbia candelabra are used to poison buck at water-holes. The main source of water is fenced off so that the animals cannot reach it. Then a pool is filled with the branches, and a scum forms on the surface. Even zebras fall easy victims to this poison, and the meat is not affected. It is interesting to note that Bushmen do not always cut away the meat round the wound in a buck which has been killed by a poisoned arrow. Some say that this part has the finest flavour!

Bushman arrows, like the poisons, vary with the localities of the clans. The reed shaft is most common in South West Africa, and bone points are more often used than metal because, according to the hunters, bone retains the poison longer. These points are detachable and are carried in separate containers; for the Bushmen know only too well the danger of accidental poisoning. Moreover, an arrow manufactured in a single piece might be torn out as a buck leaps away through the bush, and the hunter wishes to make sure that the deadly point will remain firmly in the flesh.

Feathered arrows are not unknown, but the Bushmen of South West Africa place no great faith in them. They prefer to rely on their powers of stalking, and shoot at such close range that feathering is unnecessary. While the arrows are works of art, the bows are crude but effective. It takes strength and skill to draw the sinew back to its fullest extent and when the arrow is released the hunter loses some of the skin of his thumb and forefinger. Great force on impact is not needed when hunting buck; but it must be remembered that the Bushmen have killed elephants and other great beasts with bows and arrows. That is where penetration is essential. Bushmen have demonstrated bows which will send their arrows through a one-inch plank. Early travellers who came into conflict with Bushmen found arrows in their wagon-chests, and cut off the poisoned tips inside the boxes. A Bushman arrow passed right through a horse during a fight, a light reed with a flint head.

I have also seen tiny bows no larger than a man's finger, made of gemsbok horn, A little quiver held the darts steeped in poison. The Bushman does not part readily with such possessions. They are made, not as toys for the children, but with one object – murder. This is the Bushman's "love bow", or "revolver", the weapon he selects when there is a quarrel round the camp fire over women. The arrow is usually aimed at the victim's ear while he is asleep.

It took the Germans some time to learn the ways of the Bushmen. Governor Leutwein imagined that they would make useful labourers. When he visited the Kung Bushman area for the first time in 1895 he appointed Johannes Kruger, an intelligent Cape coloured man living at Grootfontein, as "Chief of the Bushmen". Kruger was reluctant to accept authority which, he knew, would be difficult to wield; but an agreement was put in front of him and he signed. "I told the Governor that Bushmen would not readily submit to a chief, especially as I was not a Bushman," Kruger informed Union Government officials twenty years later. "The reply was that as I knew the language and the people I might have influence over them."

Kruger was paid five pounds a month, and he had to provide labourers. He collected more than two hundred Heikum Bushmen; but there was not enough *veldkos* (wild fruits, roots and herbs) for them to live on and they soon returned to the bush. German farmers settled in the district and then the real trouble started. Kruger made the following statement to the Union authorities:

"As a rule a Bushman has only one wife. They are extremely fond of their women and treat them well. The Germans took the wives away from the Bushmen and made concubines of them. The whole district is full of German-Bushwomen half-breeds. Then the Bushmen began, for the first time, to steal the cattle. One Bushman whose wife had been taken murdered the German farmer. Bushmen were shot on sight by police and German farmers and no mercy was shown to them."

Shortly before World War I the Bushman problem had become so acute that Von Zastrow, the Grootfontein district chief, was asked to report on the possibility of exterminating or deporting the whole Bushman population. Von Zastrow, a kindly man (most unpopular with the farmers), replied that such schemes did not merit consideration. He pointed out that half the farmers in the district were employing Bushmen, and would be unable to carry on if the Bushmen vanished. "Surely it must be clear that people who have wandered over the veld during their whole lifetime and have never done any hard manual labour cannot in a moment lose their habits and become efficient labourers," argued Von Zastrow. "Yet it is remarkable to observe how the Bushmen learn to plough, to cultivate tobacco, and to control oxen. Many remain for long years on the farms and become indispensable. Thefts are committed by wild Bushmen who have been farm labourers. In some cases they have been driven to commit these crimes out of motives of revenge. I consider that large areas should be left free as reserves for wild Bushmen, and by fair treatment it may be possible to entice them to give up their nomadic life and settle down as useful people."

A German police sergeant named Helfrich was murdered by Bushmen in the Grootfontein district in 1912, and that led to further bloodshed. In spite of Von Zastrow's orders, many farmers took the law into their own hands and hunted the Bushmen like wild animals. It was a repetition of the state of affairs in the Cape Colony last century, when the frontiers were pushed northwards into the domains of the Bushmen and the farmers made war on the primitive hunters. In the Cape, the Bushmen were massacred in such numbers that the race could not survive. Possibly it was World War I that saved the Bushmen in South West Africa. With the South African conquest came a humane policy.

Major Frank Brownlee, first South African magistrate at Grootfontein, reported that the Bushmen were losing their fear of white people. They were coming down to the water-holes to beg tobacco from travellers. If he sent a message saying that he wished to see a Bushman leader the summons was obeyed.

Brownlee had to send out a police patrol on camels to round up some Bushmen who had murdered a number of Okavango natives. The natives were on their way home, carrying the cloth and beads they had bought after working on farms and mines. So the police came in with their captives, fine specimens of Kung Bushmen. Brownlee sent a telegram to Peringuey, director of the Cape Town Museum. Plaster casts were made by that clever taxidermist, James Drury. Many thousands have gazed at those lifelike figures in the museum. How many have realized that the originals were murderers?

One of the merciful rules introduced since the Union occupation is a proviso which allows gaol authorities to release Bushmen if they show signs of dying while serving prison sentences. It is a fact that the tough little hunter often pines away and dies in captivity. For many, six months is a death sentence.

Court officials have noted that the Bushman is instinctively truthful. Under the law of the wild, Bushman mothers used to kill a baby if it arrived too soon after a previous child. Such offenders still come before the courts, and are dealt with leniently. Here is a little dialogue from the court records.

Judge: "Did you kill the baby to save the one on your back?"
Bushman mother: "Yes."
Judge: "Would you ever kill the one on your back?"
Bushman mother: "No, I love that one."

A Bushman cannot grasp legal procedure, of course, and there is another record of a Bushman who was sentenced to death for murder by a judge wearing the usual wig and regalia. When the Bushman was asked whether he had anything to say, he inquired through the interpreter: "I want to know what that old woman in the red dress has got to do with the matter."

Bushmen bear a grudge for a long time. Senator Vedder recently quoted a feud between Bushman clans which started with a murder a century ago, and which still leads these old enemies to snipe each other with poisoned arrows. He was pleading to the Union Senate for Bushman reserves, and pointing out that because old hatreds flourished it would be impossible to concentrate all the Bushmen in one reserve. There they would destroy one another.

Senator Vedder also pointed out that there were farmers in the north who preferred Bushman labour, while others hardly dared to leave their homes for fear of poisoned arrows. Farmers who wished to be friendly with the Bushmen had only to approach the old people and say these words: "You can go on living where you are. The water which you have been drinking you can go on drinking. Take your veld food and shoot the buck you need. If your young men come to work for me I will give them tobacco."

That is the whole secret. In the minds of the Bushmen, the farms occupied by white people are still Bushman preserves, as they have been through the centuries. They do not mind white people living there, but they guard their ancient rights jealously. Without water, hunting or roots they perish. The farmer who forbids them these necessities is the man who has good reason to expect a poisoned arrow in his ribs.

Since World War II a number of Gobabis farmers have employed Naron Bushmen with varying degrees of success. One who has become converted during the past few years is Mr. C. R. Pyper, who overcame his prejudices when no other labour was available. A young Bushman on his farm Conellan has evolved as far as driving a tractor; while others have taken charge of other machinery. Less intelligent Bushmen have learnt to milk, to do the gardening and act as household servants.

Mr. Pyper was not surprised to find that his Bushmen had no sense of time. If they went away for a week, they stayed away for a month. And in the winter months there was no holding the women who were accustomed to gather wild nuts in season. Mr. Pyper has overcome this difficulty by giving them monkey nuts, which they prefer to their own *veldkos*. For a bag of monkey nuts they will perform the "Dance of the Wind Over the Grass". The women stand in half-moon formation, singing and clapping, while the men dance and render with their voices the deeper notes of the wind.

Money is something the wild Bushman simply does not understand. Coins are given to the children as toys, or the women make ornaments of them. Rations of coffee and sugar, sufficient for a week, are consumed during a week-end. And always there comes a time when even these luxuries can hold the Bushman no longer and he returns inevitably to the great freedom beyond the last fence.

Bushmen do not peer into the future. When food is abundant they devote themselves to games and merry-making, winning the hearts of all who study them. You will see no happier people in Africa than a party of Bushmen with full stomachs.

They adore their children, and reveal their affection in many ways. In the dance of the gemsbok, for example, the fathers teach the children a lesson that saves lives during the chase in years to come. A wily old hunter takes the part of the gemsbok, holding sharp sticks to his head to represent the horns; while the children are the dogs. Every movement of a hunting drama is portrayed with such realism that the human bodies fade out, the brown man with the horns becomes a cornered antelope; the children dashing in and out, snapping and barking, are dogs indeed. The gemsbok slashes left and right fiercely, then tires, pants, struggles for life while the hunters shout and thrust their spears forward. Finally the buck goes down, fighting to the last; hunters and dogs close in and the dance ends. A young Bushman is not reckoned a man until he has killed a gemsbok or some other dangerous game, and his parents are anxious that he should not go out ill-prepared for the ordeal.

Dogs are the only tame animals the Bushmen have ever possessed. They have never owned cattle, and thus (unlike the more prosperous Hottentots) their ideas of numbers are extremely limited. ("One, two, three – many," says the Bushman.) The dogs have been their companions for centuries. Side by side they have travelled through Africa and together they have won many little victories. The finest type of Bushman hunting dog, a light brown ridgeback mongrel with a dark stripe and a trace of the greyhound in his appearance, is now verging on extinction. They are without a doubt the finest dogs in the world for the hunter's purpose, lean and savage, ready to keep a wounded leopard at bay until the master finds an opening for his spear. One of the most typical of these dogs I saw stood about fourteen inches at the shoulder with a length of body seemingly out of proportion to that height. A broad forehead, a sharp muzzle, upright ears and long drooping tail made him anything but a beauty. Yet this is possibly the oldest and certainly the most cunning breed of dog in the word.

A fugitive with his master, the Bushman dog has learnt the virtue of silence. Some declare this dog never barks; at all events there is no senseless barking to give his master's hiding-place away. The dog slinks always behind his master, taking advantage of every patch of shade, reserving his energy for the moment when he is called upon to distract the quarry's attention. Sensing danger, he will give only a warning whine. Between Bushman and dog there is complete trust and understanding. Many travellers have tried to bribe the Bushman with tobacco to part with a hunting dog, but I have yet to hear of one who was successful.

When hunting buck and ostriches, of course, the Bushman adopts suitable disguises, aided by his art of mimicry. He can walk right up to a flock of ostriches wearing a skin and feathers, supporting the long neck on a stick, preening himself as he goes. A small bush serves the purpose when buck are being stalked. At such times there is no limit to his patience. Chapman recorded meeting a Bushman who had wounded a giraffe and followed it for fifty miles. Many a Bushman has trailed a wounded animal without rest for three days rather than lose the meat.

It is natural that these primitive people should have kept alive that early luxury, the tale that is told. I once observed a Bushman who had just returned to his clan from a great distance. He squatted beside a fire and held his small audience enchanted by his narrative. "He is describing everything he has seen since he has been away," the interpreter told me. "Animals, birds, trees, the smallest living things of the veld, the remote water-holes where he quenched his thirst – every detail has a meaning for these people. For an hour or two, perhaps, he will talk and the others will not utter a word. Then, when he has finished, they will ask questions."

One of the earliest accounts of the Bushmen, written by a seventeenth-century Dutch explorer, described them as "an entirely wild nation without houses or cattle, but well-armed with bows and arrows". That, as I have seen, is true today. The search for food and water keeps them for ever wandering, so that they have no homes more permanent than a grass shelter from the wind with a fire to keep the lions away. Every old Bushman carries scars on his wrinkled stomach, signs of cold nights when he has curled up too close to the fire and been scorched. Seldom does a clan consist of more than twenty men, women and children – the struggle for food is too hard, and the Bushmen must scatter to survive.

Each clan stores water in ostrich eggs, and each has its secret drinking places; tiny wells covered over with stones and sand, not a tell-tale sign of the precious hoard remaining unconcealed. When the springs dry up in a bad season, and the ostrich eggs are empty, there are always roots and bulbs and the wonderful t'samma melons to sustain life. I noticed Bushman children with stomachs swollen to an alarming extent, the result of over-indulgence in this wild melon that is moist, but lacking in nourishment. Nevertheless, without these melons the desert would be uninhabitable. They grow always on the tops of the dunes, in great patches. The Bushmen store them in dry sand, so that the melons remain in good condition for weeks. From the crushed seeds a drink is made, the poor Bushman's coffee. All the animals, from the elephant and lion right down to the desert mice, flourish on the speckled green melon. T'samma roasted in the camp fire and then cooled, quenches the Bushman's thirst. Roast t'samma and jackal form one of the Bushman's favourite feasts.

Any other race, faced with the prospect of obtaining all their water from the juice of a melon, their food from roots and berries, would probably have collapsed and died. The Bushmen were determined to live, and so these hardy bands of hunters have come down precariously into our own time. Primitive he may be, yet the Bushman survives under conditions which would spell death for civilized man. Put the Bushman hunter in a desert, naked and empty-handed, and he alone succeeds in finding nourishment, in clothing himself, in lighting fires and making life worth living. When you see the Bushmen at home you meet man's ancestors. That is why I called them a romantic survival, "lords of the desert land" indeed.

Craft of the Magicians

THE inquiring mind of Lawrence G. Green could not resist investigation of strange phenomena such as clairvoyance, the supernatural, voodoo and other baffling so-called "wonders". The Indian Rope Trick too excited his curiosity. The tricks of the professional magician would be an irresistible challenge to his powers of detection. A friend who remembered Green in his early days as a pupil pilot in the RAF in World War I recalls his zest for practical jokes, a zest which the years did not fully quench. The snake-charmers of Cairo and the feats of clairvoyants and the secrets of African witchdoctors were to him compulsive subjects of research. In 1959 his long study of the supernatural and some baffling zoological riddles found expression in *These Wonders to Behold*. In this volume his readers roam the Continent of Africa with Lawrence Green as he introduces them to men and women who practise mysterious rites and arts. He tells them too of the puzzling features of bird migration. There is also the story of the fakir who was buried alive in a grave for 10 days . . . The chapter selected from this book discusses the ever-absorbing topic of fire-walking. South Africans are of course well-acquainted with the ordeal of fire-walking for it is practised by members of the Indian community here, notably in Natal. The chapter begins: "Whenever I hear tom-toms accompanied by reed pipes a scene of fire comes back to me down the years. It is the Umbilo temple outside Durban and thousands are moving eagerly down the South Coast road . . ." Lawrence Green writes with deep knowledge of a fascinating ritual the technique of which he explains, and quotes medical and scientific evidence to make this chapter as convincing as it is compelling.

CHAPTER III

FIRE-WALKERS OF AFRICA

WHENEVER I hear tom-toms accompanied by reed pipes a scene of fire comes back to me down the years. It is the Umbilo temple outside Durban, and thousands are moving eagerly down the South Coast road. Some white people are there, but it is a bare-headed, black-haired Indian crowd, garlanded, robed in crimson and saffron and other brilliant colours. This is the day of the fire-walking ordeal.

Fire-walking was regarded by many until fairly recently as an occult performance. It is no longer a complete mystery, as you will see. I have watched this ancient ritual at both ends of Africa, in Cairo and Durban and Cape Town. They say the technique is easily acquired, but in this matter I have not the courage of my convictions and I shall not risk my feet on the hot embers.

Tom-toms and reed pipes, incense and jasmine . . . the crowd had gathered round the fire pit now. Six tons of wood have gone into blaze. It has been spread out over the pit fourteen feet long and ten feet wide; a fierce pit which hurts your face and eyes when you approach the rope barrier thirty feet away.

Strange effigies are borne aloft by devout Hindus following their priests. I can see the supreme being Brahma, with his manifestations Vishnu and Siva. There are village goddesses, too; Annamma, the presiding deity, Chandasveramma, Mayesveramma, Maramma the yellow-clad goddess of cholera, Udalamma the goddess of swollen necks, Kokkalamma the goddess of coughs and Sukhajamma the goddess of smallpox and measles. There is a short *puja*, a saying of prayers by the priests.

Now the tempo of the drums and pipes becomes faster, the crowd roars, the fire-walkers are coming. One is an elderly man with white beard and hair. Several of the younger men have steel skewers through their tongues, and their chests are pierced by dozens, by scores of silver hooks; and on some of the hooks small limes are hanging. It looks like torture, but the most of the *Soutris*, the Hindu fire-walkers, show neither pain nor fear. One man is moaning. He has chosen to walk on nails driven upwards through the soles of his wooden sandals, and for him the fire will come as a relief.

The music rises and falls as the fire-walkers circle the pit. Then the oldest man leads the way over the carpet of fire, glowing in the breeze. All follow without hesitation. Some make the journey twice. One man passes over the whole fourteen feet of the pit three times. Then a woman with snow-white hair saunters across the pit.

Durban's chief of police and two white doctors are present. Carefully they examine the feet of the *Soutris*. Not a burn, not a blister this year. And not a drop of blood where the skewers and hooks pass through the flesh. But it is not always like this. Devotees have died or suffered painful burns in the flames while others have emerged untouched.

Fire-walking must be almost as old as sun worship in Egypt. My dragoman Ahmet, a good dragoman who knew my liking for the odd, strange and marvellous, took me to the Mousky in Cairo one day to see a performance by a marabout.

It was the season known to Egyptians as the "Scent of the Breeze", that sweltering period which corresponds with spring in more favoured lands. Spring, heralded by the burning *khamseen* wind from the southern desert, and sandstorms that filled Cairo with fine dust. Spring, with a rising temperature and breathless nights. Spring that brought a dryness which made the nose tingle and irritated the skin. I could not imagine a more inopportune time for a display with fire; but I went.

It was a street performance. The marabout was a Moslem, an elderly giant in a turban and long blue linen *galabiyeh*. Before him was a large brazier, which a boy was stoking with twigs and tending with bellows. At one side were the musicians with flutes and drums. "Al-lah! Al-lah! Al-lah!" chanted the marabout as he swayed to the orchestra and hypnotized himself for the show.

At last he threw off the *galabiyeh*, and I saw the scars of a lifetime of self-inflicted punishment. His eyes were glazed and he groaned as he stepped up to the brazier. Suddenly he seized fragments of burning wood in both hands and beat his huge, lacerated body from neck to waist.

"He is a holy man who has been many times to Mecca," my dragoman explained. "Such a man feels no pain."

The boy heated an iron rod in the brazier. It was white with heat when he raised it to the old marabout's face. And the marabout licked the rod. As a finale the boy tipped the brazier over, and the marabout walked with bare feet among the glowing twigs.

"He has done well," summed up Ahmet the dragoman as I gave my piastres to the boy assistant. "Such a marabout is not to be seen every day. Wallahi! From Suez to Siwa you will not find such another holy man."

Ahmet told me that Moslems of both sects, the Sunni and the Shia, look upon fire-walking as a form of remorse for the deaths of old rival leaders killed during a conflict over the succession to the Caliphate. One of the leaders was Husain, a descendant of the Prophet Mohammed, and both sects mourn his death. Religious fire-walking ceremonies are always held as the climax of *Muharram*, the mourning period during the first ten days of the Moslem year.

Fire-walking is not confined to Hindus and Moslems in Africa. It may be seen among primitive African tribes, such as the Wakimbu of Tanganyika. Wakimbu fire-dancers will walk through fire, cover themselves with embers, rub their faces with blazing branches and bite pieces out of the glowing wood.

One of the Wakimbu witchdoctors went further than this. He placed his head in a small pit lined with red-hot stones, and kept it there for twenty minutes. White officials in Tanganyika watched this queer performance and timed him. The Wakimbus collect certain leaves of shrubs and trees before a performance, and chew them into a paste. They claim that this *dawa*, or magic medicine, when smeared over the body, protects them against fire. I wonder.

The fire-walker I watched in Cape Town was a white man who called himself Karas, the "white yogi". It was a genuine performance, with red-hot coals spread out on concrete in the garden of a Sea Point hotel. People sat round drinking beer. In the absence of the emotional atmosphere which is usual at these displays, the show did not seem at all impressive. An excited oriental crowd makes fire-walking far more mysterious.

Nevertheless, this man sauntered over the live coals without going into a trance. His feet were examined, and they were neither protected nor blistered. Late in the evening a volunteer or accomplice came on the scene. Karas made passes as though hypnotising him, and the newcomer then walked along the fire-path without hurting himself. A little polite applause followed, but I missed the tom-toms and reed-pipes.

I said there have been deaths and lesser casualties during fire-walking displays. Lieut.-Col. R. H. Elliot, the surgeon who studied various forms of magic, traced a number of inquests held on fire-walkers who had been fatally burnt.

Durban newspapers reported a serious accident during a Good Friday fire-walking ceremony a few years before World War II. The young Indian "penitent" fell when he was half way across a twenty-foot pit of white-hot ashes. Four men had already made the journey safely when this young man staggered and found himself on his hands and knees. It seemed that no one could help him. He crawled to the edge of the blaze, and then people reached out and dragged him into safety. They laid him in a shallow trench of water at the end of the pit, and then he was taken to hospital with severe burns. Other fire-walkers told the newspapers that the man fell because he had come out of the ecstatic trance which protected him when he entered the pit.

Why do some escape and others suffer or die in this queer and ancient ordeal? No doubt there are chemical treatments which would confer some protection. Doctors and scientists have examined the feet of fire-walkers so often, however, and found no sign of treatment that this explanation can be ruled out. People with tender feet would probably be burnt, while those with hard skins would stand a better chance. But the secret of successful fire-walking must be sought elsewhere.

Is this another example of mind over matter? Only to a limited extent. Nervous people who are foolish enough to play with fire in this way are nearly always burnt. Hypnosis, religious ecstasy, supreme confidence – these states of mind will take the walker over the fire without hesitation or floundering, and that is essential.

Hindu fire-walkers in Natal will tell you that they follow a strict vegetarian diet for ten days before the fire-walking, and a system of prayer and pious thoughts, baths and special exercises. On the morning of the ordeal there is a long temple ceremony and total immersion in the nearest river. The ordeal is faced as a penance for some evil deed, or to carry out a vow made during illness or some crisis. A young Indian girl at Pietermaritzburg was afflicted with a painful stomach complaint. Someone told her that if she tested her faith three times in the fire she might be cured. This she did at an Easter ceremony a few years ago. After a week in the temple, living on fruit and milk, she walked down the fire-path without a tremor. Her feet revealed no trace of burns. She claimed that her ailment had vanished completely.

Faith is essential. Some theorists have suggested that the fire-walker waits until an insulating layer of ash has formed before stepping on to the flaming pathway. This is not correct. Kuda Bux, a Kashmiri, demonstrated fire-walking before a number of doctors and scientists in England some years ago. He brushed the ash away before his walk, and proved conclusively that he preferred the red embers of the log fire.

Kuda Bux walked fairly quickly. The fire-path was twenty-five feet long, three feet wide and twelve inches deep, about the average size used in India. Doctors found that Kuda Bux's feet were normal, with a fairly thick skin. His feet were washed, swabs were taken and examined; and the medical committee was satisfied that no preparation or chemical had been used to render him immune from burns. After the final walk there was not a suspicion of a blister.

One curious point about Kuda Bux's demonstrations was that he wore a black cotton frock coat and his trousers came down to his ankles; yet his clothes were not scorched. It took him about sixteen seconds to traverse the embers on each occasion.

The late Dr. T. W. B. Osborn, the South African medical authority and Member of Parliament, studied the Natal fire-walkers and came to the conclusion that there was no adequate physiological explanation. He pointed out that in fire-walking you have heat without blistering. A hypnotist could produce blistering without heat, by handing his subject a cold penny and telling him that it was red-hot. Thus it seemed that the fire-walker was in mental control of the situation. Possibly the sympathetic nervous system was in full activity owing to great excitement. At such times the blood vessels became constricted and the blood clotted more quickly, so that the danger of bleeding was minimized.

Dr. Osborn recalled the parallel feats of Indian yogis who were able to withstand great cold for long periods. These men sit naked on the ice of a frozen river for hours on end. Some of them lived in caves among the Himalayan snows without fires, clothed only in loin cloths. Normal physiology could not survive such exposure. But in the East such feats were regarded as the natural fulfilment of a religious way of life.

Professor David Waterston of St. Andrews University attended a fire-walking demonstration in Fiji, arranged for members of the British Medical Association. The Fijians walked with bare feet upon stones heated to a temperature high enough to set paper alight. The professor suggested that by training and practice and repeated exposure of the soles to heat, the performers were able to endure without severe pain a temperature which the untrained person would find intolerable. In the same way children could become accustomed to walking over sharp gravel. The threshold to pain had been raised.

Sir James Purves-Stewart, another medical delegate who witnessed the Fijian ceremony, disagreed with the professor. He thought the immunity to heat was brought about either by auto-suggestion by the performers themselves or hetero-suggestion by their native chief or priest. Religious ecstasy, he declared, was capable of temporarily banishing sensations of pain. Both these medical authorities were satisfied that the performers were not drugged, that their feet had not been treated, and that the soles of their feet were not abnormally tough.

So far there has been a grain of truth in many of the theories, but the whole truth has not yet emerged. I believe the man who discovered the secret of fire-walking was an American doctor of philosophy named Mayne Reid Coe of Florida. By sheer chance Coe read a physics book published towards the end of last century and giving details of a forgotten discovery known as Leidenfrost's phenomena.

When liquids are thrown upon incandescent metal surfaces they present remarkable phenomena which were first observed by Leidenfrost. If a tolerably thick silver or platinum dish is heated to redness and a little water, previously warmed, is dropped on to the dish, the liquid does not spread itself out and moisten the dish as it would at ordinary temperature, but assumes the form of a flattened globule.

It rotates rapidly on the bottom of the dish. It does not boil. In fact, its evaporation is only about one-fiftieth as rapid as it would be if it boiled. Liquid in the spheroidal state does not actually touch the red-hot surface on which it dances. It is kept away by an insulating cushion of its own vapour.

Coe tested Leidenfrost's phenomena in his own laboratory and confirmed the scientific principle involved. He had the courage of his convictions, for he walked barefoot on red-hot coals and metal plates. Coe, indeed, fortified by scientific knowledge, went so far as to place his tongue on a red-hot steel bar.

So that is the real secret of fire-walking. No drugs. No hypnotism, though the walker must have sufficient confidence to follow a steady course. No anaesthesia, and no trickery. All that happens is that the feet sweat, and the spheroidal state of the moisture protects the feet from the flames. In just the same way, the fire-eater is protected by the saliva in his mouth.

Now you know why Kuda Bux brushed the ash away and walked on red embers. If the embers are not hot enough the insulation breaks down and the walker is burnt.

Probably there are very few fire-walkers who are aware of the principle which gives them immunity. They do know, however, that a long walk is dangerous. Twenty feet is safe, and twenty-five feet is about the maximum. The point is that each foot is in contact with the embers for less than half a second, and each part of the moving foot touches the embers for a small fraction of a second. This brief contact is the fire-walker's salvation. The man who loses his nerve, stands for a second or turns back is lost.

Houdini used to put a man in an oven with a raw steak. The

steak cooked, for it could not perspire. The man came out gladly, but unharmed, saved by the cooling effect of evaporation from the skin.

Watch a woman testing her iron with moist fingers and you have an everyday example of the fire-walker's magic. Water vapour between the hot iron and the skin prevents burning. Any plumber will provide a more daring example by directing a flow of molten lead with the moist palm of his hand.

So almost anyone can become a fire-walker. It is not a fake. The ability to walk on red-hot embers is not confined to fakirs. Wipe your hand with a damp cloth, dip it into molten lead and you will come to no harm as long as the temperature of the liquid metal is greatly above its melting point.

They still hold fire-walking ceremonies in Natal, but the old Umbilo temple has been abandoned. It is a ruin, a place of weeds and snakes. But this temple looked down on great ordeals, year after year, when the fire-walkers gathered there unafraid.

One memorable day three young white girls threw off their shoes and followed the Indian fire-walkers over the glowing coals. Many people in the crowd screamed when they saw the girls on the fire-path. It seemed incredible that white girls should possess the faith and the nerve to venture into that red heat. Pipes and tom-toms played a weird tune for them that day. And all three girls came through the flames without a mark or blister, protected by their own boldness and an obscure scientific principle that has eluded many qualified scientists.

Breathing a Love of Cape Town

AFTER Lawrence G. Green's death a friend remarked reproachfully "He was Cape Town's *own* author and the city did nothing about him". The years indeed will deepen the Mother City's debt to Lawrence Green for he more than any other writer, past or present, captured the spirit and animation of the city he loved and would never leave for good in his lifetime. Green's cameos from the past, his description of the city's quaint streets with their haunting sounds, the cries of the hawkers and the plaintive liturgy of the muezzins, his gift for uncovering the true often sad stories of odd characters whom all preoccupied passers-by saw but did not know – history will always be grateful to him for preserving the past to delight the present. In terms of memory he snatched old, gracious Cape Town from the maw of the bulldozers and the demolishers. Green's three books on Cape Town *Tavern of the Seas, Grow Lovely Growing Old* and *A Taste of South-Easter* form a brilliant trilogy.

All breathe Green's love for Cape Town, his feeling for its ever unfolding past. No Lawrence Green anthology would be valid or complete without a chapter from at least one of these three haunting books. But the problem bedevilling the task of choice was "which one" because so many chapters justified inclusion. My choice of "Cape Town Characters" comes from *Grow Lovely Growing Old* which was published in 1951. This chapter reflects Green's innate feeling for the ordinary man. He saw the real pathos behind the quayside antics of "Charlie Chaplin" (Lawrence Arthur Hollern) which amused mailship passengers of yesterday. So he brought a forgotten character back to recollection. Posterity will be thankful. Lawrence Green was bored by the pompous struttings of the social high and the mighty. Yet in the characters he chose for this classic chapter there is one rich man – a fascinating eccentric who could not really hope to escape Lawrence Green's perceptive pen.

CHAPTER IV

CAPE TOWN CHARACTERS

CAPE TOWN has seen a long gallery of strange characters, and historians have often revived such odd personalities as Joseph Suasso de Lima, poet and publisher, Moses the money-changer and "Queen" Rebecca, the ex-slave who thought she was heir to the throne of England. Within living memory there have been others, and I am inclined to place Wallagie near the top of the list. Wallagie, a Malay woodcutter who lived at Claremont, died about twenty years ago. He was Cape Town's champion trencherman, probably a world champion if he had been put to the test.

Wallagie means "wonderful," and his appetite is still discussed in tones of awe by those who knew him. He was a huge, muscular man, but not a fat, paunchy type. As a rule, he ate normal meals. Then something would move him to give those legendary displays which earned him the name of Wallagie.

One day his employer sent him out to work in the suburbs and gave him a chit asking a shopkeeper to supply Wallagie with food for his lunch. Wallagie had a strong and peculiar sense of humour. After a healthy morning's work chopping down trees he presented his chit and ate one of his more remarkable lunches. When the bill came in Wallagie's employer refused to pay. The case came before the Civil Court at Caledon Square, and the shopkeeper declared that Wallagie had eaten the food in the shop before his eyes. The magistrate refused to believe this evidence, and judgment was given for the small amount tendered by the defendant. Only when the case was over did Wallagie confess to his employer that he had eaten everything claimed by the shopkeeper.

The meal that is still remembered by the Malays was a feast arranged for sixteen guests, including Wallagie, at the end of Ramadan. Tables were spread with the usual lavish array of dates, "buba" soup, rice cakes, pastries, curries with atjar and blatjang, sweet potatoes in batter, chickens and rice – the Moslem menu of the year. Smilingly the host invited the redoubtable Wallagie to see what he could do before the other guests started. Wallagie accepted, and began eating in his usual deliberate manner, with obvious relish. He cleared the tables. All the food for sixteen people vanished down his throat, and a fresh meal had to be cooked. By this time Wallagie had recovered his appetite and made another hearty meal, though he was considerate enough to leave something for the others.

Wallagie could polish off watermelons as though they were strawberries. Once he encountered a farmer with a wagon-load of watermelons, and laid a bet of £1 that he would eat the lot. He ate fourteen, and then the desperate farmer called the bet off. There are other tales of Wallagie's prowess with hardboiled penguin eggs and crawfish, but the figures are fantastic. Hadji Amor Arend, well-known in his day as a race-horse owner, vouched for one of Wallagie's feats, carried out in his presence. That was when Wallagie drank 144 large bottles of sweet ginger-beer at a sitting.

A café owner named Effendi, of Station Road, Claremont, once challenged Wallagie to consume a twenty-pound tapioca pudding. Wallagie not only finished the pudding, but topped off his meal with two large loaves, a bucket of ice-cream and a paraffin-tin of lemonade. It is said that in his heyday Wallagie ate up a whole café, so that the owner went insolvent. Buns, biscuits, fruit, sweets, mineral waters – Wallagie was on his mettle and he left the shelves empty.

In a pancake and pumpkin fritter contest at Claremont, the cooks were worn out before Wallagie stopped eating. He ate steadily and relentlessly and when no more food was forthcoming he washed down his meal with all the minerals in the café.

Wallagie's last great feat was performed in a Long Street café. This was another challenge, and the Indian proprietor put out a hundred polonies, an eight-pound cheese, four sandwich loaves and four dozen bottles of ginger-beer. On this occasion Wallagie did not finish the repast; but the challenger was afraid he would, and begged Wallagie to leave some of the food untouched.

After these displays Wallagie never suffered from indigestion.

He died as a result of an accident. No one has ever explained his powers but shrewd Malay businessmen who watched him eat were sorry that they did not organize an overseas tour for him. No doubt Wallagie's achievements have been exaggerated since his death, but there is little doubt that he would have made the hotdog and hamburger champions of Coney Island look like patients on a strict diet.

Much more widely known than Wallagie was Lawrence Arthur Hollern, the "Charlie Chaplin" of Cape Town's pavements and waterfront. It was easy to discern pathos in Hollern's way of life, but there was more of it than people realized when this frail old man scrambled for coins during his last years.

Hollern was eighty when he died in Groote Schuur hospital in September, 1946. American by birth, he started his career as a circus contortionist; and he performed as an acrobat on board Mississippi showboats. Between 1895 and 1921 he appeared in almost every music-hall in Britain. George Robey, Marie Lloyd and Harry Tate were among his friends.

Hard times in the vaudeville world drove him to South Africa in 1921, but it was not until 1925 that he appeared in the bowler and baggy trousers of Charlie Chaplin. On board the outgoing mailboats there were often music-hall artists who had known Hollern during his better days; and at the docks he made enough to pay for his cubicle at the Salvation Army Metropole.

Sir Seymour Hicks once watched Hollern's antics with tears in his eyes. He threw half-crowns on to the quay whenever Hollern's back was turned – eight half-crowns before the ship drew away. "I was at his wedding," said Sir Seymour Hicks. "I was a struggling young actor and he was a comedian in one of London's most successful shows. Now he has to do this for a living." He waved, and Hollern waved back. "I admit nothing," said Hollern when he was questioned after this dramatic meeting. Forgotten by all but an actor at the top of the tree, Lawrence Hollern still had his pride.

It was in 1938 that Hollern met with the accident that many had expected for years. The ageing acrobat often performed dangerously on the edge of the quay. One afternoon he leant backwards too far, and fell, still clasping his bowler hat and cane.

He fell on to the timber fender between the *Balmoral Castle* and the quay. A dockhand and a quartermaster from the ship climbed down to the rescue, but they had difficulty in controlling Hollern. Injured though he was, the old stager kept shouting: "Let me up – I must give my show." When the ambulance arrived a stretcher was lowered by crane and a sadly-bruised "Charlie" was taken to hospital. "My downfall was not due to being overambitious," Hollern explained afterwards. "I slipped in a pool of oil."

He was in bed for a month, and then he resumed his quayside antics until World War II closed the docks. After that he had to earn what he could by entertaining cinema queues. Though he was a familiar figure to many thousands of people, only a few knew that the face beneath the thick grease-paint was the face of a tragic old man.

It is often like that with pavement entertainers. Carlo Lotierzo, the harpist, was playing in the streets of Cape Town for years while Hollern was impersonating Charlie Chaplin at the docks. Lotierzo had been a regular musician at Government House, Adelaide. He had played at State balls and conducted his own academy of music. The "talkies" finished him, and he took to wandering with his harp.

Between the wars, too, there was Charles Ham, the old street violinist. A musician nearly all his life, he was once leader of fashionable orchestras all over Britain and the Continent. Then he went to sea as violinist in the old *Carisbrook Castle*, came on shore in Cape Town after a number of voyages, served in the Cape Mounted Rifles for seven years, and went back to the violin in a circus band. Ham had played in cinema orchestras, too, but like Carlo Lotierzo the "talkies" sent him into the streets.

Street singers are uncommon in Cape Town, though everyone knows Arthur Edward Patrick Rowley, with his tall, distinguished appearance, handsome features and grey hair. Rowley's cultured speech is not a pose. He once told me that he was Lord Kitchener's interpreter in the Sudan during the Fashoda incident, which means that he is well on in the seventies.

Some years ago Rowley used to take his seat in a leading café and intimate that he was prepared either to eat a free meal or sing – and he got his dinner. The proprietor finally appointed Rowley commissionaire, a post which he filled with dignity – for a time.

In court he was unpredictable. Charged one day with singing and breaking a globe in his cell, he replied: "As there was no electric bell and no parlourmaid, I had to make a noise to call the warder. You see, I wanted to shave."

He always referred to his singing as "my professional operations" and declared that he gave full value for money. "Have you ever felt the real pangs of cruel hunger?" he once asked a constable who arrested him for begging.

Rowley spoke to me of his occasional absences from the Cape Town streets. At the Salvation Army Social Farm he had to rise at 2 a.m. daily and milk a hundred cows. "I am now an expert cow milker," he remarked. He spent a long period in a Transvaal work colony, and returned with an exemplary discharge. "Work and Rowley do not agree, but anyone who escaped from that place was liable to be eaten by lions," he explained.

Commenting on a recent spell in Roeland Street gaol, he declared: "The food was better cooked in the old days, and there was more of it."

Rowley exists on a South African War pension of £9 10s. a month. "I pay the Salvation Army £4 a month for board and lodging, and the rest is pocket-money," he told me.

Another character of the streets known to everyone in Cape Town between the wars was George Woollends, the boot-black. Woollends was a Londoner who went to New Zealand at an early age and took part in the Second Maori War – hence the medal which he often wore. He was a sheep-shearer. Early this century he was earning a living in South Africa as a horse-breaker; and when horses went out of favour he became a boot-black. Though this is now a dying craft, there were once a dozen bootblacks in Adderley Street, and Woollends could make five shillings a day without difficulty.

A few years before World War II he had to use his wits again, for no one seemed to want their boots polished. So at the age of 85, Woollends took to making hammocks, tennis nets and other network. He slung his hammock on the Standard Bank railings and lay there watching the crowds hopefully. One day he confided to me: "I am the only man who has ever had official permission from the City Council to sleep in Adderley Street."

Cape Town's most eccentric citizen within living memory, I should say, was Michiel Hiddingh of Newlands. For nearly forty years his whims and unpredictable largesse were a cause for wonder among all who came in contact with him.

The first of the Hiddinghs, a judge, arrived at the Cape from Holland early last century. His son, Dr. Jonas Michiel Hiddingh, was a wealthy medical practitioner who bought Newlands House and the large surrounding estate in 1859, rebuilt the old brewery, and added greatly to his fortune by the sale of beer.

Dr. Hiddingh was married but childless. He wanted an heir who would carry on the business and also maintain the beautiful estate as one of the show places of the Cape Peninsula. So he sent to Holland for a nephew, Michiel Hiddingh, who was seven years old when he landed in 1867. It would have been better for little Michiel if he had remained in Holland and led a normal life, free from the influence of the riches which were to have such disastrous effects on him. His uncle and aunt bullied him and instructed his schoolmasters to cane him on the least provocation. The luxurious atmosphere of Newlands House was for him a scene of youthful misery. It changed his character and ruined his life.

Michiel had brains, however, and did well at college in Cape Town and England as an agricultural chemist. He also became a first-class shot. After he had qualified his uncle made him work in the brewery – a task for which he had no inclination. At the age of twenty-one Michiel made one sensible move when he informed his uncle that he wanted privacy and asked for the Red House, a single-storeyed house of eight rooms near the southern boundary of the estate. This request was granted.

During a visit to England the unhappy young man met a girl he wished to marry. His future was in the hands of his uncle, however, and the uncle opposed the engagement. Michiel Hiddingh returned to Cape Town more warped than ever. He withdrew into himself, studied many subjects, and acquired such a wide medical knowledge that friends in the profession described him as "nine-tenths a doctor."

Dr. Hiddingh died in 1888, too late to release the twenty-eight year-old Michiel from the complexes of youth. Although part of the estate was entailed, Michiel became heir to a great deal of valuable property and a very large income.

It is clear that Dr. Hiddingh was proud of historic Newlands House, his private park where fallow deer roamed, his flourishing brewery and chain of "tied houses". He had hoped that the whole property would remain in the Hiddingh family, and that Michiel and his descendants would live there in grandeur for generations.

The estate had been laid out by William Adriaan van der Stel as far back as 1700 to supplement the supply of vegetables to ships. Governor Ryk van Tulbagh built the original house in 1750 and entertained the Abbé de la Caille and other distinguished visitors there. Stavorinus wrote of a huge apricot tree that shaded twenty men beneath its boughs. Bougainville, in 1769, described the high hedges and planted some of the oaks that still stand.

Newlands House, indeed, with its white gables and twisted chimneys, is one of the oldest and finest country houses in the Cape. Sir David Baird and other early British governors lived there. Las Cases, former secretary to Napoleon, wrote an ecstatic description of his three months' stay. "It might have been accounted a pleasant residence even in Europe," he declared. "When left to ourselves in this delightful place we felt we had been suddenly removed from a prison to Paradise. The elegantly furnished apartments; the dovecots, the birds, flowerbeds, groves and delightful walks, the silence and solitude all presented a magical effect that reminded us of Zernire and Azor."

Lord Charles Somerset tried to build a second storey, but the roof fell in during a storm. Newlands House was rebuilt in 1828, and soon afterwards it was sold to Mr. W. J. Louw at the bargain price of £3,025. He sold it to Mr. J. Cruywagen, who disposed of part of the estate. Nevertheless, there were still twenty-nine morgen round the house when Dr. Hiddingh bought it.

Michiel Hiddingh cared for none of this. He liked the doctor's Jersey cattle and attended personally to their ailments. But he refused to be bothered with the brewery and rented all the public houses and canteens to Anders Ohlsson for £2,300 a year.

After the death of his aunt Michiel Hiddingh could have lived amid the splendour of Newlands House. He preferred to let it. (Newlands House again became a temporary Government House for a period, and during the First World War it was used as a nursing home. A later tenant was Gwelo Goodman, the artist).

Not long after his uncle's death in 1888, Michiel Hiddingh began exhibiting those peculiarities which baffled his acquaintances. One day he decided not to have a fire in any of the grates in the Red House. For the rest of his life his winter guests shivered.

Argumentative and suspicious to a degree, he lost friends who had given him no provocation. "I am a man of moods," he often admitted. But this was a deep-seated abnormality of outlook, far more serious than moodiness. You could not call him a hermit, for he was fond of entertaining in his own queer way. He did not lack public spirit, for he was Mayor of Claremont in 1894, and a shrewd and conscientious mayor he made. It was just that no one could fathom the twisted mind. For this reason he had no close friends, and though often there were many people round him he was essentially a lonely man.

In the hall of the Red House stood a number of marble statues, selected by Dr. Hiddingh. Michiel had no appreciation of any form of art, and the statues remained for years draped in pink muslin. The house was literally the Red House; solidly built, it needed no paint, but Michiel smothered it in fresh red paint every year. When electricity became available he refused to have the Red House wired. All his life he used paraffin lamps. Though he kept a number of electric torches handy, friends going out into the darkness were given lighted tapers. No telephone was ever installed. There was a bath-room in the house of course, but Michiel had the bath taken out. He preferred to have a hipbath brought into his bedroom every morning.

Works of art adorned the walls; but Michiel was contemptuous of them. If a newspaper article appealed to him, however he would have it framed and hung up. Articles with a special appeal for him were those denouncing or ridiculing doctors. No doubt he was still angry with his dead uncle.

Visitors were inspected through a slit at the side of the front door. If Michiel did not like the look of them, a servant handed them a slate bearing the words: "If anybody wants to see me on business, please don't come and bother me at my house." Sometimes he sent friends away and whistled them back. Those who gained admission to the Red House experienced hospitality on a crazy scale.

Michiel's wine cellar would have stocked a large hotel. He ordered scores of cases of whisky and champagne at a time, and never bought a consignment of less than sixty thousand expensive cigars. All his entertaining was done round the dining-room table. The drawing-room remained closed. At meals an astonished guest would find a whole chicken, or even a whole turkey on his plate; and Michiel was offended if any portion was left. Glasses were replenished the moment the level fell. Michiel had no use for bells when he wanted his servants – he summoned them to his table by a blast on a police whistle.

Something of an epicure, Michiel's favourite dish was curried penguin eggs. He employed Cape coloured women as his cooks, and they served the traditional Cape dishes to perfection. Cooks and other servants did not easily adjust themselves to Michiel's queer ways, however, and only one remained loyal. He was a coloured man, William, who served his eccentric master for twenty-three years. William survived many shocks. One day Michiel accused him of stealing a gold tooth-pick. Next day Michiel found his tooth-pick in his dining-room chair, and made amends by doubling William's wages and handing him a glass of whisky.

Michiel pressed whisky on all sorts of people. When coloured flower-sellers came to the door he bought all their flowers and sent them away with bottles of whisky and boxes of chocolates. Yet he decorated his home with ugly artificial flowers.

Ministers of religion who called with subscription lists were baited unmercifully. Michiel pestered them to drink with him, and usually refused to part with his money unless they did. "Can't you take your drink like men?" he would demand angrily. Once he managed to send a clergyman off a little the worse for wear, and he was delighted.

He kept twenty cats at the Red House, and fed them royally in the dining-room. Nevertheless, he insisted on great cleanliness in his house, and a guest who dropped cigar ash on the floor was snubbed immediately.

When one of his coloured servants broke a wrist Michiel attended to the injury himself. He made the servant sit down at the dining table, cut up the food and fed him. Yet this same tall, hearty-looking Hollander was for ever lamenting the fact that slavery had been abolished. Michiel treated everyone alike – coloured servant or a visiting doctor. But no one ever knew what the treatment would be. Once a man came with a request for £1 to buy a pair of boots. He went off with a new hat, a case of whisky and a box of cigars – but still without the boots.

For a long time after motor-cars arrived Michiel would have nothing to do with them. He often drove to Hout Bay by dogcart, and organized gorgeous hunting trips to Stellenbosch and Somerset West. It meant leaving Newlands at three a.m., but the picnic hampers were sumptuous, and the farmer who invited him could rely on a case of vintage champagne. Last century Michiel held deer shoots on the estate; for the herd had to be thinned out from time to time. He was a crack shot himself, and if one of his guests wounded but failed to kill a deer there would be no second invitation. In the end, however, this lover of animals sickened of shooting and sold the herd of fallow deer, about a hundred head, to a Somerset West farmer.

Mountaineering, chess and bridge were among his pastimes. For a period Michiel was a well-known figure on the Cape race courses; but he gave it up suddenly and was seen there no more. He spent hours peering into his microscope. His favourite text book was an obsolete work on poisons.

At last Michiel took up motoring, but never as the owner of a car. He spent at least £1,500 a year on the hire of cars at one suburban garage alone. The drivers loved him.

Among the Claremont shopkeepers he was known fondly as "Old Mike." He would stalk in with a bag of sovereigns and place orders such as no man before or since has given. In some ways a child, he found it difficult to pass an interesting shop window. Again and again he bought up the entire stock of a food shop and gave everything away to the poor. He would load his hired car with springbok, pheasant, partridges and hams – and hand them out in the street.

Often he revealed a childish sense of humour. He saw some fly papers in a shop-window, turned to a hopeful group of street urchins and told them to plaster each other with the sticky papers. He stood roaring with laughter until the fight was over, and then gave each child half a sovereign. Michiel always carried a walking stick, and he liked to deliver a whack with it if he saw a coloured man bending over some task. When the astonished man straightened up a sovereign would be pressed into his hand.

His gifts were always on the grand scale. On a farm one day the farmer's son mentioned that he would like to take up shooting. Next time he called Michiel brought with him a rifle and 50,000 rounds of ammunition. Many of his gifts were foolish rather than generous. Yet the strange Michiel also did good by stealth. He lured doctors out for drives with him and took them to the sick poor. He paid for operations – which he regarded as a last resort – and supplied the dying with every imaginable comfort. He hated publicity. Hundreds of appealing letters reached him, and these he scrutinized with the utmost care and made a close personal investigation of some which seemed genuine.

His favourite author was the German philosopher Schopenhauer. Many who would have preferred whisky received copies of Schopenhauer's works.

For some years before his death Michiel Hiddingh suffered from heart disease. When he knew that the end was near he refused to go to bed, for he had always said there would be no deathbed for him. He sat up in his revolving-chair, as jolly as it was possible for him to be, entertaining friends to the last. Thus he died, on September 11, 1927, at the age of sixty-seven, tragic victim of wealth – and a stupid uncle and aunt.

Naturally there were many who awaited the opening of Michiel Hiddingh's will with feelings of hope which could not have amounted to certainty. The will was as freakish as the man himself. He left about £40,000 to friends, but nothing to his relations. (Some of his relations were provided for under Dr. Hiddingh's will.) And he left £80,000 to various institutions and charities which he had turned down during his lifetime. For example, the Society for the Prevention of Cruelty to Animals knew him as a lover of animals, but had never succeeded in extracting a penny from him. Michiel Hiddingh put the S.P.C.A. down for £5,000.

Other bequests included £20,000 for the free dispensary, £15,000 for the New Somerset Hospital, £15,000 for the Old Men's Home, £10,000 for the deaf and dumb institute at Worcester. It was typical, unexpected, characteristic of a man who was often a fool with his money, yet who really knew all the time where his money would do the most good.

The Sinister Breakwater

GENERATIONS of writers to come will praise Lawrence G. Green and his publisher Howard B. Timmins for they pioneered the post-war boom in home-spun literature. In a partnership of skill and vision they proved at long last that the South African people did crave to read books about South Africa by South Africans. Green risked his time and his leisure and Timmins risked his money!

Tavern of the Seas from which the following chapter has been picked was the first of Green's splendid books about Cape Town and the third of his postwar works. Its success was immediate. A prescribed school edition followed several reprintings. He wrote then nostalgically of an old and vanishing Cape Town. Those who read *Tavern of the Seas* more than a quarter of a century afterwards will find that it awakens old memories even more nostalgic than ever before. For such were the spell and genius of Lawrence Green.

Any chapter from *Tavern of the Seas* would have adorned this anthology. Why have I chosen one with the grim yet compelling theme of crime and punishment? Firstly I felt that the chosen chapter should appeal to readers to whom the Mother City is remote or even personally unknown. Secondly I think this chapter dramatically lights Lawrence Green's ability, unrivalled in his generation, to discover the hidden historical treasure behind familiar landmarks which so many hardly notice any more on their ordinary occasions. Every strolling sightseer in Table Bay Docks must be aware of the old Breakwater thrusting its crooked finger into the bay. Ships' passengers and crews view it dispassionately as their journeys end in Table Bay. Here, however, Green uncovers the sinister past of this gnarled and nobbled breakwater. It is a story to enthrall all South Africans.

Moreover *Underworld of Cape Town* has a wider social implication for all thinking citizens. The dedicated penologist will forever fret over the seemingly slow pace of penal reform. This fine chapter, however, does subtly and unobtrusively preach the moral that justice in the present century has become more conscious of the quality of mercy than many people imagine. As a man of infinite compassion Lawrence Green knew this. Man, despite his awful aberrations, does become kinder by the day and the decade!

CHAPTER V

UNDERWORLD OF CAPE TOWN

For human misery in the mass and over a long period I suppose there has never been anything in South Africa to match the Breakwater Prison. Some of the warders, some of the men they guarded, are still living. The evidence is abundant.

It was in July 1846 that Mr. W. E. Gladstone presented to the British Cabinet a dispatch from the Governor of the Cape urging the need for a breakwater to protect the shipping in Table Bay during winter gales. Mr. Gladstone himself suggested that it should be built by convict labour.

The convicts were assembled. In 1860 Prince Alfred, afterwards Duke of Edinburgh, pressed a silver trigger and thus tipped the first load of stone. That was the first and last touch of luxury in the whole enterprise. For more than half a century after that white, native and coloured prisoners toiled in the quarries and harbour, carrying out one gigantic task after another. The prison became one of the most feared in the world, a place that ranked in the criminal mind with Dartmoor and Devil's Island. You can still form an idea of the terrors of this prison by walking through the open gates in Portswood Road and gazing at the treadmills and the solitary confinement cells. The gates are wide open now, but something of the old atmosphere of hardship and despair still remains within the turreted walls. Here was Old Newgate under our southern sun.

I have met several warders who were stationed at the Breakwater Prison. One of them landed in Cape Town in 1888, a penniless lad of eighteen, and became a warder for lack of anything better to do. He found himself among an odd assortment of colleagues – ex-soldiers, ex-policemen, seamen who had deserted their ships, adventurers without references. The pay was one shilling and eightpence a day, and fourpence was deducted for messing. "We fared well," the old warder assured me. "There were always a few first-class chefs among the prisoners."

The warders carried old and battered Snider rifles, but they were never trusted to load or fire. They kept tobacco in their ammunition pouches, and relied on fixed bayonets in emergencies. Only the head warders had serviceable weapons.

That was the time when I.D.B. (illicit diamond buying on the Kimberley fields) was being punished savagely in an attempt to stamp out the traffic. Magistrates could, and sometimes did, award ten years' hard labour for this crime, and the minimum sentence was five years. There was no option of a fine. Thus scores of men who were not criminals in the ordinary sense were trapped and sent to the breakwater merely for being found in possession of uncut diamonds. As one writer in 1895 remarked: "The breakwater depends entirely for its rate of progress on the output of I.D.B. convicts from Kimberley."

Many of those who experienced the full horrors of the Breakwater Prison should never have been awarded hard labour. Yet doctors, lawyers, army officers and other educated men fell into the merciless net and learned the meaning of penal servitude. There were also international crooks who had hastened to South Africa during the diamond and gold booms like vultures to a feast. Some became wealthy; most of them ended up on the long, grey stone breakwater in Table Bay. Perhaps there are a few old ones who still sit round where criminals gather and talk of the "old breakwater days" – but not wistfully.

They wore the broad arrow in those days, and each man had his number stamped on the back of his jacket. Dangerous customers marched out to work in chains. The rings were riveted round their ankles, and they lived in chains for months at a time.

At five o'clock each morning the "rouse bell" sounded. The wards, as they called the dormitories, were bare with concrete floors. Each man had bed boards with a mat, a pillow and three blankets. The doors were unlocked at five-thirty and the mealie pap breakfast was served. At six work started – quarrying and loading stone. Lunch, always stew and bread, came at mid-day. From one to five they laboured again, and at five they clumped back for their evening soup and bread. They could walk the yards for a spell, and then at eight they were herded back into the wards. It was the pitiless monotony that made men give up hope. This, they knew, would be their lot for all the years they served at the Breakwater Prison.

The wards were lighted at night so that every man could be watched. Towards the end of the century arc lamps with hissing carbons were used. Each half hour during the night a bell tolled. Then the warders on duty along the walls would chant their monotonous reports: "Number one, and all's well." And so on from post to post.

"Halt! Who goes there?" a sentry would challenge.

And back would come the inevitable cry: "Visiting rounds!"

In the early days each white convict slept with a native convict on each side of him – to reduce the risk of communication. Often there would be a thousand convicts within the walls.

Sunday was the day of services and the weekly shaves, haircropping and baths. The men were given razors until the custom became dangerous owing to attacks on warders. Then the convicts had their beards clipped for them.

On Sundays the "prison widows" and children trudged down the Portswood Road to visit the men they had not forgotten. Once a month every man was permitted to see a visitor and receive a gift of small fruits. Nothing large enough to hide a file, a knife, or tobacco was allowed. Interviews lasted twenty minutes, and the convicts remained behind wire netting.

The aristocrats of the prison, for some queer psychological reason, were the "I.D.B." men – just as in a modern prison the skilled safe-breaker is treated by his fellows with some respect. The "I.D.B.'s" always boasted that they had parcels of diamonds "planted" for the day of their release. Impostors who claimed to have dealt in diamonds when, in fact, they had been sentenced for less glamorous crimes were liable to be set upon by genuine members of the fraternity.

One day two "I.D.B." men who had just been released at the end of long sentences contrived to break the monotony. They drove round Table Bay Docks in an open carriage, lolling back like princes with cigars in their mouths. They wore gorgeous clothes, and as they visited gang after gang they waved genially to old friends and made rude gestures to the guards. Hundreds of convicts cheered them. It was the great topic in the bleak prison that night.

The law was harsh, and as I have said, there were men who should never have been sent to penal servitude. Among the victims of injustice (a warder told me) were a number of British regular soldiers whose time had expired while on active service. For refusing to obey orders when they should have been discharged, they were all sent to the breakwater. In the 'eighties of last century many criminal lunatics were treated as criminals; they, too, swelled the numbers in the ghastly prison. But the most pitiful case of all was a man who had come from a family of low mentality. He had seen someone climbing out of his wife's bedroom window, and had fired and killed the intruder. Only then did he discover that he had shot his own father.

Percy Collingwood, one of the most skilful safe-breakers of his day, served a stretch at the Breakwater during this century. Once the superintendent challenged him to open a new safe in his office. Within ten minutes Collingwood had got the door open with his bare hands. Collingwood was a well-educated man, too intelligent to attempt an escape from prison; but he helped two other men to escape. In 1918 he was deported from the Union.

Convicts recaptured after a "break" usually received six months and twelve lashes with the cat-o'-nine-tails. In later years the maximum number of strokes was reduced to ten; but it was still a punishment that scarred a man for life. The "cat", with its nine knotted thongs of whipcord, was pickled in brine to stiffen it. The prisoner was stripped to the waist and fastened by the wrists to the triangle. Each stroke was delivered with all the force a muscular warder could apply.

It sounds like medieval torture, and indeed it is nothing less. The "cat" is still a legal instrument in South Africa, and a few learned judges who are unaware of the facts still include the "cat" in their sentences.

Yet some of the men on the breakwater even risked this torture for the sake of freedom. One "I.D.B." convict, a clever malingerer, contrived to be transferred to a convict hospital outside the Breakwater Prison. From there escape was a much simpler matter, and he succeeded in reaching England. He was doing well in an honest business of his own when he met one of his old companions of the breakwater. The man was a blackmailer. At last the victim refused to pay any further money, and so the blackmailer sent an anonymous letter to the police. The "I.D.B." man was arrested. He appealed against extradition, but failed. Back he had to go to the breakwater, the place six thousand miles away which he had never expected to see again.

Special cells were built in the prison in 1891 to hold men who had escaped so often that they could not be trusted in the ordinary wards. You can still see these steel and concrete cells in the prison quadrangle. The walls are fifteen inches thick. It would take dynamite to demolish them. And you can still read the messages scraped defiantly on the walls. "Three days cells for two big smokes – this won't break my heart."

"Frenchie" Ferroli was the desperado who caused the authorities to build these cells. He walked out of the Breakwater Prison in a warder's uniform, swinging a pair of handcuffs and nodding a greeting to the sentries at the gate. He was caught while being shaved in a Cape Town barber's shop six months later, and finally he was deported. That was the only final solution of the problem of men like Ferroli.

Then there were three men who made a skeleton key, entered a room where the warders kept their civilian clothes, and walked out boldly into the yard. It was Sunday, the visitors were there, and the three men were mistaken for visitors who had wandered into the wrong part of the prison. They were ordered out of the gates, and gladly they went.

A maniac named Harry Wilson was sent to the breakwater for sand-bagging an Indian trader in Natal. He was a tall, slim man who could not bear captivity; and he escaped from the train bringing him to Cape Town. He was recaptured, but he attempted to escape so often that his original sentence of two and a half years grew to six years; and he received, at various times, a total of fifty lashes with the "cat".

They put him in one of the special cells, handcuffed, leg-ironed and chained to a ring bolt in the wall. Still he fought for liberty. One day he threw his breakfast in the face of the warder who had brought it in, and tried to find keys to fit his handcuffs. He was so troublesome that at last the prison doctor certified him as insane, and he was transferred to the lunatic asylum on Robben Island. There he found a boat one day, rowed across to Sea Point, and left a simple message. "Good-bye – Harry." That was the last that was seen of Harry Wilson.

He was one of the small handful of men who were never recaptured. Another man hid in a train at the docks and steamed off to freedom. But the most remarkable escape was that of a soldier named Holloway.

Holloway had been sentenced to death for shooting his sergeant after he had been reprimanded on parade. When the sentence was commuted to life imprisonment he went to the Breakwater Prison. After only a few days there he was placed in a waiting-room with another man until the photographer arrived to take the routine portraits. Holloway was in prison garb, but the other man was not. They changed clothes. Although Holloway was seen climbing the prison walls the guards failed to overtake him. Every ship in the harbour was searched. The hunt went on for weeks, but Holloway had vanished completely.

Among the lesser punishments at the Breakwater Prison was the treadmill. This cruel and senseless invention appears to have been in use in the old Cape Town "tronk" as far back as 1824. It was always reserved for men. There were two treadmills at the Breakwater, and though the punishment was abolished in 1905, the rusty machinery is still there. I think it ought to remain there as a perpetual reminder of the evils that appear in prisons, and the need that still exists for a more humane system.

The first breakwater treadmill was installed in the eighteen-seventies, and it held two victims at a time. A larger one, capable of holding six men at once, was built in the eighteen-nineties. The convicts called it "grinding air". They were on a sort of moving staircase which began to revolve when they stepped on, and which had to be kept going at a steady pace. If the men slackened off the planks they stood upon came up and lacerated their shins.

The treadmill was the customary penalty for laziness and petty gaol offences. A man would spend the whole day, from nine to five, climbing these endless stairs, with only five minutes' rest every half hour. Three days was a "stretch", and then he would return to the stone quarries. Men who revolted against the punishment were handcuffed to a bar, and there they hung with every turn of the mill bruising their legs.

On a cold day, with a kind-hearted warder using the brake mercifully, the treadmill was tolerable. But in summer a sadistic warder would inflict torture by allowing the wheel to run too fast.

I knew another warder who went to the Breakwater Prison in 1900 and remained there for ten years. By the beginning of the century some of the abuses had been remedied; but it was still a grim place, dreaded by all evil-doers. This warder told me it was the most interesting prison in the world, for almost every nation in the world seemed to be represented among the inmates, and some notorious criminals were serving sentences there. One was "Cuban" Jackson, who was deported to the United States. There he linked up with the celebrated Chicago May, and soon afterwards received a life sentence for shooting Eddie Guerin.

The convicts had books, draughts and chess – and a slice of cake at Christmas. In later years the steam kitchen turned out wholesome meals. The men needed it, for they did a harder day's work than any other convicts in South Africa. The huge quarry where the oil tanks now stand in Table Bay Docks was hewn out of the rock by the hard-driven convicts decade after decade.

The warder declared that it was impossible to stop tobacco entering the prison. Friends of the convicts hid it in the quarry at night; and in spite of routine searches there were always leakages. A more puzzling side of prison life was the news service. Often the convicts discussed the details of important events before the warders had heard the news.

It was not until 1923 that the Breakwater Prison was finally evacuated. Then it became a native location, and a government research laboratory was built in the old punishment yard.

The warder who was there during the first ten years of the century had served in many gaols and prisons, and he made a remark about the Breakwater Prison that still lingers in my mind. "I won't say that it reformed men," he summed up. "But it was the only prison I knew which kept a lot of men straight afterwards simply because they were afraid to come back.[

often met them in the street, and they told me so. No man ever forgot a stretch at the Breakwater Prison."

Roeland Street gaol is one of those landmarks which might be demolished without a single protest reaching the newspapers. It was built, as far as I can discover, because the *Cape Argus* rightly denounced the overcrowding of the old "tronk" on the waterfront. Ever since December 1859, Roeland Street gaol has been occupied by erring humanity, and it looks as though there will be a centenary (without celebrations) in the not distant future.

It takes a long time to abolish a gaol. As far back as 1824 the waspish but merciful Dr. James Barry visited the "tronk" in the course of her duties and faithfully reported what she saw: "In a dungeon in that place I found Jacob Elliott with his thigh fractured, without crutches, without a bed or pillows, blankets dirty in the extreme, without a single comfort, and in short in such a state of misery that if he had not been under the special protection of Providence he could not have survived. He has not been provided with any sort of medical attention which is so much required in his helpless, painful state. Only once in twenty-four hours has the jailor taken him a bucket of water and the common prison allowance."

Dr. Barry removed this prisoner and another from the "tronk" and sent them to hospital. She also exposed the medical officers who had neglected their patients.

One day, perhaps, the obsolete Roeland Street gaol will vanish and be forgotten as completely as the "tronk." At the moment it is an unpleasant reality. It is an efficient place in one respect. During the first eighty years of Roeland Street you could have counted the number of escapes on the fingers of your hands. Munnik, the murderer, went to the gallows without revealing the details of his escape; but it is believed that he scaled the high gaol wall with a rope, held in position by someone waiting outside.

The old gaol's reputation as an Alcatraz suffered its worst blow in September 1946, when eleven coloured men, all awaiting trial, sawed through the bars of a second-storey cell with a hacksaw blade and dropped into a side street.

Roeland Street is more like a railway station than a prison. No one stays there for long, though the maximum sentence of six months may be monotonous enough for those who have to serve it. But a great number of those who pass through the heavy entrance doors are on their way somewhere else. The gaol receives the man with the shortest possible sentence, and also the man who has been condemned to death, and who must be taken to Pretoria for execution.

Some years ago a prison visitor assured me that he could show me round Roeland Street gaol. I was doubtful, but I went inside with him and waited in an office. After a delay the head warder arrived. He favoured me with the most penetrating stare I have ever known in my life, then refused to admit me. Some warders, I am told, boast truthfully that they have never forgotten a face; and I feel that mine is still neatly filed at the back of the head warder's mind, and that if I turn up at Roeland Street again he will recognise me and remark with satisfaction: "Ah, you've been here before." As it was, I went out with my curiosity unsatisfied.

Only once has the austere routine of Roeland Street been upset. That was during the 1918 influenza epidemic, when the place became a hospital, the warders became nurses, and one man in every ten died. A warder who was there at the time told me of a dramatic situation which arose. Two men were due to be hanged within a few days, a white man and a native. The warder gave them all the available medicines, a nourishing diet and brandy, in the effort to save their lives. All the time he was nursing them the paradox bulked large in his mind. The native recovered – just in time to be able to walk to the gallows. The white man died, to the intense relief of his relatives and friends.

There has not been an execution at Roeland Street since 1935. In that year the execution chambers in all the provincial gaols were dismantled, and every person condemned to death in the Union has been hanged at the Pretoria Central Prison. The executioners are now salaried government officials. In the past, in Cape Town and elsewhere, casual hangmen were employed; and the results were not always satisfactory. One former Cape Town hangman was a shopkeeper, and he chose his own assistants. A fee was paid for each execution. These men travelled about the Cape according to the demands of justice, and regaled inquisitive people in the dorp hotels with tales of their prowess with the rope. Nowadays a deep secrecy surrounds executions. Nothing but the bare announcement is made. But in earlier days everyone in the town soon heard every ghastly detail.

Just before the end of last century the Cape hangman was a sailor named James King. His predecessor in office had been a drunken wretch who had been dismissed for bungling several executions. King officiated at more than a hundred executions, and was given a pat on the back by one newspaper for the "neatness and despatch" with which he carried out his task. After one painful experience, when a condemned man put up a terrific fight on the scaffold, King insisted upon all murderers walking on to the drop in their stockinged feet.

The system of casual hangmen was abandoned because some of these men fortified themselves too liberally before the ordeal, and could not always be relied upon to appear sober at the right time. I was told of a gaol superintendent who had to carry out an execution himself in the absence of the hangman. More recently two executioners refused to travel to a distant gaol unless they were given higher pay.

Once I talked to a man who had shot his wife during a quarrel, and found himself in the condemned cell at Roeland Street. He said that when every second seemed to be taking him nearer the gallows he learned to appreciate the value of life.

The condemned cell, he told me, measured only eight feet by six and a brilliant overhead electric light was never switched off. He was given curry and rice every day as a sort of treat. On a Monday morning three weeks after he had been sentenced the warders informed him that a crowd had gathered in Roeland Street. They were waiting for the black flag to be run up, and the tolling of the gaol bell. But this man had petitioned the Governor-General for a reprieve. It was the first sentence to come before Lord Buxton for review. The sentence was commuted to life imprisonment, and after ten years on Robben Island he was released.

Almost within living memory executions were held in public in Cape Town. The very last, I believe, was in the eighteen-sixties, and the late Senator Munnik often related how he played truant to join the crowd at Gallows Hill.

Gallows Hill was a mound of earth, near the present Traffic Control Depot, off Ebenezer Road. This was the "outside place of execution" of Dutch East India Company's days, selected because the people living round about the old gallows at the Castle complained vehemently (and not unjustifiably) of the bodies left exposed after sentences had been carried out. No one lived near Gallows Hill at the time, and so the place became the scene of tortures that are hideous to recall. Only a little more than two centuries ago a white woman and her black paramour were marched there for execution. They had murdered the woman's husband, and the judge of the day had devised the deaths that he thought fitting. The woman was half-throttled; then, when she recovered consciousness, the strangling was completed. The man was thrust down on a sharp stake in a sitting position. He was given a bottle of arrack and left there until he died two days later.

The execution watched by Senator Munnik was performed mercifully. A cart drove up to Gallows Hill. It moved under the gallows, where the executioner was ready. He wore a tall, belltop hat, dark glasses and a long, white false beard – a disguise which did not baffle the crowd, for his identity was well known. The executioner pinioned the man, adjusted the noose, stepped off the cart and led the horse away. The drop was sufficient to cause instantaneous death.

Not all hangings, as I have already said, were done in that way. Campbell, a visitor to Cape Town, saw the hanging of a white farmer by two natives on Gallows Hill. "I do not recollect ever witnessing so horrible a transaction," he wrote. "I think these hangmen would have killed a dog or a pig with more gentleness and feeling." Natives were employed when, as often happened, no white man would volunteer for the task.

As recently as 1877 a case came before the Cape Parliament of a man who was cut down from the gallows before he was dead, and who began to recover while he was being placed in the coffin. The hangman, assailed by a legal doubt, refused to act again until a fresh death warrant had been made out. The victim solved the problem by dying a few hours later.

Great Men of the River

TODAY travellers on the superb inter-provincial tarmac highways pause on the Great North Road to view with wonder that great inland lake, the Hendrik Verwoerd Dam. South Africa's mightiest river has been harnessed by visionary engineers and shrewd governmental planners. But what does South Africa really know of the great Orange River as it flows from the Aughrabies Falls to the sea on the last 400 miles of its meanderings from its beginnings in Lesotho? A quarter of a century ago Lawrence G. Green, for whom the Orange River held infinite fascination, uncovered many dramas of the past regarding what he described as "the river of adventure that flows below the Aughrabies Falls".

"These last bends," he wrote in a splendid chapter in *To The River's End*, "and loops, the last four hundred miles between the falls and the sea; these are the four corners where the march of the centuries has left few signs. Here are the isolated people, the weird canyons, the parts so lonely that even the prospectors have not yet scratched the rocks."

Time has not aged this chapter. Some of the dominating – and no doubt domineering characters whom Green interviewed on his roamings along the banks of the river must have passed on. But mighty men, men such as the now legendary Weidner of Goodhouse might have drifted into limbo but for Lawrence Green's determination to grant them literary immortality.

Since the days just after World War II when Green travelled on rough and dusty roads to obtain material for one of his best books the often icy fingers of progress have touched some aspects of his Orange River narrative. At the Aughrabies Falls there are now tarred roads, picnic places and an hotel. But mostly the Orange River, the great artery of the South African society, still flows from Aughrabies through remote country on which the spirits of the great characters and bold prospectors immortalised by Lawrence G. Green's gaze – or perhaps frown down.

I have not attempted to modernise *The Lonely River*. To do so would break the spell of Green's brilliant writing. All the reader need remember is that Green wrote this chapter in 1948. Little vital has happened since.

CHAPTER VI

THE LONELY RIVER

You who have only crossed the Orange River by train have no idea of the unknown river, the river of adventure that flows below the Aughrabies Falls.

These last bends and loops in the great trench, the last four hundred miles between the falls and the sea; these are the far corners where the march of the centuries has left few signs. Here are the most isolated people, the weird canyons, the parts so lonely that even the prospectors have not yet scratched the rocks.

Along these river banks, too, are the diamond terraces, the gold reefs and beryl and scheelite deposits, the copper mines abandoned after years of toil. This is the Orange River of sun and solitude, where people stagger under the dead weight of the summer heat. There is nothing in Africa to match the furnace of this valley at noon. Yet it is a river of rare dawns and bright moonlights; and I am thankful that I have slept beside it in the open and seen the first amber light upon the water, and felt the wind coming as hot on the face as the breath of a leopard. This is the wild river, the land of odd and reckless characters. Life has often been dangerous here; but life can be good, too, you can relish your food and your drinks, the wild duck you shot and the beer you have cooled in the canvas water bag.

Below the falls there are no more irrigation settlements on the grand scale. Nearly everywhere the river runs to waste. Mr. A. D. Lewis, the former director of irrigation, expressed this disastrous fact in a memorable report:

"There can hardly be a true South African, and certainly no irrigation engineer, with soul so dead that he can contemplate our greatest river tearing down to the ocean through a vast area of country which is thirsting for water, without feeling that some great effort should be made to design and carry out irrigation works for the Orange River which would rival those famous works of other great rivers of the world – Ganges, Indus, Nile, Colorado."

Mr. Lewis pointed out, however, that the low-water flow of the Orange comes from the high Drakensberg country, where there is no permanent snow on the mountains of the headwaters. Thus in the critical spring months the river dwindles. "The Orange tears steeply down in a rocky valley," emphasised Mr. Lewis. "It has always been a powerful eroder, never a builder of lands." The alluvial soil consists of narrow patches and strips, or islands which are swamped by floods.

There is enough water in the Orange to irrigate a million acres, but no way has yet been found of taking out furrows large enough to transform Bushmanland into a garden. Only here and there do you find small areas where the levels and the soil are favourable.

One successful small scheme which I visited is at Onseepkans, about thirty miles north of Pofadder. It was called Orangeville when the enterprise started in 1916; but the settlers preferred the the old Hottentot name, meaning "the drinking place for cattle."

Japie Lutz of Upington, that redoubtable planner of furrows, took a hand in the work. Now there are about sixty plot-holders (each man with about six morgen), and the settlement runs along the valley for seven miles. Mr. L. J. Collyer, the village storekeeper, formerly a member of the Cape Mounted Police, told me about the prosperity of Onseepkans.

"Our oranges can compete in any market in the world," declared Mr. Collyer. Between the wars, Onseepkans sent its navel oranges direct to England. All the tropical fruits grow well there, especially paw-paws and bananas. Wheat and melons are important crops; peas and table-grapes flourish. You get two crops of peas a year in the river silt, and in a good year a settler can make a few acres yield a profit of £1,000 after paying all expenses.

An aged Hottentot entered the store while Mr. Collyer was praising the fertility of Onseepkans. He wanted a bottle of buchu essence, favourite country remedy for pain and cramp in the stomach. Mr. Collyer keeps a register, however, and rations out this strong medicine. It contains a high percentage of alcohol.

Onseepkans, remote though it is, ranks as an official "port of entry" from South West Africa into the Union. You can have your car taken across the river in a rusty iron boat, a precarious voyage at the best of times. The people want a bridge, and they even talk hopefully of a railway line that will cross the river at Onseepkans and bring Windhoek nearly four hundred miles closer to Cape Town. At present the farm produce goes nine-five miles by road to railhead at Kakamas. Mr. Collyer knows the tracks through Bushmanland, however, and drives from Onseepkans to Cape Town, 440 miles, in a day.

During great floods the water comes almost to the door of Mr. Collyer's store. The last time that happened was in 1924, a year after he had settled at Onseepkans. As a contrast, the river dried up in 1945, and left some of the fish to decompose too close for Mr. Collyer's comfort. There had been no rain worth mentioning for six years at the time of my visit; but fortunately Onseepkans does not depend on rain. The summer heat is the dry 120 degree heat of the Orange River valley; but Onseepkans is healthy in spite of it. If anyone needs a doctor urgently, it means a telephone call to Kenhardt, 160 miles away.

Like most of the settlements in the Orange River canyon, Onseepkans has a dramatic approach. I remember a forest of kokerbooms in the sand; the koppies piled loosely with sun-baked stones; the steenbok that stood on a rock to see the car pass; and then the school and buildings of the Roman Catholic mission beside the river.

Onseepkans makes a pleasant picture indeed in the memory. Mr. Collyer putting crushed peach stones into a ten gallon cask to clear the silt-laden river water for drinking. Glossy black karakul skins drying on their frames. The fragrance of grapefruit orchards and the restful stretches of lucerne. Here at least the river does not run to waste.

Most daring of all Orange River irrigation efforts are the "one man" schemes to capture enough of the rushing waters to cultivate small patches of desert. One such place is Abbassas, not far to the east of Goodhouse, though a long detour has to be made from the main road to reach it.

Mr. H. J. C. Krapohl, the surveyor who was at work in Bushmanland forty years ago, retired to Abbassas. I am told that he selected the place for health reasons; a wise choice, for he was still alive at the age of eighty-nine when I last heard of him.

It is intensely hot at Abbassas. No rain fell there between the years 1925 and 1932. Nevertheless, Krapohl lived at Abbassas for nearly thirty years. He busied himself with wagon-making, an occupation he preferred to surveying. Krapohl was a famous botanist, and many succulents bear his name. He also grew dates, which are only now being planted on a large scale along the Orange River.

The author Rider Haggard is credited with introducing the date palm to the dry districts bordering the river. Roman Catholic missionaries were the first to adopt the idea, and there are many fine date palms at Pella and other missions.

One flourishing grove of palms not far from Abbassas owes its origin to a small military detachment stationed on the frontier at the outbreak of the 1914-1918 War. A soldier received a packet of dates in a Christmas parcel. He threw the stones away, and left to posterity a legacy of fruit and shade of which he is probably unaware. Eighty trees now yield an annual crop of two tons.

Weidner of Goodhouse – if you have never heard those names coupled then you know nothing of the Orange River.

But now, I hope, you have realised that this journey is something more than a search for adventure along the frontier. To find people in a desert is not enough. I want to know how men live on happily in isolation year after year. The life of Weidner of Goodhouse is the key to something elusive which, all too often, is apt to vanish in shimmering waves of heat.

Goodhouse is one of those places which always makes me wish I could find leisure to take up painting. In the evening light there is a contrast between the hot mountains, the sand, the sun-scorched rocks and the river greenery, a scene that has never been put on canvas. I should like to be the first to paint the spirit of Goodhouse, a picture which would be far more than a landscape. And if I had the brush of a Neville Lewis I would persuade Mr. Carl Weidner to sit for a portrait. Those two pictures would decorate the walls of my country cottage and inspire me on empty days; for I have always found at Goodhouse something which is missing in the largest cities.

Weidner of Goodhouse is not physically an heroic figure, but he lives up to his motto. *Alis Volat Propiis* – "on his own wings he flies." Seventy-eight when last I called on him; and still working and planning for the future. One of the strongest characters I have ever met; hospitable to a degree, infinitely resourceful, and as original in his own way of thinking as George Bernard Shaw. A visionary who has spent most of his life with burning deserts all round him. If you passed through Goodhouse with only a glance at this short, rotund man with the benevolent face, then you were a victim of your own stupid haste and you lost an experience.

He was born at Berncastler on the Moselle, and even as a schoolboy his palate had developed so that he was called into the cellars to taste the famous Berncastler Doktor. In his youth he moved into Belgium and found his first job at the Antwerp Town Hall. It had something to do with draining the polders, the low country reclaimed from the sea; and young Weidner sailed the Scheldt happily in a small boat, opening and closing the drains at the right moments. This work taught him the elements of irrigation, which later played a great part in his career.

Next he was offered work in a completely waterless place, the newly-founded German settlement of Angra Pequena in South West Africa. He built the first four solid houses there in 1893. Already the independent character of the man was taking shape. He fell out with a Prussian officer and was, as he told me himself, "forcibly removed". Weidner set out into the interior in an ox-wagon with two German scientists, a botanist and a geologist. He saw Lake Ngami, "a mere puddle", and also outspanned for the first time beside the Orange River at a drift which the Hottentots called Gu-daos, the "sheep ford". Both the scientists died of fever on this journey. Weidner proofed himself with rum and survived.

Gu-daos has been changed to Goodhouse on all maps. You drive through kloof after kloof, always in the sand tracks, and at last there is Goodhouse . . . and Weidner. Not so long ago the motor journey was an ordeal.

Northbound, you had to climb a hill called Kooisabees, a hill of red sand where the sun flayed you in summer and the heavy sand threatened to bring an end to your motoring. One moment's hesitation was fatal. You had to grind through it, painfully, using an instinct that is higher than skill. Or else you stuck in the sand on Kooisabees hill and hoped that one of Mr. Weidner's trucks would come and pull you out.

Southbound, there was the dead valley of the Aub River, which may flow once in a quarter of a century. Here, too, in the days before balloon tyres it was fatal to slow down. The radiator boiled and you had to let it boil.

Between these two deserts lives Weidner . . . and loves it. But it was years after the ill-fated journey that he settled there. He was in Cape Town, taking out options on the Cape Flats and planning to build a canal linking Salt River with False Bay. After that he went ostrich farming at Oudtshoorn; and as a diversion he agreed to edit the *Mossel Bay Advertiser*. For two years he brought out the newspaper every week, dashing away from his farm on a motor-cycle, hurrying back to clip the ostrich feathers.

The old settled districts could not hold Carl Weidner for long. In 1910 he was back on the Orange River, looking for farms where ostriches would flourish. He went to London, raised £119,000 for the venture, and bought farms along the river for the company – including Goodhouse. On the north bank of the river, opposite Goodhouse, he bought a farm called Haakiesdoorn from a firm called South African Territories Ltd. The agent who sold him the farm was a man with short-cropped hair, bristling moustache and spectacles. His name was Alexander Scotland, and he looked exactly like a German. In fact he was the famous British intelligence officer who served for years in the German Army, joined the German General Staff during the 1914-1918 War; and was smuggled into Germany again in 1939 to resume his perilous occupation – again on the German General Staff. You may remember that Scotland gave evidence at the trial of Kesselring in Venice. Scotland, by the way, is a nephew of George Bernard Shaw.

Weidner, of course, knew nothing of all this until recently. Weidner deplores all wars, and holds aloof from all such human folly in the splendid isolation of Goodhouse.

As a financier before the 1914-1918 War, Weidner was almost a success. He returned to Luderitz (his Prussian enemy having departed) and secured a whaling concession. Then he went to Germany to find capital; for it was laid down that the whaling company must be German. He interviewed Ballin, the shipping magnate, friend of the Kaiser; and even reached Solf, the German Colonial Secretary. Again the money was forthcoming – £50,000 for whaling along the coast of South West Africa. Germany needed whale oil to convert into explosives. The company declared a fifteen percent dividend on the first year's working. In 1913 Weidner settled at Goodhouse to develop the ostrich and citrus farms on behalf of the London company. He looked like becoming a millionaire.

"War came and finished my career as a company promoter," Weidner told me with his philosophic laugh. "The whalers were seized by the British Government – and the market for ostrich feathers collapsed. I had £8,000 due to me from the whaling, and in the end I got £284. The war anchored me firmly in the desert at Goodhouse."

Then he revealed one of his secrets, one which has a wide application. "If you live in a desert there is only one thing to do," declared Weidner. "You must turn it into an oasis."

Misfortunes with money he dismissed lightly. "What is lost is lost. As long as I have enough I do not care. And what lovely times I have had . . ."

I had known Weidner (and his beer-cooling apparatus) for a long time before he revealed another phase in his character. After the 1894 wagon trek, it seems, he sat down one day and worked out the amount of alcohol he had consumed in his life. Still in his twenties, he estimated that he had taken as much as an ordinary man would drink in twenty years. So for the next twenty years, until 1914, he remained a teetotaler. Having worked off these liquid arrears he poured himself out a glass of beer; and he still enjoys his moderate daily allowance.

It was in April, 1913, that Weidner settled down to create his oasis at Goodhouse. He had to take everything with him. Before leaving Cape Town he bought harness; at Paarl he found a cape cart, and he selected the horses at Klapmuts. Elsewhere on the road he bought a market cart, Clanwilliam provided more horses, and at Van Rhynsdorp he added a wagon and mules to his cavalcade. Weidner's trek to Goodhouse gave work to many a farrier and put money into the pockets of wayside farmers with forage to sell. After weeks on the road he reached the river bank and made his home there. Goodhouse gave him complete happiness for many, many years.

He brought up the river water with a crude oil pump, and soon had more than a hundred morgen under irrigation – a hundred morgen of orange and grape-fruit trees, vines, pawpaws, mangoes. The government would not build a road to Goodhouse, so Weidner cut his own track and sign-posted it. When prices of everyday commodities rose after 1914-1918 War, he opened a store on his farm and sold the necessities to his labourers at pre-war prices. Abraham Morris, the Hottentot leader, was among his workmen.

Not long after his arrival he built the pont which has carried so many thousands of travellers over the Orange River. One day the pont sank, and an angry motorist stormed into Weidner's homestead.

"How far did you get before it sank?" inquired Weidner politely.

"Midstream – my car's in the middle of the river," raved the motorist.

"Ah, midstream," exclained Weidner. "Then I'll tell you what – you pay only half price."

Weidner has his own eccentric sense of humour. He loved political discussions, and corresponded with many politicians. General Hertzog alone he regarded with admiration, and they exchanged Christmas cards for years.

There was once a Minister of Mines for whom Weidner had nothing but contempt. After some difference of opinion over prospecting rights, Weidner wrote a letter in which he compared the offending minister with a baboon. The minister's secretary replied, pointing out that the phrase was objectionable. Weidner retaliated by giving a pet baboon the name of the Minister of Mines. For months visitors heard the story, and then Weidner would shout the name and the baboon would come leaping out of its box.

A former Governor General of the Union visited the Warmbad district of South West Africa, territory of the Bondelswart Hottentots, many years ago. This was before the Bondelswart rising in 1922, and the Governor-General made a speech which filled the Hottentots with pride. At the end of the speech the Bondelswart brass band played a tune which all the members knew, and which seemed to them appropriate. It was "Deutschland uber Alles". And when Weidner heard the details of the speech he wrote a letter applying for naturalisation as a Bondelswart.

Weidner once travelled to Cape Town to ask the Minister of Railways for a line to Goodhouse. He put the case eloquently and finished by expressing the pious hope that he would see the railway built before he died. "That depends on when you choose to die," remarked the Minister of Railways. The line has not been built yet, and that was one of the rare occasions on which Weidner did not have the last word.

Ten years ago I found Weidner still eagerly absorbing the political columns of the newspapers; but he confided to me that he had become "less cantankerous" in politics. This was a notable transformation. I learnt to respect his political forecasts, however, and I know that he has in his possession a letter from a former Prime Minister of the Union sadly admitting the accuracy of one of Weidner's shrewdest prophecies. When I was last at Goodhouse in 1947, Weidner was still denouncing certain political figures, though less bitterly than he had done in the past.

"It's hard to find anyone high up with a sense of humour," he remarked. "If there had been one in Europe, just one, there would have been no war."

Weidner's own sense of humour has startled many an impostor. A prospector came to Goodhouse with a marvellous sample of gold quartz, and expected Weidner to be deeply impressed.

Weidner picked up the heavy nugget and stared at it. "Gold

all right," he said. "In fact, I can still see the King's face on it."

Caught off his guard, the prospector grabbed the nugget and gazed anxiously at the specks of gold. Later he became indignant and threatened an action for defamation. Weidner was not alarmed, and he heard no more of it.

Goodhouse is known to the general public, of course, not as an oasis but as the hottest spot in South Africa. For many years Weidner was the official weather recorder there; and he published his views on the climate in a famous pamphlet in which he attacked the Schwarz rain-making scheme. One night, after a magnificent dinner of roast goose, he explained to me why Goodhouse is so hot.

Weidner always has a hearty laugh when the Cape Town newspapers report a heat wave with a maximum temperature of ninety-eight degrees. He looks at his Stevenson screen and finds a day temperature of 114 degrees (or more), with ninety-eight in the evening.

Goodhouse is only about six hundred feet above sea level. North and south, however, the land rises sharply to three thousand feet; so that the low river forms and air pocket – a hot-air trap – from which there is seldom any release. Cool sea breezes nearly always pass over Goodhouse. Fortunately the super-heated Goodhouse air is intensely dry; otherwise the climate would be intolerable.

The hot Goodhouse air often rises in the later afternoon and battles with cooler down-draughts. A westerly wind springs up as a result, sometimes amounting to a gale. At sundown the wind slackens, and a gentle breeze may reduce the temperature to seventy-four degrees. Goodhouse accepts this mercy gratefully – and sleeps well. Weidner infinitely prefers the dry, hot weather to the moist, cloudy days when the thermometer remains obstinately at ninety-eight.

Although Goodhouse is ninety miles from the sea (in a direct line), the sea exerts its influence even on this distant furnace in the Orange River valley. When fog banks appear on the western horizon, the temperature drops thirty-five degrees within a few hours.

The pay of an official weather observer, I must add, is five shillings a month. Weidner faithfully recorded one of the weirdest climates in the world for this reward. He resents any suggestion that there are hotter places in Africa; he has temperatures at his finger tips and I would not care to debate the matter with him. Many an opponent has been floored by the fact that the thermometer at Goodhouse, night after night, has registered ninety-five degrees.

Only once has the heat driven Weidner away from Goodhouse. That was in the burning February of 1945, when the mean maximum was 109 degrees and when throughout one ghastly night, the temperature remained at 102 degrees.

Lambs and calves were dying in the heat. Cattle were losing their hooves in the hot sand. Only then did Weidner decide to escape, taking his thermometer with him. He found sanctuary in what he called a "Namaqualand refrigerator" – a four-roomed mat house at the foot of the Kamiesberg within twenty miles of the sea. "This type of construction surpasses anything mechanical air-conditioning could produce – an ideal abode for asthmatics, chest sufferers and people with nervous breakdowns," Weidner wrote to me. "Yet, to be honest, I am beginning to long for a little more sizzling in my old frying-pan."

One of Weidner's greatest friends was Fillis, the circus proprietor. Fillis once offered Weidner a job as a clown; and I believe he thought seriously of taking it. Always a jolly man, with the right build, he would have kept his audience roaring in the big tent.

I was on my way to Goodhouse in 1947 when I asked someone whether he had seen Weidner recently. The man shook his head. "I heard he was dead – getting on in years, you know, and he must be dead by now."

This disturbed me, though I could hardly believe it. Then I drove down the long, sandy approach to Goodhouse and steered the car cautiously on to the little pont. As the Hottentots hauled the pont across the river I was relieved to see the familiar, portly figure reclining under a reed shelter on the north bank. His wife had died a few years before – a heavy blow – and he had sold the famous Goodhouse farm. But he was still Weidner of Goodhouse to all who knew him, though he was building up a new estate at Haakiesdoorn, exactly opposite his old home.

Seventy-eight, and still full of plans, and the energy to carry them out. He talked to me of the old days in Luderitz, and the irrigation canal that would turn Haakiesdoorn into a paradise. Weidner was constructing a new pont of welded metal, capable of carrying fifteen tons across the river. After that, he wanted to drift down the Orange River in a flat-bottomed boat from Goodhouse to the sea, taking photographs as he went.

"*Alis Volat Propiis.*" That fits him better than his dark suit. He talks of leaving Haakiesdoorn and ending his days on Tristan da Cunha. If he did, it would be a different island; for Weidner leaves the mark of his personality on a place. I cannot think of him living out of sight of his beloved Goodhouse. "The heat suits me," he remarked before I left. That heat would knock out men half Weidner's age. But his secret is not to be found in the climate, for Weidner would have mastered the Arctic.

I think that when Weidner first settled at Goodhouse he realised that it is impossible to live in two worlds at once. Goodhouse became his world, and he made it a comfortable and fruitful world. The other world came to his door often enough. He listened to thousands of travellers and remained secure in his own philosophy. I wish there were more Weidners in this world, for he achieved more in his own, hot little world than the statesmen have done with all their wide horizons.

Not far west of Goodhouse is Vioolsdrift, the last irrigation scheme on the river. Set among the mountains you come upon pockets of rich soil here and there for twenty miles. It was in 1932 that a band of white road-workers, despairing of life on relief schemes at 3s. 6d. a day, decided to build their own water furrow at Vioolsdrift.

Following the earlier example of Cannon Island, they did not approach the government, but simply set to work. First they built hartbeeshuisies for their wives and families. Then, having cut up the irrigable land into erven to their own satisfaction, the men returned to road making to raise capital for the enterprise.

It was a brave idea. While the men worked on the official roads, the women and children made a precipitous road of their own to the site where the Vioolsdrift dam was to stand. Whenever possible the men joined them and blasted the long irrigation furrow out of the rock. All this, mark you, without proper capital or skilled assistance.

Here, as at Cannon Island, government officials were so deeply impressed by the initiative of the settlers that the people of Vioolsdrift were allowed to remain on the land they had seized. Money was voted for a complete scheme – £75,000 which grew to £114,000 before the work was finished.

I should like to provide a happy ending for this story of toil in the wilderness. Unfortunately, as the years passed, it became apparent that Vioolsdrift was a fiasco. Experts visited the place and found too many people on the tiny plots. The settlers, cut off in that distant valley, had no markets and no reasonable transport facilities. The government decided that it would be a waste of public money to go on bolstering up a settlement without prospects.

So the settlers who started work with such high hopes are drifting away from Viooldrift. And the muddy, intractable river tears past the abandoned erven on its remorseless journey.

When Mr. A. D. Lewis explored the course of the lower Orange River in 1912 he did not encounter a single white man between Raman's Drift and the sea. He started from Pella intending to ride on horseback. The police advised him to walk, with Hottentots as carriers; they said it would be impossible to ride continuously along the river bank, and they were right.

Lewis travelled on foot during the most severe December heat for half a century. The pace was too fast for the Hottentots; their velskoens wore out, and Lewis had to bribe them with tea and tobacco. Even then he had to engage fresh carriers whenever he came to Hottentot huts. The carriers knew only their own language, and Lewis had to make signs. He had food for a fortnight, and he was determined to follow the river down to the ocean.

Sometimes he was able to hire a riding ox, but most of the time he plodded along the edge of the water on foot. Often the day's march included climbing; for he came to grey-topped mountains rising sheer from the river for several thousand feet. Granite terraces revealed bands of bright red, yellow, green and black minerals – interesting specimens for a man with a scientific training if only the temperature had not remained steadily above the hundred mark.

Fresh leopard spoor was common enough. At one place some large animal rushed towards Lewis and his party from the river; they could hear tree branches crackling, but they never saw the animal. The carriers dropped their loads and ran up the mountainside. When they returned, they told Lewis a hippo had charged them. Lewis doubted it, though there were still hippos in the river.

At Aussenkehr he found the ruins of an early irrigation scheme with a queer story. Two brothers named Petersen, owners of the Crocodile Hotel in Liverpool in 1887, had sold their business and settled in this incredibly remote spot. One of the Petersens was a consumptive, and his main object was the recovery of his health. Why he should have selected Aussenkehr, an almost unheard-of spot in the no-man's land of the Cape frontier, remains a mystery. The brothers hauled a steam engine and pumping machinery by ox-wagon from Port Nolloth to Aussenkehr; and for ten years they produced good crops of fruit and vegetables. Then the consumptive died. A mechanic named Nipper, who had been employed by the Petersens, decided to take over the enterprise, but he went bankrupt. Then a retired policeman, Price, went to live at Aussenkehr. Price departed, and from the beginning of this century, I believe, Aussenkehr has seen only occasional visitors – police, prospectors and Hottentots. It is a beautiful stretch of the river, an ideal place for an extreme isolationist.

Only when Lewis approached Sendeling's Drift did he find the Orange River emerging finally from the mountains and entering the coastal plains.

The prospectors know the Orange River canyons better than any other travellers. The late Mr. S. Rabinowitz of Steinkopf a prospector almost up to the day of his death in 1947, often told me of the journeys he made in the silent world of the lonely river; and of his sufferings when supplies ran short and the heat was a burden.

"King Solomon of the Richtersveld," they called Rabinowitz He first trekked into that wilderness with pack-donkeys in 1905 meeting only the poverty-stricken Hottentots, the people who live on goats, dassies and wild honey. Over the border the Germans were at war with the Hottentots. At that time Rabinowitz often crossed the river on trading expeditions; and one day he rode to the nearest German garrison and sold a wagon-load of oats.

As he was returning to the river that night, he and his Hottentot guide entered a deep kloof. "There are men in the kloof", whispered the Hottentot. "The horses know there are men here."

Rabinowitz could see no one in the moonlight. Next day, however, a German patrol was ambushed and wiped out by the Hottentots in that kloof. Long afterwards the Hottentot leader told Rabinowitz that the white blaze on his horse's head saved him in the kloof. They were just going to fire when they recognised him.

That was Rabinowitz's narrowest escape, though he had another when his wagon skidded on the steep track up Hell's Kloof in the Richtersveld. He fell clear, but wagon and donkeys were hurled down the mountainside. The grim scene is still called Rabie's Fall by the Hottentots.

Rabinowitz made many expeditions in search of the legendary "mountain of copper" near the Orange River. Once during the 1914-1918 War, when copper was £130 a ton, a Bushman offered to lead him to the spot. After days in the mountains they met another Bushman. Next morning the guide informed Rabinowitz that he had changed his mind and decided to keep the secret of the "copper mountain." Rabinowitz argued with the Bushmen, made them tempting offers of tobacco; but he had wasted his time. He always firmly believed the legend. And indeed, there is a huge boulder of pure copper at Kuboos in the Richtersveld, too large to move. This is regarded by prospectors as a signpost to the copper mountain which no one has ever found. Tap the boulder with a hammer, and it rings like a bell.

Moderate wealth came Rabinowitz's way in 1926, as a result of a queer experience that stuck in his mind. Thirteen years previously he was out riding near the Orange River mouth when his horse plunged into quicksands on the south bank. Rabinowitz fell spread-eagled on the sand; but he still had his sjambok and he lashed the horse until it emerged. He could not mount it, so he grasped the tail and was pulled to safety.

Rabinowitz rode southwards along the coast until he came to the dunes known as Buchuberg. There he rested and hung out his clothes to dry. While lying there he noticed indications of diamondiferous gravel. He did not follow the clue at the time; but in 1926 he went back and prospected the area thoroughly. Before long he found one of the fossilised oyster shells which are typical of the rich Namaqualand deposits. There was something better than a pearl in that oyster – a diamond. Rabinowitz and his partners might have become millionaires if they had worked their claims themselves. Instead, they sold to Dr. Hans Merensky. I believe Rabinowitz's share ran into many thousands of pounds.

He bought three farms in South West Africa, 65,000 morgen altogether near Karasburg, and stocked them with four thousand karakul sheep. "Black diamonds are better than ordinary diamonds," he declared. He sold the store at Steinkopf, where he had lived for many years between prospecting trips. And he brought his wife and family to live in Cape Town.

I used to meet Rabinowitz on the seafront at Sea Point occasionally, and he seemed restless. A world tour failed to reconcile him to city life. In 1937 he returned to the Richtersveld. He had a scheelite mine within sight of the river, and he tunnelled into a mountainside to bring out the tungsten ore. Rabinowitz was happy again in the Orange River heat. When he died he was prospecting for diamonds again by special permit near the Namaqualand coast. He was a man who had endured great hardships, but who still preferred life in the open.

Heyes was another prospector who knew the Richtersveld from end to end. He was famous for the journeys he made on foot in that area, covering great distances in a day when there was no other way of reaching water. I remember his seamed, suntanned face, and the way his blue eyes would shine when he spoke of the riches waiting to be uncovered.

Ernest Heyes started his career as a prospector early this century, trekking along the Molopo with "Scotty" Smith. He was at Luderitz in the early days of the diamond discovery. Then he drifted south to the Richtersveld and spent years in

THE LONELY RIVER

the territory to which the old missionary Richter had given his name.

One of the stories Heyes told me emphasised the loneliness of the Richtersveld. Heyes reached the Orange River at a shallow part and saw a man wading towards him from the South-West African side – a young policeman, unkempt and in distress.

The constable told Heyes that he had reached the verge of insanity. His two companions at the outpost had gone off on duty, and he had been entirely alone for two months. He had not seen a white man during that time. His rations were almost exhausted; in fact, he had nothing left but a little mealie meal. As a result of this experience, he said, he had decided to buy his discharge.

In 1925 Heyes explored the "Wondergat," the mysterious cavern on a koppie near Anniesfontein, three miles south of the Orange River. He took a winch and wire cable to the spot, and was lowered into the darkness.

The cavern, I may say, is avoided by the Hottentots. It would be a danger spot if it was not so remote; for the hole is about twelve feet in diameter, it goes straight down, and the baked earth round the edge crumbles underfoot. The Hottentots call the hole "Heiji Eibib," and they say it is a tunnel leading to the river, inhabited by white bats and various ferocious monsters. Long ago, according to Hottentot legend, fire and smoke came out of the earth and the cavern was formed by this eruption.

Scientists do not accept this volcanic explanation, for there is no lava anywhere near the entrance. Water action seems improbable, though it may have been the "eye" of a spring in the far-off days when this desert was a garden. You can hear a rumbling noise near the mouth of the "Wondergat." Sulphur and mica are found close by.

Heyes went down for about sixty feet and landed on a ledge. The bats that flew in his face were the ordinary brown specimens. There were none of the "stones that sparkle like fire," which the Hottentots had assured him he would find if he survived the anger of the monsters. He noticed tunnels leading out of the shaft, but he could not reach them with the wire cable restricting his movements. The air smelt sulphurous. Heyes gave the signal, and returned to daylight with only a sample of guano to show for his exertions.

The "Wondergat" was explored again in August, 1947, when the Diamond Detective Department in Namaqualand were following every clue in an effort to round up diamond smugglers. They received information that the source of one rich haul was the "Wondergat." Sergeants de Kock and Le Roux went to the spot with a coloured constable; and the constable volunteered to descend with an electric torch and see what he could find. Like Heyes, the constable was unable to reach the bottom. The heat was intense, the bats that Heyes encountered were still there, and there were no diamonds. Take a long wire with you if you go to the "Wondergat."

I am glad that the name of Cornell is now to be found on the map of the Richtersveld, for this poet and prospector made many valuable geological discoveries in the great bend of the river. Those who followed profited by the written information he left. Cornell's Berg in the Richtersveld is his memorial.

Oldest of all the Richtersveld prospectors was Mr. William Carstens of Port Nolloth, who is still alive at the age of ninety-one. In another work I have described how Carstens and his sons discovered the first diamonds in Namaqualand. In 1892 a Hottentot brought a few small nuggets of gold into Port Nolloth. Soon afterwards a doctor who had been out vaccinating the Hottentots returned with the news that he had seen two fair-sized nuggets in the possession of a chief known as Ou Links. "There must be mountains of gold in the Richtersveld," said the doctor.

Carstens decided to trace the gold to its source. After a long wagon trek he found Ou Links and gave him a sovereign apiece for the nuggets. Then he asked him to reveal the position of the gold. "If I find enough gold I will build you a proper church," Mr. Carstens promised.

After much hard travelling, however, it appeared that Ou Links had no intention of giving the secret away. A young Hottentot crept up to Carstens one night and offered to guide him to the right place. The Hottentot displayed a lump of quartz and yellow mica which, he said, had come from the source of the gold.

Carstens was led up a creek about twenty miles from the Orange River. "Within a few minutes," he told me, "I had picked up a nugget the size of my thumb from the blue shale."

Some weeks later he returned to the spot with the magistrate to verify the discovery, and a "cradle" for washing gold. The magistrate panned eight sacks before he found a "colour"; then two nuggets came to light. Carstens recovered enough gold to make two rings for his wife. The magistrate, however, decided not to proclaim the area as a diggings – he considered it too remote and waterless.

Was this the real source of the Hottentots' nuggets? It is doubtful. Indications of gold have been found in other parts of the Richtersveld since then. Rabinowitz traced a gold reef; and there were rumours at one time that Germans had crossed the river and were taking gold back with them.

The most persistent search for gold in this area was made by Mr. Thomas Billingham, a Yorkshireman. He had been prospecting for seven years when I met him there, and he had just sunk three shafts to the north of Kuboos, over the mountains.

"Wild country – but a treasure house of wealth," declared Billingham. "I have seen leopard spoors right up to the labourers' huts. The boys will not stay there without guns. Scorpions, too; they are always getting bitten by scorpions. But it is not a bad place. There is a fine large spring of water, and I can grow all sorts of vegetables in my garden."

Billingham and his assistant were two of the three white men in the area at that time, and there was some doubt about the third. It was said that he was a Swede, an old sailorman who had come inland and had made his home in a cave in the face of a cliff near the river. Over seventy, according to the Hottentots, and living on a diet of baboons and insects. A cave man with long hair and a red-grey beard, shunning civilisation.

Wherever you go along the more remote parts of the Orange River you will hear tales of the Great Snake. At first I regarded it as folklore. Now I have gathered so much evidence from reliable people that I believe the Great Snake is something more than legend and imagination.

The Rev. H. C. V. Leibbrandt, first Keeper of the Archives in Cape Town, mentioned a personal experience with the Great Snake. He was brought up on the banks of the river, and natives told him of the snake and its weird powers. Once he was shown a spot where, according to the natives, the snake had been resting among the reeds. "There was a clear impression of a great body, for the reeds had been flattened," recorded Leibbrandt. "However, there were still elephants in those parts, and they may have been responsible."

The powers of the snake, I may add, include a mysterious influence over all who behold it. Those who express disbelief suffer ill-health or death; while those who respect the snake can reckon on good fortune – especially along the river diamond diggings. The snake can read your thoughts and entice you into the water. Its breath knocks a man down yards away.

So much for the fairy story aspect. Now here is the evidence of Mr. G. A. Kinnear, a general dealer who claimed to have seen the snake in 1899, while on a trading journey in the Upington area. He bartered his goods for sheep, goats and skins; and brought the stock across the river in a flat-bottomed ferry boat.

"The boat had just been fully loaded with goats and was about ten yards from the bank when the head of a monstrous serpent emerged from the stream," declared Mr. Kinnear. "The head, in which were set two large blinking eyes, was from seven to eight inches in width, and the eight to ten feet of body it reared out of the water could only have been about a quarter of its length. Only for an instant did its head appear before it dived again. I waited in suspense for its reappearance as I naturally expected it would make for the boat, but that was the last I saw of it. Hendrik, the boatman, was terror-stricken, and the other natives holding the goats were screaming in their fear."

Probably the most authentic account of the Great Snake was given by Fred Cornell. He was camping about twenty miles below the Aughrabies Falls with two companions in

1910, one of them an American named Kammeyer. The Orange River was in flood. One day Kammeyer was bathing in a quiet backwater, where cattle were grazing at the water's edge.

Suddenly Kammeyer cried out in terror and ran back to Cornell. Kammeyer said that a wave had surged past him, and that the open-jawed head and tremendous body of a huge snake-like monster had emerged to a height of twelve feet. The snake had pounced on one of the calves and disappeared with it. Cornell confirmed the fact that a calf was missing.

Kammeyer stuck to his story. He declared the snake's body was as thick as a barrel. Hottentots employed by Cornell said they had seen the Great Snake on several occasions, and had shot at it – but the snake was immune to bullets.

Further down the river the late Father Wolf of Pella Mission told me that years ago the Hottentots kept complaining to him that a huge snake was preying on their stock. Father Wolf was impressed by these reports, and led an expedition into the mountains along the river in search of the monster. He found nothing.

Next the snake appears in the Richtersveld. Heyes, the prospector, assured me that he saw it in 1929 where the Gooiniet River joins the Orange a few miles east of Sendeling's Drift. "I was three hundred yards away when I saw it, but my Hottentots ran for their lives," declared Heyes.

Finally a police sergeant on duty near the mouth of the Orange River told me a queer story.

"There is a large snake or something in the river," said the sergeant. "I have never seen it, but not long ago I caught a coloured shepherd in a place where he had no right to be. All the country above the high flood level on the north bank of the river is out of bounds – it is a diamond area. The shepherd knew the law well enough, but he told me that he had just seen the Great Snake and dared not go near the river with his flock."

It is not easy to deceive a hard-bitten sergeant of the South African Police with a fairy story. The sergeant, however, made immediate inquiries among the natives employed by the police to patrol the river and report trespassers. To his astonishment he learnt that his men had not been out on patrol that day. They reported that they had seen the Great Snake among the trees, and pointed out the spot to the sergeant.

"These were trustworthy men," summed up the sergeant. "They had seen something that very morning. I sat watching the river for a long time, but there was no trace of it."

It is significant, perhaps, that Sir James Alexander, the explorer who visited the mouth of the Orange River in 1838, wrote in his book: "Here an immense snake is occasionally seen whose trace on the sand is a foot broad."

Cornell suggested that the Great Snake might be a new species of giant reptile. I do not think it is necessary to go beyond the known snakes, however, to find a reasonable explanation of the Orange River monster. The average large python is seventeen feet in length, and museum authorities admit that twenty-five foot specimens have been observed. Surely that is a Great Snake, large enough to have been responsible not only for the fairy tales but the true accounts of reliable eye-witnesses.

Obviously there has always been more than one Great Snake in the Orange River. Large pythons do live in the rocky, inaccessible defiles of the unexplored mountains that drop sheer into the river. Pythons are great swimmers – and deadly adversaries when they meet small animals and slow-witted, or unfortunate humans. The pythons of the Orange River created this legend, and they are still keeping it alive.

At many places on the Orange you will also hear the legend of the poisonous lizard that comes out only at night, utters a high-pitched sound, and kills children with its teeth. No such creature exists, of course, for the South African lizards are all non-venomous. But there is a harmless lizard in these regions which may be heard calling at night.

The most fearsome looking lizards of the Orange River mountains are the monitors, or leguaans. These are giants indeed, especially the green water leguaan which sometimes grows to more than six feet in length. Rock leguaans seldom exceed four feet. The Bondelswarts hunt them and use the fat in their medicines.

A cornered leguaan can be a nasty customer, but its strong,

sweeping tail is more dangerous than its teeth. The rock leguaan goes to earth during the cold South-West African winter, and remains secure in its burrow unless a ratel finds it.

Yellow tarantulas swarm in the Orange River gorges at certain seasons. Sometimes they drive you from the campfire, and then you are fortunate if you can wade through a side-stream and find an island.

One of the finest sights in the summer is the migration of the Namaqua partridges in search of water. "Kelkewyn!" they call. "Kelkewyn!" The air is filled with brown coveys; there are so many thousands of them that the beating of their tiny wings creates a sound like a high wind in the canyon. Hawks follow the little grouse (they are "partridges" in name only) and take their toll. Often the grouse outfly their pursuers.

Some of the fish in the Orange River might well be mistaken for monsters. The mud barbel, for example, grows to six feet in length and weighs as much as 130 lb. Burchell named it *Silurus Gariepinus*. These sluggish fish are found in slow moving parts of the stream. Dark green above and white below, they have no scales. It is the largest fresh-water fish in South Africa.

When the river dries up, the barbel retreats deep into the moist mud. Special breathing organs attached to the gills enable it to remain alive for months, until the river flows again. You can hook them with worms or meat as bait. The Hottentots spear them in shallow pools at low river. Mud barbel, however, is not much of a dish unless you have been living on tinned food for a long time. The flesh is tough and reddish and rich in oil.

In spite of the intense summer heat in the Orange River canyons, the mud barbel will remain alive for a full day out of water. Return it to the river after hours of exposure to the sun, and it will revive immediately.

The favourite fishing spot on the Orange River last century, and long before that, was at the end of the Aughrabies canyon. There the Hottentots angled with bone hooks and set their karee-wood fish traps. Wikar found a whole tribe living there on a diet of fish, wild berries and wild beans.

Far up in the northern Richtersveld you will see, across the Orange River, the end of a long tributary, the Fish River. Trudge up the dry bed of the Fish for about thirty miles and you come to the weird health resort called Ai-Ais.

Hundreds of farmers and their families trek to Ai-Ais every winter. A tent and wagon town arises in a bowl among the black mountains; and all the people wallow in the hot radio-active mud of the river bed. Miraculous cures are reported from this distant, desert spa. The water bubbles up out of fissures in the black clay at 131 degrees Fahrenheit, and every day from May until August the wagons and cars come down through the mountain passes and stop near the healing waters. In summer Ai-Ais is abandoned, for the heat is unbearable.

These last great loops of the Orange River have drawn many men beyond the limits of civilisation and held them there. Beside the life-giving waterway the terrifying deserts to the north and south are forgotten.

This indeed is South Africa's "lost world." Otters in the river, baboons in the dark gorges, monkeys swarming among the mimosa trees; and a path along the river bank so narrow that only a pack donkey can follow it. Sometimes there are gaps in the mountain barrier, where old, dry watercourses reach the great river. But most of the way there are only the flanking peaks, and below them the rock terraces baking in the sun and polished by the sands and winds of a thousand years.

The heat comes in powerful waves. Sun helmet and dark glasses cannot shut it out; this temperature would grill a snake in the sand. Only a Hottentot or a Bushman really fits into this landscape – the land of red, hog-backed mountains, weird trees, the sound of the waters and the smell of woodsmoke from the campfire.

No mountaineer ever took greater risks than did the Bushmen when climbing these mountains in search of honey. Sometimes along the Orange River you will notice a pile of stones at the foot of a precipice. This was not a surveyor's beacon. Look up, and you may still see the great hive which some Bushman marked as his own property.

Bees nest for centuries in these inaccessible cavities. Mountain hives are often extremely rich; the hoard of honey becomes so large that the bees are unable to consume all of it. You need a chopper to break up the outer mass of hard, sugary wax.

The Bushmen intent on robbing a hive, and unable to find footholds in the rock, thrust sharp sticks into cracks – just as the modern climber uses steel "pitons" as a last resort. These tough Bushman pegs remain jutting out of many a steep rock face, decaying tributes to the daring of the little men who displayed supreme skill in reaching the hives. Many a Bushman was killed, many were crippled during these desperate climbs. Not only the heights, but the infuriated bees opposed them.

They climbed like baboons, they surmounted the most formidable overhangs with poles and crazy ladders. They got their honey and lowered it in the shells of ostrich eggs. Alpine rope would have helped them as they traversed precariously downwards, but they made the descent with their own sure feet and hands. And that night, you may be sure, they danced beside the Great River.

Pioneers of the Swartland

LAWRENCE G. GREEN's love of the Western Province may have unconsciously stemmed from the fact that so many of the province's grandest landscapes are within sight, even if only a dim and distant sight, of Table Mountain. To Lawrence Green the mountain and the Atlantic Ocean far below it in all the sea's unpredictable moods symbolized home to an inveterate traveller, "an incorrigible wanderer" as he described himself on the title page of his last book *When the Journey's Over*. He described *Beyond the City Lights*, which was published in 1957, simply as the "story of the Western Province". Let no one imagine that this work resembles a dry travel brochure or a chronological literary stew into which Green tossed the left-overs of other or lesser writers. Lawrence Green loved the Western Province too much to be slovenly in his depiction of the cradle of civilisation in South Africa. Chapter after chapter of this fine work abound with quaint historical details which must have been the harvest of infinite and patient research. He captured in his own inimitable style the spirit and the traditions of the gracious and serene old Cape. But for the genius of Lawrence Green much of this history of the Cape would have remained lost, unwritten, and unknown. In deciding which chapter to print in this anthology I was influenced by Green's own enchantment with the wheatlands of the Cape. He takes his readers through the famous Swartland to the wild-flower paradise of the Darling district and tells the story of the great families with their roots deep in its profitable soil. Listen too to these sentences which light up the majesty of Lawrence Green's description of a colony of flamingoes he saw at the Yzerfontein Salt pan: "I stopped my car in wonder and walked cautiously through the reeds to the edge of the vlei. Everywhere my eyes rested on the coral of the flamingoes. Some strode through the waters, grotesque bills curving downwards, necks coiling like snakes as they raked the mud for their food". This chapter too recaptures in an unwarm world of clinics, specialists and medical benefit socities the tasks and the character of the old-fashioned country doctor who rode on horseback to visit his patients. The adventures and the dedication of one of these splendid unselfish men, Dr Louis Biccard, will surely live on as valuable Africana.

For the kindly old-fashioned country doctor with his worldly wisdom and simple remedies is a vanishing figure on the South African scene that Lawrence Green has saved from limbo.

CHAPTER VII

IN THE WHEAT BELT

People of the Western Province wheat belt have an unmistakeable *bry*, a rolling of the letter "r" in a manner subtly different from any other Afrikaans accent. General Smuts always gave as perfect an example of the famous Malmesbury *bry*, in English or Afrikaans, as any son of the Swartland ever born. I am told that this *bry* is a Huguenot legacy, and that other Afrikaners sound more German when using "r" words.

The land of the *bry* runs for a hundred miles and more, from the very outskirts of Cape Town to the Piketberg district. Wheat is grown in other areas besides this irregular plain between the mountains and the sea. Nevertheless, the Swartland is the greatest wheat belt in South Africa, the stretch that produces a million bags in a good season.

I once attempted to explain the name Swartland by the fact that the *renosterbos*, all too common there, darkens the ground when it turns black in winter. No one has contradicted me, but I have since heard a theory that the first white explorers to reach the Malmesbury site, the military patrol under Corporal Wintervogel, found coal black soil round the mineral spring and gave it the obvious name. Elsewhere in the district the unploughed land is usually a reddish-brown colour.

Hunters were sent into the Swartland during the first half century of the Cape settlement. In the *Oude Wildschutte Boek* you may read the names of the men who relieved the meat shortage by bringing down such vanished game as eland and hartbees. (The largest buck I ever shot there was a duiker on Klaver Vlei.) About forty elephants roamed the valley called Groene Kloof at that time, but they were tuskless and the hunters left them alone. Groene Kloof has become the Darling district in the course of time, and I find it hard to imagine that land of spring flowers and cream as elephant country.

Salt pans were discovered by the early hunters, and some of these valuable pans are still being worked after two and a half centuries. Burgerspan, Koekiespan, Rooipan, Kompanjiespan, Swartwater, Ysterfontein, Grootwater and Reeboksfontein all appear on early maps. Kolbe, the old traveller, found slaves loading wagons with salt. He said it was fine white salt, enough for the whole Cape garrison and for export.

It was the Yzerfontein salt pan which presented me, in August 1956, with one of the most vivid scenes in the whole world of birds. The pan was full of fresh rain water, and hundreds, if not thousands of flamingoes had gathered there. I stopped my car in wonder and walked cautiously through the reeds to the edge of the vlei. Everywhere my eyes rested on the coral of the flamingoes. Some strode through the water, grotesque bills curving downwards, necks coiling like snakes as they raked the mud for their food. Others showed grace and beauty even when standing on one leg. Here was a pageant of massed flamingoes. They came down from the sky like flames, scarlet bands under their broad black-edged wings mirrored in the vlei. Here was a living rainbow. Blazing squadrons of birds streamed overhead, long necks and long pink legs stretched out in line.

This was a noisy sanctuary, for the air was filled with the beating and whirring of wings, the piping and rustling, croaking and crying and gaggling of the exquisite flamingoes. Other birds were there: pelicans and wild geese, sandpipers and wild duck, white egrets, herons, snipe and reed warblers, waterhen and reedhen. But always the scene was dominated by the splendour of the tall flamingoes.

Farms in this area were given out very early in the eighteenth century. Klaver Vlei, my favourite, a place of happy memories for me, was among the earliest farms in the district. Tweekuil (1703) to the north of the present town of Malmesbury, was the first Swartland cattle post to be established. One year later Klaver Vlei was being used by the bold and rebellious Henning Huysing as a cattle run. Huysing left the Cape to denounce Governor Willem Adriaan van der Stel in Holland, and the farm passed to the governor's henchman Starrenberg. The farm reverted to the Dutch East India Company later and was used for horse-breeding. But it was not until Sebastian van Reenen bought the farm from the Company in 1791 that the gabled homestead, large stables and bell tower were built. This explorer and adventurer, and his brothers Johannes and Jacob, were responsible for many enterprises, and they introduced woolled sheep into the district.

William Duckitt, the English agricultural expert, was the next owner. He exchanged his farm High Constantia for Klaver Vlei in 1815 and lived there happily until his death ten years later. Duckitt, a most intelligent and observant man, started a diary in which each day's work at Klaver Vlei was carefully recorded. The huge leather-bound volume was shown to me by Mr. Martin Ruperti, a descendant of William Duckitt and until recently owner of the farm. The keeping of the diary has become a Klaver Vlei tradition. For a century and a half each day's work and events have been conscientiously recorded without a single break. Prices received for wheat and livestock, wages paid to labourers, quantities of grain planted and reaped, details of the ploughs and sickles and scythes used, the vagaries of the seasons and all the whims of nature are to be found in volume after volume. It is a priceless record and microfilm copies are preserved in the Cape archives.

Wine made by William Duckitt was praised by Lieutenant James Holman, R.N., the blind traveller who rode about the Cape on horseback in the eighteen-twenties. Holman attended a birthday party given by the Duckitts on the Ganse Kraal farm in honour of Jacobus van Reenen, son of the man who had been sent out in search for the Grosvenor survivors. Many guests came from distant farms, and a sumptuous dinner was served.

When the health of the host was proposed a *bokaal* was put on the table, a half pint wine glass kept for state occasions. It was filled to the brim, and the guest was expected to empty it at a draught. Thus the glass made the round of the table. "It was by no means a disagreeable penalty when it is filled with such fine old hock as was drunk on this occasion, made on Mr. William Duckitt's estate," remarked Holman. "After a few songs the ladies retired, and the *bokaal* reappeared to do them homage."

Duckitt nearly lost his home the year after he bought it. Slaves lived in the loft, and one night they set the thatch on fire by accident. Fortunately the house had an exceptionally thick *brandsolder* of clay bricks, and that prevented the fire from spreading down below. But the front gable was lost, and the builder who replaced it failed to match it with the fine curves of the end gables.

The farm passed to William Duckitt's eldest son William. Duckitt's widow lived there until her death in 1843. She had been Mary Whitbread, a daughter of the well-known English brewing family. Her father had helped to finance King George III. A silver candle snuffer bearing the mark G III R is among the heirlooms on the farm. It seems that a Miss Duckitt was among Queen Charlotte's ladies-in-waiting. Another interesting relic of a different sort is a model of the famous double-furrow plough invented by William Duckitt of Esher in Surrey, father of the Duckitt who settled at the Cape.

Duckitt the settler brought three sons to the Cape with him: William, already mentioned, Frederick and Charles. Frederick owned the farm Groote Post adjoining Klaver Vlei. He married Hildagonda Versfeld; and one of their daughters was the Hildagonda Duckitt who wrote the most successful Cape cookery book ever published, Hilda's "Where is It?"

My own happy memories of Klaver Vlei are of days in the veld, walking many miles to shoot a buck or guinea fowl. I remember the south-east wind on my face; the snorting of the horses; grilled mutton and pork chops, with a choice of sherry, brandy, red wine or beer when we met the wagon at lunch time. Jannie Kirsten, with his old-fashioned high collar and leggings and hammer-gun, divining for water with twigs of *wildedagga*. Martin Ruperti, our host, talking about his favourite dish – tortoise pie. The gables of the homestead glowing in the late afternoon sun as we trudge in line uphill through the heavy sand along the river bank.

In this countryside there are pleasures that never change. I can understand why that English gentleman, William Duckitt, became rooted on this lovely farm. "Mr. Sebastian van Reenen's wheat was by far the best I saw in any part of the country," Duckitt wrote when he first saw the farm which he was to own later. "The land is uncommonly good, a blue colour, strong loam. Sebastian van Reenen has given two thousand dollars for an English stallion and three hundred and ninety-six dollars for a young Dutch bull. This shows a desire to get forward, and in a few years when the country is better inhabited it will be found wonderfully productive."

In the family museum at Klaver Vlei you can see Duckitt's watch, the furniture he brought from England, and a miniature revealing the man himself: a clean-shaven man with a long, thoughtful face and brown eyes.

It is hard to imagine the Darling district without this great farmer's descendants. When the centenary of Darling was celebrated in the spring of 1953, Miss Charlotte Duckitt, aged eighty-seven, impersonated her aunt Hildagonda. She remembered her aunt collecting the *balseminie* (nemesia) seeds in the district and sending them to a firm in England. Before long the delicate flowers were being cultivated in gardens all over the world; but they are still seen at their best growing wild along the edges of the Darling wheatfields. No wonder old Doctor Lichtenstein observed: "A man could scarcely explore this country without becoming a naturalist."

Darling village, like many others, was founded when the Dutch Reformed Church bought the farm Langfontein for a new church and dorp. Charles Darling was governor of the Cape at the time. The cream for which Darling has become renowned was first made on a commercial scale by two Swedish dairymen, Möller and Threnström, who settled in the village at the end of last century.

Only thirteen miles south of Darling is the Moravian mission village of Mamre. The new road by-passes the thatched cottages where two thousand coloured people live snugly amid their fruit trees and oaks and gardens; but now and again I take the old road through the village. You may envy the people of this quiet old backwater when I tell you that they pay a property rate of twenty shillings a year for a building lot and ten shillings for each land or garden lot. A fee of twenty shillings is collected on a thousand bundles of thatch, but a householder may gather firewood for his own use free of charge.

At one time Mamre was one of the chief sources of Cape Town's domestic cooks. Many of the younger women now prefer factory life. Housewives of a certain age sigh for the days when it was only necessary to drive out to Mamre to secure a good servant who was happy to accept a wage of three pounds a month.

Malmesbury town started on the farm Kersfontein, round the mineral spring with the black soil which I have already mentioned. As far back as 1745 the widow Van der Westhuizen accepted £175 so that a church could be built on Kersfontein. About twenty people were living there at the time; and more than half a century later, when Burchell passed that way, the village was only just beginning to take shape.

I have mentioned the two prime ministers, General Smuts and Dr. Malan, as sons of the Malmesbury district. Riebeek West claims both of them. Smuts was born at Boplaas (also known as Ongegund) at one end of the village; while Alles Verloren where Malan was born is three miles away at the other end. A fact which is not so widely known is that a third prime minister, General Hertzog, was born only thirty miles away and spent part of his childhood on his father's farm Amoskuil in the Swartland.

I know a white-haired doctor who rode to his patients on horseback in the Swartland before the end of last century. He is Dr. Louis Biccard of Durbanville, a member of the oldest medical family in South Africa. His grandfather's brother was a surgeon in the Batavian Army at the Cape in 1802; and his uncle, Dr. F. L. C. Biccard, wrote the first South African medical book: "Volksgeneeskunde voor Zuid-Afrika", published in 1866 by J. C. Juta, Cape Town.

"My uncle grew up in the Swartland and practised at Malmesbury, but I first met him when he was medical superintendant on Robben Island," Dr. Biccard told me. "His book of home remedies was my first medical text-book. He pointed out that nothing specially applicable to South African conditions, local ailments, climate and the way of life of the people had ever been published. The book instructed remote farmers on the treatment of face pains, headaches and hypochondria, and the way to deal with poisoning by such things as mushrooms, bitter almonds, honey, crawfish and mussels. He also had treatments for the bites of mad dogs, scorpions, spiders and bees. He recommended certain Cape plants and herbs, such as crushed buchu leaves and wildedagga; and a mouth-wash of Hottentot's fig juice for toothache. His snakebite treatment consisted of binding the limb, sucking out the poison and then burning the wound with a red-hot iron."

Thus inspired, young Louis Biccard studied at Edinburgh for five years and went on to Vienna before returning home as a qualified doctor. It was in 1897 that he rode out of Hopefield to attend his first Swartland patients. In his saddle-bags were a few simple but useful drugs and medicines, morphia, laudanum with bismuth and chalk mixture for stomach troubles, and a cough mixture. He had an old-fashioned horn type stethoscope and the essential surgical instruments.

"When the doctor was wanted, someone galloped to Hopefield on horseback," Dr. Biccard recalled. "On two occasions I had to eneucleate an eye to save the other eye – kitchen-table surgery without the aid of a nurse. I had to give the chloroform myself. Both patients recovered. I could not send them into hospital in Cape Town, for that would have taken more than a day. In fact, country doctors rarely sent a patient into town. There were no ambulances. The drive would have injured many patients. We dealt with everything on the spot, for the practice of medicine was much simpler in those days and there was nothing the Cape Town hospital staffs could do that we could not do."

Dr. Biccard looked down the years on the emergencies he had faced alone on those distant farms. Children with diphtheria struggling for breath while he carried out the tracheotomy. The triplets he delivered at Hopefield long ago without a midwife's aid. (They all grew up to be healthy adults.) Arms and legs amputated. The problems that had to be solved alone, with the nearest medical consultant four hours away by Cape cart. German measles or scarlet fever? Sometimes an ailment could be diagnosed by the odour. The country doctor gained experience in the hard way, and gathered knowledge which has yet to appear in the text-books.

"It was do or die," Dr. Biccard went on. "Fractured legs were always treated at home, splinted with a board from the farmyard and a sheet, kept in position with the aid of a cotton reel and a sandbag. In many serious illnesses, however, the means of diagnosis did not exist. We spoke of a 'kink in the bowel' instead of appendicitis, and often there was nothing we could do about it. People did not live as long as they do now. And yet, I believe the cancer percentage may have been smaller. People lived on simple diets and they were more sober. Old people took one small tot of brandy, and perhaps a glass of wine at dinner. Life was less complicated and healthier. Farming was on a smaller scale and the farmer had more leisure."

It was not always such an easy life for the doctor, however, and Dr. Biccard found that it often took half a day to visit one patient. He charged ten shillings an hour for such visits; then he would return home, change horses, eat a hasty lunch, and ride off again. Dentistry was a sideline. He pulled out thousands of teeth before regular dentists arrived. Farmers also expected him to act as veterinary surgeon, and he helped many a cow-in-calf and sow.

Once a year in June all the doctors of the Swartland gathered on the cattle farm Langefontein near the Langebaan Lagoon. Dr. Biccard met his colleagues from Malmesbury, Darling, Vredenburg and Moorreesburg; and for a week they went out shooting every day and sat discussing patients every night. The farm was owned by the father of Dr. Steyn of Moorreesburg. During one such week the doctors shot forty steenbok. "It was our only holiday, and somehow our patients survived until we got back to work," smiled Dr. Biccard.

Hopefield is about the same age as Darling, and it was named after two Cape civil servants, Hope and Field. The village was laid out on the farm Langekuil, along the bank of the Sout River. It was the natural choice, for the main road from Cape Town to Saldanha Bay passed over the site.

The district is a dune world, and many farmers have to fight the sand. Hopefield people talk about *duineveld* and *bog-grond*. The *duineveld* is covered with reeds and *taaibos* shrubs, with the large candle-bushes standing alone like trees. Rain sinks into this sandy soil quickly. But the *bog-grond* is different; thorns and a smaller type of candle-bush grow there, and the rain runs off and forms pools.

Vredenburg has been peaceful for a long time now. When the village was established about a century ago, however, two neighbours named Baard and Loubser quarrelled violently over the division of the ground and went to law. The lawyers did well out of it, and the new dorp became known as Prosesfontein. Long after the legal processes had ended a meeting of church authorities decided to change the name to Vredenburg.

Piketberg is a name that goes back to Isbrand Goske, governor ten years after Van Riebeeck, who set up a military outpost there (a *piket* in Nederlands) while he was having trouble with the Hottentots. The farms Heuningberg and Groenvlei were given out early in the eighteenth centrury; and the early farmers lived a dangerous frontier life, with Bushmen, stray Hottentots and runaway slaves raiding their cattle. Once every farmer had to clear out and make for Cape Town. In a fight that followed, more than sixty Bushmen were killed. Not until the end of the eighteenth century were the Bushmen finally driven away into the north.

From range to range the Piketberg valley is an ocean of wheat. If you drive up the Piketberg mountain, however, a new scene opens before you and you are in a secluded world of dog-rose hedges, orange trees and fruit orchards. Behind these mountain farms there is a romantic story, told in various forms. I had the authentic narrative, however, from Mrs. Jessie Bucton, a daughter of the Versfeld who built the famous road up the mountain.

According to local legend the first white men to live on the mountain were two sailors, an Englishman and his Dutch shipmate, who deserted and found sanctuary in this wilderness. After them, in 1780, came Mouton, the first real farmer. He settled at the place known later as Mouton's Vlei, planted oaks and made a garden. After his death the place became derelict. Years passed, and a number of adventurous farmers tried to make a living on the mountain, but nearly all were driven out. Leopards were troublesome. The lack of a road led to bankruptcy.

J. P. E. Versfeld, the man who turned the mountain into a paradise, was born in 1838 at Klaasenbosch, the Wynberg wine farm. He was related to the Van Reenen's of the Darling district, and he lived on several of the Groene Kloof farms before he left school. Mr. Riley, a tutor on one of these farms, composed a ballad referring to Versfeld:

But see who comes, now ladies all take heed,
Ruperti's rival, killing John indeed!
Those sunny auburn locks upon his brow!
My muse says 'carrots!' Muse, you're vulgar now.

Versfeld was musical, with a good voice, and fond of poetry. As a young man he took charge of a Caledon farm, and while he was there he met and married a Miss Elizabeth Metcalf. Then he moved on to an uncle's farm Preekstoel, near Malmesbury, saved a few hundred pounds and bought a flock of merino sheep. He often declared that his father had never had to give him anything except a horse.

One day in 1867 Versfeld saw that a farm named Langberg was for sale on Piketberg mountain. Many wise heads were shaken when Versfeld bought it, for no one had made a success of farming in that remote area. Versfeld moved in with his young wife and two small daughters. A springless wagon carried their goods up the rough track to the heights of the mountain. The Versfelds and their servants walked.

Among the servants were Dantjie Engelbrecht and his wife and children. Dantjie had worked for Versfeld as a shepherd at Caledon. Another coloured couple left Preekstoel with the expedition, and remained with the Versfelds. Large sections of the coloured population on the mountain to-day trace their descent from those two faithful couples.

Langberg cost Versfeld three hundred pounds. The house had mud floors. It was without ceilings and there was no glass in the windows. However, a new wagon had been abandoned there. The previous owner had lost his cattle owing to *lamsiekte*, and he had no oxen to draw the wagon. Versfeld had learnt at Caledon that cattle did not die of *lamsiekte* on veld that had been grazed over by merino sheep. He looked forward to his new enterprise without fear, and even when a leopard jumped into the kraal on the first night and took a sheep, he was not dismayed.

Versfeld had many encounters with leopards, and one or two narrow escapes. As a rule he shot the marauders with *lopers*, and sometimes he set gun-traps. It was a primitive life in many ways. All the babies born on the mountain were carried down the bridlepath by the servants to be christened in the Piketberg church. That was a journey of three hours. The village was without a doctor when the Versfelds settled on the mountain, but the magistrate, the clergyman and the schoolmaster lived there. On the mountain there was the Lukas family at Platberg, making the celebrated roll tobacco which still bears their name. It was longer and thinner in the leaf than the so-called boer tobacco of the period, and it had a typical aroma. The cured leaf was twisted in a rope for the roll. Versfeld learnt the process, and for many years tobacco and sheep were his mainstays.

After two years at Langberg, Versfeld bought the farm Voorste Vlei not far away and established another flock of sheep and a tobacco garden. During a bitter winter the sun did not appear for a fortnight, all the lambs died and Mrs. Versfeld's health appeared to be suffering as a result of the climate and the remote life. Versfeld drafted advertisements on several occasions with the idea of selling his farms. Mrs. Versfeld tore them up. One of her sisters came to stay with her. The farms prospered. In 1872 Versfeld was able to buy Mouton's Vlei and build a new house there for his family.

"Mouton's Vlei was a little paradise after Langberg, which had a finer view but which was rather bleak and exposed," Mrs. Bucton told me. "Mouton had left eighty tall, thick-stemmed orange trees in a grove, mighty pears of the sweet saffron variety, a row of walnut trees, a large peach orchard, apricots, almonds, figs and apples, quince and pomegranate hedges, clumps of bamboo and poplar, and a vineyard. And the whole place cost only eight hundred pounds."

Versfeld planted more trees. His oak avenue, which he completed in 1887 from the house to the lower garden, was called Jubilee Avenue in honour of Queen Victoria's Jubilee. Versfeld's own family grew, and this good-hearted man also made himself responsible for a number of other children whose parents had met with misfortune. Nevertheless, there was a large and happy crowd of children up at Mouton's Vlei. A governess arrived from England to preside over the schoolroom. Dances were held every Friday evening in winter, with the coloured labourers playing their fiddles and concertinas. Every child learnt to ride.

During one of his journeys to Saldanha Bay to buy salted

snoek for his labourers, Versfeld bought day-old ostrich chicks. He paid twenty pounds apiece for eight of them, and they formed the nucleus of a prosperous venture. Versfeld went into partnership with his brother-in-law Peter van Breda, acquired Geelbek farm on the Langebaan lagoon, and sent the young birds there. (I saw their descendants running wild on the farm eighty years afterwards.) Before long Versfeld was making a thousand a year from ostrich feathers alone. He bought a town house at Wynberg and took some of his family there – a journey of two days from the farm. He also invested in grain land near Piketberg to keep his elder sons busy.

When the feather boom collapsed in 1885, Versfeld took his family back to the mountain farm. No one lamented the return, for all regarded Mouton's Vlei as their home. Four years later Versfeld built the pass which was the greatest achievement of his busy life. He thought it would be a long and expensive business; but the shale surface proved easy to work and his twenty coloured labourers were full of enthusiasm.

Every morning Versfeld rode off at dawn on his grey horse Moscow, returning after dark. He took a day off when his son Jack was born, and that day's work had to be done over again, for the men had made the gradient too steep. The stroke of genius which made Versfeld's Pass famous was the design which turned three hairpin bends into loops. A road with sharp corners would not have been safe for ox-wagons. In three months Versfeld's road was an accomplished fact, and only in very recent years have the engineers been able to improve upon it.

Sad to relate, Versfeld's health failed and he was sent to England for treatment. Nothing could be done. He died in London, far from his mountain home, at the age of fifty-eight. His widow had to bring up the younger boys without him; and she remained at Mouton's Vlei until 1923, the year of her death.

Piketberg was the ancestral home of that strange and somewhat mysterious race known as the Griquas. Originally there was a pure Hottentot tribe, the Grigriqua, and these people seem to have become a mixed group as a result of early contact with the regiments of Germans and others in the service of the Dutch East India Company at the Cape. In time the half-caste Griquas produced leaders, shrewd men who spoke Dutch and were largely civilised. Adam Kok was the first of them, a slave who may have had a white father. Born in 1710, Adam became the Governor's cook; hence the surname Kok. He cooked so well that the Governor rewarded him with his freedom and a loan farm in the Piketberg district. There, in 1746, a son Cornelius was born. Adam Kok also gained possession of land farther north, in the Kamiesberg, and so a migration started which kept the restless Griqua clan moving across the face of South Africa for so many years. The first Adam Kok, who reached the age of ninety, was the great-great grand-father of Adam Kok III who led the great trek of two thousand followers into the unknown country of which Kokstad became the capital.

Evidently there were wealthy coloured people in the Piketberg district at various periods. Court records show that in 1882 a coloured woman named Georgina Novella disappeared. Her son, eight years old at the time, applied in 1909 for leave to presume death. The order was granted, and the son inherited ten thousand pounds which had become due to his mother.

"*Swak, swak, Piketberg!*" That is the expression Piketberg has supplied to the Afrikaans language, and the origin is to be found, in an amusing true story. In the 'eighties of last century a Hollander artisan wandered from farm to farm doing odd jobs. When he had saved a little money he would visit Piketberg and spend it at the hotel. Not far away was the cemetery. One Saturday night the Hollander went to sleep among the tombstones, unaware of his strange resting place. Next day was Easter Sunday, and a coloured brass band passed the cemetery at daybreak playing religious music. Up sprang the Hollander, and when he saw the graves all round him he imagined that the Day of Judgment had come. Soon afterwards he realised that he alone had risen from the dead. "*Swak, swak, Piketberg!*" he called mournfully. "*Slechts een rechtvaardige!*" (Weak, weak, Piketberg! Only one righteous person!").

Ancestral Home of All Afrikaners

LAWRENCE G. GREEN would always whimsically shrug aside any complaint that he devoted too much space in his works to food and wine. He believed that most people shared his delight in memorable meals, exotic dishes and fine wines. Even those who have never sampled these gastronomic delights must still gladly become second-hand gourmets under the guidance of Green. In this chapter from *In the Land of Afternoon*, which deals appealingly with traditional country hospitality in the Cape, passages about food and wine abound. Yet do not fear that in this fine chapter Green poses as an egalitarian Mrs Beeton rattling off menu after menu and recipe after recipe. The full book itself, which is rich in humour and strange legend, takes readers into the mellow Cape countryside which Green described as the "ancestral home of all Afrikaners". Hospitality of course is an instinctive tradition among all countryside Afrikaners. The weary traveller or passing friend may today find that hospitality on the farm stoep or in the cool, lofty *eetkamer* has become more sophisticated and stereotyped than it once was. Who will criticise if the can opener today has become an indispensable utensil in the loneliest farm *kombuis*! But the value of this chapter goes deeper than the magnificent entertainment it undoubtedly provides. Lawrence Green has rescued from the oblivion of lost memory much lore of the farmhouse kitchen and indefatigably he even tells his readers why *koesisters* are called that. He recalls too in the alluring manner of an author in love with his topic simple farm recipes and avers that Namaqualand partridge biltong, a delicacy becoming rarer by the decade, is the finest biltong one can eat – if biltong anyway does not offend one's taste.

This is indeed a charming chapter about the Cape countryside. written in 1949.

Green contends that "old Cape cookery at its best can stand up to some of the world's finest dishes". I cannot argue. All I know is that if this anthology did not reflect Lawrence Green's intense interest in good food and fine wine I would sense that he would be reproaching me in that literary Valhalla where his spirit must dwell. So with Macbeth I can only say: "May good digestion wait on appetite and health on both!"

CHAPTER VIII

COUNTRY HOSPITALITY

COUNTRY AIR gives me an appetite which has often to be curbed. And here on my stoep nothing pleases me more than the wine of the country and the traditional farm food. I say after much thought, and despite foreign experience, that the old Cape cookery at its best can stand up to some of the world's finest dishes.

Perhaps it is because my home is in the Cape. Nevertheless, I do not think my palate has led me far astray. The meals I remember with most pleasure are those I have enjoyed within sight of the Cape mountains.

I was listening not long ago to an aged wine farmer describing the land of plenty in the Drakenstein valley where he had spent most of his life. "Those farmers and their families were Nature's aristocrats," he declared. "Every evening their tables were spread for many times the number in their households; almost every evening they entertained people they had never seen before. They did not get much for their wine or fruit. The oranges went to Cape Town in large, square baskets on ox-wagons and fetched two shillings a hundred. Yet nothing could be more delightful than the hospitality of the old Cape countryside before the days of motor-cars."

Farm labourers (went on the old farmer) were better-nourished in those days. They earned a shilling a day and their food. Wine farmers slaughtered sheep and cattle and made their own bread, long loaves baked in ovens sealed with clay. A labourer's slice was four fingers thick. Salt snoek was the breakfast dish, with meat in the middle of the day and more fish at night.

That was the time when every farmer made three liqueurs for household use – Jan Groentjie (peppermint), aniseed and Van der Hum. They were known as "the green, the white and the brown," and the guest had to taste all three before he departed.

Probably the finest wine ever made in the Cape was the sweet red wine they kept in small casks on top of the large vats in the cellars. After a quarter of a century this wine became syrupy and valuable in sickness. It warmed the whole body as you drank it. No doubt some of these casks survive, but you will not find them easily.

The Hugos of Brandwacht, in the Worcester district, had a famous wine of this type. It was laid down by Jacobus Francois Hugo (known as "Oom Koos Mostertpotjie" because of his fondness for mustard) in 1786. The casks were replenished from time to time; but there was still a little of the original wine left when samples were sent to a Paris exhibition in 1878 and gained a bronze medal.

Bismarck, the "Iron Chancellor" of Germany, received several bottles of this wine on his seventieth birthday. He liked it so much that he secured a further supply. When the Crown Prince was ill in 1882, suffering from a sore throat, Bismarck sent him a bottle of Hugo's wine; and the Crown Prince found that it comforted his throat.

Wines of that age are seldom drinkable today, but they have a marvellous aroma. Major Piet van der Byl has some very old wine in his cellar at Fairfield in the Caledon district. His most venerable bottle was laid down by an ancestor in 1777. And his grandmother made several bottles of Van der Hum every year, following different recipes. He opened one bottled in 1865 a few years ago and was captivated by the mellow graciousness of the liqueur.

Here and there a stubborn wine farmer clings to the *trapbalie* and has his grapes pressed by human feet. Machinery does a quicker job, but old-fashioned methods often pay in the wine industry and I would be the last to denounce such a picturesque scene as the tramping out of the grape juice. Some experts say, too, that the modern "eggrapoir" presses the stalks and pips too hard, and gives the wine an acid flavour.

They sang as they walked round the *trapbalie* – the great vat into which the baskets of grapes were thrown. It looked primitive, but that was once the method in all the great wine countries and memorable vintages were pressed in that way.

Young wine, not matured but about six months' old, is

known as *Vaaljapie*. This is the favourite everyday drink of the Cape coloured farm labourer; and in some districts it is difficult to get the heavy work of harvesting or shearing done without regular tots of *Vaaljapie*. It takes its name from its tawny colour; though some varieties are red. *Vaaljapie* can be a sound and refreshing drink, in strict moderation. But a raw *Vaaljapie*, undiluted with water, has unpleasant effects.

The wine of the Cape which give me greatest pleasure is one which I can buy only when I have a railway dinner. It is the dry red wine of Zonnebloem, near Simondium, made by John de Villiers who was killed in a motor accident in 1948. John de Villiers knew that the Cape soil and climate favour red wines rather than white. He approached his task with a scientific mind and within a few years he was taking all the important prizes at the Paarl wine show. That young man was on his way towards the production of a wine that would have stood up to many a French burgundy. I hope that his secret has not been lost, for there is inspiration in a glass of Zonnebloem.

Wine and cookery go together. In a previous book, "Tavern of the Seas," I recalled Hildagonda Duckitt's grand books on Cape cookery and her fondness for wine in her recipes. She was the pioneer in this literary field. Her "Hilda's Where is It?", a recipe book of Cape, Indian and Malay dishes, first appeared in the 'eighties of last century.

Soon afterwards, however, came the earliest Afrikaans effort – "*Kook, Koek en Resepten Boek*" by Mrs. Dijkman. It was printed by the Patriot Press in Paarl, and was followed in 1904 by an English edition. Mrs Dijkman based her work on a book in Nederlands, "Aaltjie, de Zuinige Keukenmeid", which was the standard work in country kitchens during the latter half of last century.

The peculiar merit of Mrs. Dijkman's book is to be found in an appendix in which she preserved for posterity a number of old and little-known household medical remedies. She explained in her preface: "It is not my intention to play the doctor or to deprive him of his dues, but simply to be of help while he is being called. The good, kind doctor always found what I had done in his absence to be the correct thing. This gave me courage."

Mrs. Dijkman's remedies and notes on invalid cookery were praised by the late Dr. C. Louis Leipoldt. He did not like her ordinary recipes so much, however, but preferred the authentic Cape *skottels* and *bredies* of Hilda Duckitt's books.

This century's authority on Cape dishes is Jeanette van Duyn (Mrs. H. M. Slade), who is known in every corner of South Africa as a demonstrator. Born in Porterville (Cape), she first became a typist and then joined the staff of the Transvaal "Agricultural Journal." At this time she knew little about cooking; but she had to provide recipes for her journal and she tested each one in her own kitchen before printing it.

Her work was noticed by General Louis Botha, and at his suggestion she was sent to universities in London, Canada and the United States at government expense to qualify as a dietician. This was money well spent, for in later years Jeanette van Duyn was able to solve many of the South African country housewife's problems.

Jeanette van Duyn demonstrated the old Cape recipes at Wembley. When one of the ostriches there laid an egg, she was able to bake a cake and prepare *melktert* and *poffertjies* for Queen Mary and her ladies-in-waiting. Jeanette also made sosaties, bredies and bobotie, served with maize-rice. Queen Mary took samples and a recipe for *koesisters* away with her.

"Miss van der Hum" is a nickname Jeanette earned because of her weakness for a dash of the liqueur in some of her sweet recipes. She has added considerably to the range of Cape cookery. Watermelon toffee is among her own creations. At a period when most of the railway chefs were foreigners, she gave special lectures on the preparation of Cape dishes. Her cookery books have done much to revive this art in South African households.

Bobotie is an ancient dish, and Dr. Leipoldt once told me that he had discovered something very like bobotie in a collection of recipes dated 300 A.D.

Mrs. Dijkman made her bobotie from minced meat (cooked or raw), bread, butter, onion, milk, pounded almonds, lemon juice, eggs, curry powder and a small bunch of orange leaves. The mixture was baked and served with boiled rice. Medieval recipes do include a similar dish, but saffron was used instead of curry powder.

One dish brought to the Cape by prisoners who had served their sentences in Dutch men-o'-war, was called "wentel jeefjes." It consists of bread soaked in milk and eggs and fried – rich and rare fare for men who were little better than galley slaves.

Crawfish usually appears cold nowadays, with mayonnaise. Dr. Leipoldt preferred the method of taking everything out of the shell, pounding and stewing it with sherry, and then replacing it in the shell and pouring a curried egg sauce over the rich flesh. Mrs. Dijkman served her crawfish baked, with breadcrumbs. Both these methods produce dishes of finer flavour than any mayonnaise.

Sweet potatoes are reverenced in the platteland to a degree unknown in the towns. For centuries the "patat" has ripened in patches of dark green vegetation towards the end of June. In the wheat belt the standard winter breakfast consists of sweet potatoes, boiled snoek and coffee.

They boil sweet potatoes in their skins on the farms. You can fry them in boiling fat for a change; or serve them chipped with cinnamon sauce; or soak them in brine and embody them in a curry. A sweet potato salad with pickled fish is typical of the Cape cuisine.

Three varieties are grown in the Western Province. Largest of all is the "white," which runs up to nearly thirty pounds. The Port Natal patat is smaller, and has a more subtle flavour. Very sweet and yellow is the borrie patat.

Van Riebeeck had the patat (but not the ordinary Irish potato) planted in the Company's garden very soon after his arrival. As early as 1655 this resolution was passed: "So too shall 'Pattattissen' be planted on Robben Island, in order to determine if the dry soil will not allow them to grow better than they do here, as we find to our astonishment that they are of an extraordinarily excellent kind, each weighing as much as four or five pounds, wherefore all diligence must be applied to their further cultivation." Van Riebeeck secured the patat from Java.

The patat, of course, belongs to an entirely different family from the Irish potato, though both appear to have their origin in America. Irish potatoes were growing in Angola long before they reached the Cape; and even at the end of the eighteenth century the Cape farmers concentrated on sweet potatoes and left the Irish variety to their slaves. It was not until the middle of last century that Irish potatoes became plentiful at the Cape.

Pumpkin is the great standby in the country districts, though as a staple diet it has no great value. Those pumpkins you see ripening on so many roofs are usually boiled to a pulp, mixed with meal, lard and salt, and served with mutton.

Bean soup is a well-known farm dish. Known as *boontjies en mielies*, it is often served as thick as porridge. *Kluitjiesop* is a heavy dumpling soup. They also make thrifty soup embodying the fins, tail, head and backbone of a geelbek, with onion, curry powder and lemon leaves as flavouring; and this is accompanied by boiled rice.

Boerewors is another farm product which some still make in the old way. It may be defined as a game sausage dating back years before the Great Trek; a sausage in which the meat has been pounded with a wooden stamper rather than minced.

Modern *boerewors*, which is not to be despised, is usually a mixture of lean beef with pork fat, seasoned with wine or vinegar. It is a dry sausage, made without the addition of water. Sheep-tail fat may be used instead of pork. On the veld the sausage is grilled. At home it is usually heated in boiling water.

Koesisters are doughnuts of Malay origin, but the derivation of the name is not so easy. Some say that a mother was busy in the kitchen one day when her little daughter asked her what she was making. "*Koek, sustertjie*," was the reply – hence the name. In the East Indies these doughnuts are dipped in coconut, and the Malays of Cape Town still observe the custom at their weddings.

Cake is not served at morning tea on Boland farms, as a rule. That is the time for the special konfyt called "teewaterkonfyt," composed of whole fruit such as figs, oranges, nartjies and apricots. During the afternoon come the oblietjies, soetkoekies and melktert. Buckwheat cakes are typical of the Montagu district, for the buckwheat flourishes there. The flour is nearly white and makes a softer, stickier dough than wheat flour. Buckwheat has a delicate cereal flavour.

Coffee is not the only beverage enjoyed on the farms, as some city people imagine. It is customary to serve coffee in bed, at breakfast, after lunch and at four in the afternoon. Tea comes into its own at eleven in the morning, at dinner, and at nine at night.

The coffee varies, as any country traveller will agree. Certainly there are country-dwellers whose stomachs appear to be as strong as coffee-pots; they take it so often and so concentrated that the visitor can only marvel.

Roasted wheat, crushed peas, even peach peels are used to form distinctive blends of which various households are proud. In hard times mealie coffee is the substitute. I have also heard of "ghoo coffee" made from wild almonds. The roasting takes the poisonous element out of them, but the drink is more like cocoa than coffee.

For more than twenty years the great coffee-drinking centre of the Cape was the Afrikaner Koffiehuis in Church-square. It was really the Dutch Reformed Church Hall, built to serve as a Sunday school hall and for church events. But in 1916 a new hall was built elsewhere, and the Koffiehuis restaurant was established.

At one period you could see many famous politicians and Afrikaans authors and poets in the Koffiehuis – Langenhoven and other celebrities. There at least the coffee was beyond reproach. The building was demolished in 1938.

Biltong is the most famous food of the veld, and the Cape produces the finest of all biltong – the bird biltong of Namaqualand.

You seldom see it nowadays, for the Namaqua partridge no longer arrives in millions when the spring rains fill the vleis. They use only the breasts. Early this century the trek-boers caught the birds in nets and filled barrel after barrel with the dried, salted flesh. It is so tender that it crumbles between the fingers. Partridges in other parts of South Africa do not lend themselves to this treatment, and so the Namaqua partridge biltong, pale white in colour, remains a local and vanishing delicacy.

The queer name biltong is derived from two Afrikaans words – "boud" (haunch of venison) and "tong" (tongue). Strips of biltong hung up to dry look like tongues.

I have found mention of biltong in books published early last century; but there is an earlier name – "tasalletjies" or "tasaaltjies." The modern "tasalletjies" are strips of meat, peppered, salted, laid in vinegar, then dried in the wind and finally grilled. Going further back, however, one finds the Portuguese word "tassalho," meaning "preserved meat." It appears that the first biltong made at the Cape was called by the Portuguese name, which was later embodied in the Afrikaans language.

Biltong, of course, is known by different names in many lands. It is a first cousin of the Canadian pemmican, made from bison; and it is similar to the charqui on which the Chilean army climbs the Andes. Springbok and blesbok make the best antelope biltong in South Africa. Here is a voortrekker recipe:

Cut out the shoulders and haunches of the buck and dissect out the muscles carefully. Then prepare the pickle with four gallons of water; put a raw potato in the water and stir in salt until the potato floats. Add a handful of coriander and boil. Remove and stand until cold. Then place the meat in the pickle and allow it to stand for twelve hours. Hang from the rafters in a room where the biltong is in a continual draught.

Much biltong is dried in the sun, but the connoisseur declares that this method robs it of flavour. Properly cured, biltong lasts for decades and matures like wine. I have a record of an auction sale of 1897 biltong, held in 1918. The biltong had become hard as stone and fossilised in appearance. When filed down, it revealed a blood-red interior, the very essence of concentrated nourishment.

South African literature is full of biltong stories, but the most amusing anecdotes I ever heard were related by that great biltong lover, the late Colonel Deneys Reitz. While serving in the trenches in France during the First World War, he received a parcel of biltong. Reitz kept cutting off strips and munching them until he heard an English officer remark: "What a hog that man is for tobacco."

Reitz also told me of President Kruger's affection for biltong. The president had a large supply hanging from a tree in his garden in Pretoria when the generals met at his house just before the South African War opened.

A grave discussion was in progress when the servant girl

thrust her head round the door. "Oubaas!" she called excitedly. "Someone has stolen the biltong!"

The president left the room hurriedly, followed by General Louis Botha, in a desperate effort to catch the thief.

Beef biltong is not in the same class as springbok biltong, though it is a sound product when skilfully prepared. Ostrich biltong is tough and oily. Nevertheless, thousands of ostriches were killed and turned into biltong during the feather slump in Oudtshoorn and after.

Biltong does not lack medical support. Years ago the leading London hospitals ordered quantities for convalescent patients. The late Dr. C. Louis Leipoldt described to me the tests he had carried out with South African biltong and Canadian pemmican when Shackleton was planning his last Antarctic expedition. The biltong was proved to be more nourishing. Shackleton took hundreds of pounds of biltong south with him.

Dr. Leipoldt treated duodenal ulcers with biltong. He declared that a pound of biltong was equal to three pounds of fresh meat, and that a stick of biltong was sufficient food for a man on a long day's march. Biltong has cured some people who were unable to eat anything else owing to seasickness.

Probably the most convincing recent testimony in favour of biltong is that given by Jimmy McLoughlin, a Scottish soldier who returned from a German prisoner-of-war camp broken in health. The doctors in Glasgow tried various diets and finally despaired of his life. Jimmy then took his life in his own hands and emigrated to South Africa with his wife and two children.

He settled on the Transvaal farm of "Oom Hans" van Rensburg, and there he first tasted biltong. It saved his life. Jimmy McLoughlin sent parcels of the life-giving biltong to friends in Glasgow; and they thought so highly of it that Jimmy decided to set up in business as a biltong merchant. Recently he was reported to be dividing his time between his family in the Transvaal and the insatiable, biltong-hungry grocers of Glasgow.

It is not generally known, perhaps, that biltong may be served hot. First you heat it on red-hot coals, then pound it with a wooden mallet until the sticks are crushed flat, and fry for five minutes in sheep-tail fat. That makes a crisp and crumbly dish.

Shredded or grated biltong goes well with fried eggs. As a

sandwich filling it is excellent. I have also seen biltong omelette, a clever combination.

In 1937 it became illegal to sell game biltong in the Cape Province; the Transvaal and the Orange Free State had already set an example. The ban was necessary. It slowed up a slaughter which had been in progress ever since the modern rifle reached South Africa. It put the "biltong farmer" (also known as the "biltong jackal") out of business.

All the "biltong farmer" needed to make a comfortable living was a rifle and many cartridges, salt, and a car. He sold biltong and hides; and even the bones of the buck went to a fertiliser factory. These men were exterminating the game of the country. If they were caught exceeding the "bag limit" imposed by their shooting licences they paid £25 fines cheerfully – and went on shooting. When foot-and-mouth disease broke out they were allowed to shoot "unlimited wildebeest"; and they shot thousands and prospered. Some of them have defied the law for more than ten years. One who was caught not long ago was fined £120. He pleaded that his biltong was beef – but the magistrate knew the difference.

Just as typical as biltong is the country *braaivleisaand*. This form of hospitality is now so widespread that many people have sheltered fire-places built in their gardens; open-air ovens, tables and benches reserved for this special meal.

You do not know how much meat you are capable of eating until you have stood round the long wood fire at a *braaivleis* and grilled your own mutton chop – and then another and another.

Tradition demands wooden plates at a *braaivleis*. You should hold the meat over the flames on a pointed stick, and eat it with your fingers. Boerewors, sosaties, jacket potatoes; all these provide variety. There is sure to be coffee, and the drinks may include anything from whisky to *witblits*.

Among the rare country dishes is eel – not smoked eel from Holland but fresh eel caught in one of the eastward-flowing rivers and fried or stewed with wine. Mrs. Dijkman does not often recommend wine in the kitchen, but she makes an exception of eels. She also tells you how to serve boiled eels with parsley and butter sauce, and eel pie.

Eels have been found in the vleis of the Cape Flats. They

migrate overland in suitable country, and conger eels are sometimes caught by the trawlers on the Agulhas Bank. I have still to see one on a fishmonger's slab.

There are centenarians among eels, running to eight feet in length and a girth of twenty-four inches. Large eels have been caught in the Dwars river, Ceres. For some reason which has never been discovered, eels do not enter west coast rivers. That is where you find the barbel with its hideous whiskers, but with a flavour as delicate as an eel if you have the right recipe.

Truffles, the underground edible fungus which pervade other foods with their fragrance, are found in the dry, northern Cape districts. Some dogs detect them in cracks in the hard earth. You can boil them and eat them with butter, pepper and salt; but they are at their best when cooked with chicken or spaghetti.

Both Mrs. Dijkman and Hilda Duckitt are silent on the subject of snails. Nevertheless, there are edible snails in the Cape. They are not the burgundy snails that are bred so carefully in France for the table; these snails are the ordinary garden snails which appear after rain. Starve them for a week, then boil in flavoured water, extract from the shell and serve with a sauce of chopped garlic, parsley and artichoke fried in butter.

You may complain that snails are not typical of the old Cape cookery. Well, here is a dish that is much older than the white settlement at the Cape, one which every farmer knows. It is tortoise, the geometric tortoise of the Malmesbury district. Many country people firmly believe that because the tortoise grazes on medicinal herbs, its flesh has a special value. They make omelettes from tortoise eggs which is harmless enough. But if they go on eating the tortoise itself at the present rate, the geometric species will certainly become extinct.

Perhaps you would prefer a strip of biltong, or a *koeksister*, to these last dishes on the country menu. I think you are right. Weird dishes are all very well as an experiment, but give me the choice and I shall order *tamatie bredie*.

Secrets of the Kombuis

Dr C. Louis Leipoldt, who is mentioned in the previous chapter, and has been described by Lawrence G. Green as "greatest of Clanwilliam's sons", will always occupy an honoured place in the pantheon of Afrikaans culture. He was a pioneer of Afrikaans prose and poetry. By profession he was a medical doctor and often startled conventionalists with his original views and theories. With Lawrence Green, Louis Leipoldt shared a love of good food and fine wine. Leipoldt himself was a cook in the *cordon bleu* class. Green though he could cook an adequate breakfast and a light lunch preferred to rely on the culinary crafts of others!

In *On Wings Of Fire* Green recalls the story of Clanwillian and the celebrated Leipoldt family. Dr Leipoldt described Clanwillian as "a minature paradise with the tree of knowledge left out". For space reasons I have reluctantly left out Green's main chapter *In The Leipoldt Country*. But I have included the shorter chapter *Leipoldt the Chef* because it not only satisfies the space problem but also because Green learned from Leipoldt in his lifetime some of the lore and the secrets of the *kombuis* in the old and gracious Cape. It is right I think that these secrets should be revealed to a wider audience than ever before. The Nortier to whom Green refers in this unusual chapter was Dr Peter Le Fras Nortier, an early Rhodes Scholar and Leipoldt's greatest friend, whose name also will always be honoured in Clanwilliam's history. An agricultural researcher of repute and achievement Nortier among other triumphs discovered the secret of cultivating *rooibos* tea seeds. He too was a medical doctor. All admirers of the works of Lawrence Green have always been intrigued by his zeal for writing about food and wine.

He himself, I repeat, was quite unrepentant about this preoccupation! I am sure this short chapter will appeal also to those many South Africans who stifle for reasons that may be many and personal their boredom with three dull plain meals a day.

CHAPTER IX

LEIPOLDT THE CHEF

"Remember that every man who has been worth a fig in this world as poet, painter or musician, has had a good appetite, and a good taste."
                                        WILLIAM MAKEPEACE THACKERAY

I FOUND Leipoldt and Nortier at the "O. M. Bergh Garden". That was the name of Nortier's small farm outside Clanwilliam, and the two doctors were bending over the succulents when I arrived. Leipoldt was a tall, intellectual, clean-shaven man with a wide smile that reflected his peculiar sense of humour. It was too friendly to be mischievous, though Leipoldt delighted in leading pompous and opinionated people into carefully-devised traps. Nortier was shorter and rather stout, but there was no mistaking the brain in the fine head, with its broad forehead, grey eyes and grey hair brushed back. His deep tan spoke of long years under the strong Clanwilliam sun.

I had come to ask Nortier about the *rooibos* tea seeds which a Hottentot woman had found in the underground larders of the ants, a remarkable discovery. Dr. Nortier told me the whole story*. From *rooibos* tea the conversation moved on to other drinks and dishes, strange and familiar. Leipoldt dominated this part of the discussion, as I hoped he would, for this was his favourite subject; even closer to his personal taste, perhaps, than medicine or botany. It gave me the chance of asking Leipoldt where he had learnt the art of cooking.

"First of all I learnt in my mother's kitchen in Clanwilliam, for here the old Cape cookery flourished," Leipoldt replied. "I studied the oriental touch in the kitchens of the White House

---

* I gave the story of this discovery in my book *In the Land of Afternoon*, published by Timmins.

and the old Royal in Plein Street, Cape Town, where the superb Malay cooks followed recipes that had never been written down. Finally I graduated in the international cuisine while I was a medical student in London, washing dishes at the Savoy and other great hotels to pay my fees at Guy's Hospital. Yes, I was a pupil of Auguste Escoffier, that master chef and inventor of new dishes, the most celebrated artist of all time in his chosen profession."

Leipoldt spoke of the little-known sea foods he enjoyed as a boy when the family trekked down to Lambert Bay to escape the Clanwilliam heat. Mussel soup with milk and cream was one dish; mussel fritters was another, the shellfish blended with parsley, curry powder and wine. They ate the albatross in those days, known as *malmok*, that large and splendid ocean bird. It was hung for days, marinaded in wine vinegar, and braised with onions. Leipoldt said a *malmok* cost a tickey and was not at all fishy. Also very palatable was the white-breasted duiker. You plunged it into boiling water, pulled off the skin, feathers and all, and roasted it in an iron pot. Curried limpets appeared on the table at Lambert Bay and fish cakes with almonds and chutney. Leipoldt's favourite sea fish were the rarer sorts; the butter-fish that the fishermen take home with them and which should be fried in butter; the *baardmannetjie* with its thick snout and delicious flesh; the *bamboesvis* or sea bream which feeds on seaweed and is caught in river estuaries; the young and dainty *elf;* the dark-veined *galjoen* grilled on the beach; the beautiful roman, and the windtoy that appears before gales and is caught only in winter. Leipoldt spoke longingly of the *tambryn* or John Brown, and *kliptongvis*, a rarity with the best flavour of all. I wish that I had questioned him about the *kliptongvis*, as it must be a local name, unknown to Barnard and other authorities.

When the famous Araucaria pine was cut down outside St. George's Cathedral in Cape Town the timber provided Leipoldt with a round section which he used for cooking delicate fish such as the *baardmannetjie* and butter-fish. The plank was grooved, with a well to catch the gravy. He brushed the plank with butter, placed the fish on it, and baked it in a hot oven. Silverfish, hottentot and stumpnose were best served as *mootjies* slices grilled brown with melted butter and parsley. Leipoldt did not object to the common fish such as *snoek*, but only the rarities appealed to his imagination, for example the scorpion fish known as the sancord, a winter delicacy. He had a contempt for electricity and gas, and declared firmly that fish should be cooked on an open wood fire. When he covered a fish in clay and baked it in the coals he thought of the treat for days afterwards.

Dr. Nortier put in a word for the freshwater yellow fish and barbel from the Olifants river, and Leipoldt agreed, though he pointed out that the muddy flavour was a disadvantage. He had caught them during his boyhood, using fruit or sweet potatoes as bait; and he said that nightlines with dead rats on the hooks were most effective in luring these huge fish. Such fish, he said, had to be marinaded in vinegar to soften the bones. They were grilled or baked whole in the pan. As a contrast Leipoldt used to catch the minnows of the Cedarberg streams in a pillowcase. These slender little fish, no larger than tadpoles, were fried in deep fat and tasted rather like the whitebait of Europe. But carp were the best of the river fish, grilled carp flavoured with herbs. Eels were unknown in the Clanwilliam area, but at the White House he had tasted marvellous eel sambals and eel pancakes.

Leipoldt recalled a peculiar sport of the Clanwilliam coloured people in his youth. Just before the swallows migrated in March they were fat and luscious. The men armed themselves with long bamboo whipsticks baited with feathers. Swallows were easily killed during a *swawel-slaan* outing, and one man might take home a couple of hundred birds. Grilled, stewed with onion and potato or roasted, the tender swallows made an excellent dish, reminiscent of the ortolans of Europe. Leipoldt said you could pickle these small birds in wine or vinegar and eat them raw as hors-d'oeuvres. "All birds are edible." Leipoldt remarked. "Starlings are good provided you eat them fresh. Cranes and herons were often on sale at the old Darling Street market, where the Cape Town city hall now stands. I found them palatable, though you had to be careful not to break the heron's bones or the whole dish became fishy. Before the flamingo was declared royal game we used to feast on this splendid bird. Nothing in the world of birds can compare with breast of flamingo – except perhaps the grey lourie. Flamingo does not need much bacon. We used to fry the dark flesh of the breast and sometimes we made a rich flamingo soup, tasting rather like wild-duck soup." Leipoldt also spoke with enthusiasm of *dikkop* for the flesh was not so dry as that of many game-birds. It was the smallest and most delicious of all the bustards. Robben Island is a haunt of the *dikkop*, and there he had eaten the birds stuffed with orange, a dish that lingered in his memory. He liked the green pigeon best, especially when it had been feeding on wild figs; it was more tender than the Cape rock pigeon. All pigeons, he said, should be baked in clay with their feathers or roasted in hot ashes. Guinea fowl was another bird that varied greatly in flavour according to its diet. Namaqua partridges, too were usually palatable, but at times they were uneatable. Wild duck was tough. Cape quail soon decomposed and should be roasted at once with fat bacon, green vine leaves and green chillis inside.

Leipoldt said that hippo meat was on sale occasionally at the Darling Street market at twopence a pound. He had also eaten it when he was a medical inspector of schools in the Transvaal early this century, and thought the flavour was like a blend of pork and beef. Hippo fat, of course, was the finest of natural cooking fats. He knew the giraffe, too, and liked the tongue. Wildebees, apart from the tongue, was not worth eating. Zebra was the best of the horse tribe. Eland was his favourite antelope, fat and beefy. Kudu had memorable marrow-bones but the meat of the springbok was much better. Leipoldt had few prejudices at the table; he loved frogs and snails, gypsy dishes such as squirrels and hedgehogs, and he described the taste of snake flesh as "peculiar, smooth and oily, reminding one of terrapin flesh". Lizard flesh he found delicate. But when I mentioned dassies Leipoldt seemed to be more interested in the historical aspect of this odd little relative of the elephant. Leipoldt was, of course, an authority on Van Riebeeck; and he recalled the meal at which the governor had said that the dassies sent to him from Dassen Island were more delicious than any other meat he had ever tasted, better than the lamb on the table that day. Dassie, declared the governor, was "more delicate than a prime young cock from the Mother Country". I gathered that Leipoldt would have chosen the lamb.

Sorrel was a plant close to Leipoldt's heart, though many

South Africans have never tasted it. Sorrel was the first Cape plant to arouse the interest of learned men in Europe, for it saved the lives of sailors who called at Table Bay suffering from scurvy. Dutch and English crews, weak and ill, staggered on shore and filled baskets with sorrel on the Table Mountain slopes. Van Riebeeck and his men planted the indigenous Cape sorrels in the Company's garden. Leipoldt gathered sorrel along the Olifants river and bought sorrel leaves in the Cape Town market at a penny a bunch. Sorrel soup had the flavour of chestnuts. Sorrel softened and improved all vegetable stews. Leipoldt mentioned the shrub called *bobbejaanuintjies* that the shepherds brought into Clanwilliam at one hundred little bulbs for twopence! After twenty minutes in boiling water they tasted like new potatoes. He spoke, too, of *jakkalskos*, the fruit of a parasite growing on euphorbia roots. It had an unpleasant smell but jackals and baboons loved to dig it out. Leipoldt used to put it through a sieve to get rid of the bitter pips and make a souffle with sherry and cream. Treated in this way, it became a luxurious dish. Leipoldt, who thrived on argument, often annoyed some people by stating emphatically that there were practically no typical South African dishes. He proved conclusively that the troubadors in the south of France eight centuries ago enjoyed a mould of mince flavoured with almonds and baked with an egg custard coloured with saffron – in other words, bobotie. Early manuscript recipes in Europe mentioned bobotie by that very name. All the *bredies*, according to Leipoldt, were almost identical with the *ollas* of Spain and Portugal. However, he was prepared to admit that a *jakkalskos* dish was unique and truly South African.

Paw-paws were grown in many Clanwilliam gardens, for the heat suited sub-tropical fruits. People called the paw-paw "bobotie fruit" because this finely-cut curried meat was often served with paw-paw leaves as a flavouring. Horses were given the leaves to make their coats shine. Leipoldt thought the pawpaw tasted at its best when mashed in a pudding with sugar and spices, ginger and eggs, and steamed in a cloth. The sauce he preferred with this pudding was made of *skilpadbessies*, the astringent berries that grow wild on the dunes. They also made a paw-paw soup in Clanwilliam, using the green fruit, and they never failed to add the right amount of sherry. Avocado pear also went into a satisfactory soup. Pomegranates were grown in Clanwilliam and made a grand stuffing for meat. Prickly pears were dried in the sun and packed flat in fruit jars; they made a useful preserve. Poor people mixed the dried and roasted prickly pear peels with their coffee beans.

The *boerewors* of Clanwilliam, I gathered from Leipoldt, possessed qualities such as city butchers have never been able to achieve. Beef gave it bulk, though pork and mutton were added; and it was flavoured with such things as powdered ginger and mace, cloves and nutmeg, fennel and coriander, thyme and rosemary, sage, mint and garlic. Wine, vinegar and brandy were worked into this heroic formula and then the whole mixture was forced into the long skins. Leipoldt declared that *boerewors* should be grilled in the open on a fire of *renosterbos;* but in Clanwilliam the sausage was sometimes sun-dried like biltong and eaten on buttered farm bread.

I also took a note of Leipoldt's own recipe for tomato *bredie*. No doubt this classic method will appeal to those who wish to follow one of the greatest authorities on Cape cookery. Peel two pounds of ripe tomatoes, cut in quarters and add a few green tomatoes. Take two pounds of thick rib of mutton, as fat as possible, cut in pieces and dust with flour. Place the meat in a shallow saucepan with one pound of sliced onions, three sliced leeks, half an ounce of green ginger, a few cardamoms, coriander seeds, peppercorns, fennel seeds and some crushed thyme, marjoram and garlic. If you like it hot, add a crushed chilli and black pepper. Braise all this with sheep fat and when the meat is nicely browned, add the tomatoes. Cover closely and simmer for several hours, shaking often. Then add salt to taste, a teaspoonful of chutney sauce, a tablespoonful of moist sugar and let it simmer for another two hours with the lid off, until it has thickened. Add a glass of wine and serve. It should then have become a well-spiced tomato puree with tender pieces of meat impregnated with flavour. A proper tomato *bredie* is never watery or greasy.

I think Leipoldt acquired a taste for curry in the East, and he was certainly an authority on all these dishes, from the *rystafel* of Java to the *kerries* of the Cape Malays. He said that curry and rice was originally the meal served after funerals at the Cape, hence the *begrafnisrys* still found in recipes; rice dotted with raisins and coloured with turmeric. As a doctor he recommended curry because the condiments stimulated the digestion. "A fine curry is the highest form of a blend," declared this epicure. He enjoyed the interesting side-dishes that accompanied curry; the indispensable rice, plain or with borrie; the lightly-fried eggs, bananas and sambals of apple, quince or cucumber. Leipoldt collected rice recipes wherever he went, for he had the true South African longing for rice at almost every meal. He found yellow rice in Turkey, where the cooks use saffron instead of borrie. I will not give you Leipoldt's recipe for rice with penguin eggs, because only the most influential people can now be sure of their penguin eggs.

Some gourmets pick at their food but Leipoldt had a huge appetite. I sat next to him long ago at a lunch in the Groote Constantia cellars, a lavish affair in honour of visiting Members of Parliament from Britain. Everything was of the best, and Leipoldt's capacity for wine and food astonished me. It was a treat in another way, for he commented so wisely, with such wealth of detail, on each course and each wine, that I left the cellar with the back of my menu covered with priceless notes. No one, not even Hildagonda Duckitt, knew half as much about the Cape dishes as Dr. C. Louis Leipoldt. Years ago a Cape Town newspaper approached Leipoldt at Christmas and asked him to suggest the ideal menu. Here is his effort:

Green pea soup
Roast muscovy duck and cucumber salad
Rice, stewed peaches, steamed
marrow, potato puree, broiled
yellow butter beans
Cold Christmas pudding and sweet sauce
Melktert   Fruit salad
Green fig preserve
Mealie bread
Coffee

It was hardly orthodox, of course, but Leipoldt was never orthodox. I have no doubt that he would have gone through that menu course by course, missing nothing, and keeping his wine glass filled.

Clanwilliam farmers made some good dry wines last century, until the phylloxera destroyed the vineyards. Some of the old wine remained on the farms in Leipoldt's time and he spoke wistfully of these lost growths. However, there has been a revival in wine-making which would have gladdened Leipoldt. Those old farms Zeekoe Vlei and Die Berg are pressing grapes; and the stein wine from Die Berg is a well-known table wine. The copper kettles which once produced *witblits* in the Clanwilliam district are now museum-pieces. I believe that the only farm with a permit is Zeekoe Vlei, where the brandy Leipoldt loved is "stoked" in the old-fashioned way.

Enigmas of Dassen Island

To many South Africans who live inland or far from the Tavern of the Seas where the spirit of Lawrence G. Green will always abide, Dassen Island is a speck on the map north of Table Bay. On a clear day, however, Capetonians who live on the slopes of Signal Hill can see the diffused coastline of this distant island which is remarkable for its penguin colony and which a naturalist has called "the eighth wonder of the world".

Lawrence Green in his yachting days often visited Dassen Island and so absorbed its story and its atmosphere of remoteness. Natural history always intrigued him and in this chapter from *So Few Are Free*, published in 1946, Green in his incomparably readable manner introduces you to the penguin colony and to the inhabitants of the island. Epicures and older Capetonians will read this chapter with welling inevitable nostalgia. Once penguins eggs, a great Cape delicacy, could be bought freely and cheaply from Cape Town's provision merchants. Then as the colony of penguins dwindled and eggs became scarcer the delicacy disappeared from the shops. Rationed supplies became available now and then from a government department. Today even that source has gone. Dassen Island remains remote and enigmatic; its lighthouse beam guides mariners to safety. Oil pollution from uncaring giant tankers threatens to reduce further the unique colony of penguins. Lawrence Green wrote *So Few are Free* over a quarter of a century ago. History ought to be grateful to him for preserving this picture of a Dassen Island now endangered by pollution – the monster problem of modern society.

CHAPTER X

EIGHTH WONDER OF THE WORLD

OF ALL the islands I have seen, one which a naturalist called the "eighth wonder of the world" remains among my happiest memories. Dassen Island is still an unknown wonder. It is austere compared with the tropic isles, but I can sail there again and again without making the bleak discovery that its fascination has dwindled.

You will find Dassen Island looking like a starfish on the chart, thirty-six miles north of Cape Town and five miles from the coast. It lies in the path of a mighty, freezing, ocean current that sweeps up from the Antarctic, and then runs close inshore for more than a thousand miles, all the way from the Cape to Angola. This icy stream robs the landward breezes of their moisture so that the vapour turns into fog instead of rain. It controls the climate and makes a sandy desert of the west coast and the islands. But the great current also brings riches. It carries with it the life of the Antarctic – the whales and the penguins.

Dassen Island, through this current, is really an outpost of the Antarctic. South Polar explorers have stated that nowhere in high latitudes are penguins found in huge colonies such as those which flourish on Dassen. It is the chief breeding-ground of the Blackfooted or Jackass penguin, and at times there are probably fifteen millions of them on the four square miles of Dassen Island. A wonder isle indeed, and not only for the naturalist. The tale of human beings on Dassen is full of strange episodes.

I had an air glimpse of Dassen as far back as 1919, from the window of a twin-engined wartime Handley-Page converted for passenger flying in South Africa. It looked like a white starfish that day, and in fact the old Portuguese navigators called it "Ilha Branca", because of the white covering of guano. In later years I sailed to the island in small yachts, lying securely at anchor in House Bay while the south-easter whipped up the combers all the way southwards to the half-submerged blue mass of Table Mountain.

Even now there are old fishing skippers who speak of Dassen as d'Almeida's Island. Many an isle has been named after a man, and the original d'Almeida was a young Portuguese naval officer serving in a gunboat which called at Table Bay about the middle of last century. He went down with typhoid and was left behind. During his convalescence he sailed with fishermen, landed on Dassen Island, and decided to make his home there.

Although the low-lying, windswept island is not, at first sight, inviting in appearance, d'Almeida had chosen wisely. Large deposits of guano awaited export, and there was always a ready sale for the penguin eggs. So d'Almeida built a house, married, and lived there all his life. His son inherited the bird sanctuary, but left after some years. The grandson, Antonio d'Almeida, first became a farmer, then a miner; but when the post of headman on Dassen fell vacant, the authorities remembered Antonio and offered him the billet. Thus the third of the line returned to the island and re-established the dynasty. He is a good-humoured giant of a man with the dark hair and olive skin of the Portuguese, but a South African in speech. I could not have found a finer guide to the island and the birds. Among the fowls and sheep round his house I noticed two tame baboons. "My grandfather kept a zoo on the island," explained d'Almeida. "He had many different varieties of buck, and made a study of the smaller South African animals."

Antonio d'Almeida can answer any question about the penguins. There are six colonies of them on the island, and each penguin uses the same burrow year after year. This has been tested and proved by "ringing" experiments. The sandy areas of the island are honeycombed with burrows; elsewhere, any shelter is better than none, and penguins are to be found wherever there is a fragment of whalebone or wreckage or an overhanging rock. Burrows are usually lined with seaweed and grass, but some tough penguins use pebbles. Paths from the burrows to the sea are well-defined. Indeed, the penguins have been in possession of Dassen for so long that even the rocks have been worn away by the tracks of millions upon millions of penguin feet.

There is no more approachable bird than the penguin, but I would not advise anything more familiar than an approach. Extend a coaxing hand, or let your foot slip into a burrow by mistake, and you may receive a vindictive jab from a beak as sharp as a pick. If you wish to lift a penguin, first watch d'Almeida. The technique is similar to that used with snakes. Put your foot deliberately on the penguin's neck, then seize it before the beak can be turned against you.

A penguin is more like a boat than a bird, and it makes astounding voyages. When the wanderlust calls the Dassen Island penguins and they depart on their mysterious migrations, they range all over the Southern Ocean. The fat little creatures you see on the island beaches, looking like peevish, clumsy old clubmen, have flippers that propel them at the rate of a hundred miles a day in deep water. They have seen the fjords of far Kerguelen, the ice-clad mountains of South Georgia and the cliffs of the Madagascar coast. But they always turn back before reaching the equator. North of the line you will find penguins only in zoos.

Sometimes a rare Rockhopper penguin waddles on shore at Dassen. It is smaller than the Jackass, and you can tell it at a glance by the yellow plumes on its crested head. The nearest Rockhopper breeding ground is the Tristan da Cunha group. Jackass penguins, by the way, take their name from their own braying sounds; it is like listening to an enormous herd of donkeys. At long intervals an albino penguin is found among the black-and-white millions. Such an oddity leads a desperate life, for penguins are intolerant birds and they peck the albino, strike it with their flippers and pursue it in the water.

Prowling among the grey, furry young penguins on Dassen you will see the Sacred Ibis, a sinister bird from Egypt. The ibis not only steals eggs but plunges its long beak into tasty chicks. It is a distant relation of the stork. Coloured labourers on the island call them "chimney sweepers" because of their naked black heads and necks. In flight they are more attractive, for the white wing feathers are tipped with green. The ibis pest is a serious problem; they nest among the other birds and if you attack one, all are disturbed.

The penguin has other enemies. There is the southern black-backed gull, a determined robber; and young penguins, not yet at home in the water, find the long arm of the octopus reaching out for them. Man-eating sharks are common off Dassen Island. If you see a pathetic one-legged penguin using a flipper as a crutch, you may be sure there has been an escape from a shark.

Although the penguins dominate the Dassen stage, there is a wealth of other bird life for those who seek it. On the island may be seen the largest and smallest of all the web-footed birds – the famous wandering albatross with wing-span up to seventeen feet; and the tiny black Mother Carey's Chickens with their white rumps. Both are petrels and lovers of the open sea. The albatross shuns the mainland and does not often visit Dassen. Those observed on the island had doubtless flown without effort all the way from their breeding place on uninhabited Gough Island, south of Tristan da Cunha. Mollyhawks, the small albatrosses, also visit Dassen. The Cape fishermen often catch them on hooks for food, and call them "see kalkoen" (sea turkey). Then there are the terns, known on this coast as "mutton birds", laying their eggs on the bare ground without a semblance of a nest. The plovers are more careful; they hide their eggs under the sand. Another wading bird from the northern hemisphere which winters on Dassen is the curlew. You will also find oystercatchers, wagtails and larks among the penguins.

Cormorants inhabit the outer rocks of Dassen Island in vast numbers. This voracious fish-eater is known in South Africa as the duiker (diver), and there are four kinds – the trekduiker, bank-duiker, the small, dark-brown reed-duiker and the white-breasted duiker. Trek-duikers are by far the most common, and you have only to see them on the wing to realise that they have been well-named. Strung out low over the water, they go past in cavalcades which cannot be counted but which must run into millions. They pass Dassen in "treks" several miles in length with hardly a gap between each formation. Unlike the penguins, they fish in organised flights, driving the shoals into shallow water and devouring them. Each duiker, it is estimated, eats its own weight in fish every day.

Duikers and penguins have one taste in common – they prefer the soft fish, and catch those with scales only when other varieties are scarce. A gluttonous duiker trying to swallow a fish too large for its throat is one of the alarming spectacles of Dassen Island. On a rock, with wings extended, the duiker becomes an heraldic emblem. They are all comparatively tame when nesting, but at other times they fly off as one approaches.

Finally there is the gannet ("malgas" in South Africa), a handsome bird which nests on other islands and comes to Dassen only for the fishing. A gannet in search of food gives a sensational display. Flying at two hundred feet, it will suddenly take aim and then fall headlong, with folded wings, upon its victim. This gannet is almost identical with the British solan goose except for the tail feathers. It receives full protection as a valuable guano bird; but the fishermen catch them illicitly by trailing bait on a board painted the colour of the sea. The terrific impact kills the gannet.

Dassen had several names in early days. Joris van Spilbergen, the Dutch seaman, seems to have been the first man to report the island. He was there in November 1601 with three ships bound for the Indies; and he called it Elizabeth Island. It seems probable, however, that the French were ahead of him. Spilbergen left it on record that he found a grave with a cross and some bottles, apparently of French make, on the island. He salted penguins and conies for ship's provisions and sailed away.

Four years after Spilbergen's visit the first English ships touched there, the Tiger and the Tiger's Whelp, and General Sir Edward Michelburne of the English East India Company went on shore with several companions. A storm drove the ships off, and the visitors had to wait on the island, with their upturned skiff as shelter, for two days and nights. "Upon the said island is abundance of great conies and seals, whereupon we called it Cony Island," wrote Michelburne.

Now the coney of the Bible, which is what Michelburne certainly saw, is known in South Africa as the dassie or rockrabbit. (Both names are incorrect, as the dassie is not a rodent, but a small relative of the elephant.) Here arises a little mystery of Dassen Island which I have never been able to solve. Van Riebeeck, the first Dutch Governor of the Cape, sent many sealing expeditions to the island; and these men named it Dassen because of the numbers of dassies they observed. ("Das", in Nederlands and Afrikaans, means a coney; "dassie" is the diminutive form and "dassen" the plural.) The men killed a number of dassies for food, and declared they had never eaten more delicious meat. So there is no doubt about it – the island was once populated with dassies, which have now entirely disappeared. I shall return to this mystery later.

Van Riebeeck ordered the first settlement of Dassen Island in 1654, for it seems that he feared intruders. Jan Woutersen was the leader of the party, and he was warned that he must appoint a successor if he "took ill, became melancholy or died." The thoughtful Van Riebeeck also sent a Hottentot beachcomber to the island to learn Dutch, so that he could accompany trading expeditions into the interior as interpreter. This man often appeared in later records; he was Klaas Das, probably named after the island.

The men on Dassen Island built a loopholed stone battery with two cannons and a stone house. A well yielded good fresh water. Vegetables were planted, and aided by the rich guano, the settlers soon had a flourishing garden. Four free burghers, who had bought a large boat called the Penguin from the Company, became coast traders and carried the produce of the island to Table Bay – sealskins, seal oil, dried seals' flesh and penguin eggs. Later in the century the Company had five hundred sheep grazing there. The island was also used as a place of banishment for a burgher's wife found guilty of "slandering an honest woman". Her term of exile, however, was only six weeks.

There is a long gap in the records of Dassen Island during the eighteenth century, but it is clear that men were stationed there from time to time to prevent foreign poachers from raiding the seals. The first recorded shipwreck occurred in 1801, when six men from a cutter owned by Tielman and Roos lived as castaways for twenty-six days. An account of their adventure states that they ate "rabbits and penguin eggs". Please remember the rabbits.

The next wreck was more dramatic, and a lively description of it was given by Mary Molesworth, daughter of Major-General Arthur Molesworth of the Madras Army, in a letter to her father. I was fortunate in discovering a copy of this letter in Cape Town. Miss Molesworth left England in the ship Lady Holland late in 1829, bound for India. She describes the commander as a very disagreeable man. "You may form some idea of his character when I tell you that in consequence of some slight misunderstanding between him and a young officer at the cuddy table he threw two full bottles of wine at the gentleman's head, and nearly killed him."

One night in February 1830 the ship was beating against the south-easter, trying to make the Cape, when the passengers heard the unpopular captain shouting: "Helm hard down! Breakers ahead!" The ship struck at seven knots and lay rolling on a rock. The captain lost all authority. Seamen plundered the spirit store. Amid this confusion Mary Molesworth went to her cabin and saved her watch and a few trinkets. One passenger put guns in the boats for fear of landing among savages. There was a heavy surf running, but some of the seamen had remained sober enough to launch the longboat. The women were put out of a porthole, helped along the side of the ship to the stern, and lowered by a rope into the boat. In this way Mary Molesworth with thirteen other women passengers landed on Dassen Island.

She was taken to a hut which she describes as a "Robinson Crusoe abode, constructed of bones of whales and covered in with turf. There was a little lamp burning on one side, which threw a dim light on us as we crept in and made us appear more ghastly than our fright had already done. The walls were made of half-dried seal and rabbit-skins, which, with the bad oil in the lamp can easily be fancied not to emit a very refreshing smell. Fishing tackle, tobacco pouches and an old torn garment took up one corner, another was occupied by a rude image of the Virgin Mary. It only contained ten persons in a sitting position."

At daybreak Mary Molesworth walked out and found the island "covered with hares and penguins". (First, conies, you remember, then rabbits and now hares.) Winifred, a blue greyhound, had swum ashore from the wreck; and Mary Molesworth records that the greyhound caught seven hares, which they ate with rice and onions. They also boiled a ham on a fire of seaweed. The ship had carried three hundred pipes of Madeira. One came ashore. "This was a great comfort to the gentlemen and sailors in their toils."

The castaways found the island littered with large shellfish, which they used as drinking vessels and spoons. The hares, they noted, fed on ferns. The three men on the island were not permanent inhabitants; they were there for a few months collecting penguin eggs. Not one life had been lost in the wreck, and, as the hut was overcrowded, some of the ship's company threw sails over a whalebone and slept in this tent. Mary Molesworth found the island climate an ordeal. "Our faces and hands were without any skin on them, our eyes red and inflamed with the white sand on the island, and our feet were so swollen and blistered that it was with much difficulty we could walk . . . Our captain was a quiet, unobtrusive spectator of the whole, pitied and despised by most of us."

Meanwhile the ship's doctor and the second mate had rowed to the mainland for help. The doctor, aided by a Saldanha Bay farmer, had gone to Cape Town on horseback with the news; and Sir Lowry Cole, the Governor, sent H.M.S. Falcon immediately to pick up the castaways. Within a week of the shipwreck Mary Molesworth's troubles were over.

You will have observed, of course, how Mary Molesworth has complicated the mystery I am still trying to solve. I put all the facts in front of Antonio d'Almeida recently, and left him puzzling over it. In his grandfather's day, he told me, there were hordes of rats which must have come from a wreck. His father imported cats to kill the rats; and years afterwards the cats which had run wild became a nuisance.

Antonio d'Almeida took white rabbits to the island. Some escaped from the hutches, and their descendants are still living in penguin burrows. But the dassies? Antonio said there were many dassie colonies on the mainland opposite Dassen, and so it is reasonable to believe that there were dassies on the island centuries ago. But he had never seen one there, and his father and grandfather had never mentioned dassies. For the moment

I must admit defeat. I found tortoises on Dassen . . . but no answer to the riddle of the dassies.

Penguins are easily irritated, and there have been long periods when the numbers of birds on Dassen Island have dwindled. Some years ago fishermen off Marcus Island, one of the group to the north of Dassen, made a habit of catching penguins and using them as bait. Forthwith the outraged survivors deserted the island, and the whole revenue from eggs and guano was lost. When the lighthouse was being built on Dassen Island in 1893, the penguins and duikers resented the invasion of their stronghold by workmen, and for a long time they would not settle down. For many years it has been necessary to obtain a permit to visit any South African guano island; the birds are so valuable to the State that no risks can be taken. All the islands are guarded by headmen. Some naturalists believe that the periodical dwindling in the numbers of birds is due to the balance of nature being upset; the birds increase to such an extent that they cannot obtain enough fish. Then a certain number of birds die, and the balance is restored. The penguin, of course, is seriously affected by any shortage of fish, as it has to swim in search of food and has only a limited range during the breeding season. Hungry, and harried by fishermen in search of bait, the penguin has no chance of settling down comfortably in a burrow on Dassen Island.

The egg-collecting season in normal years begins in February and lasts until the end of June. One private contractor organised the work for more than twenty-five years, paying the Government a "royalty" on each egg collected. The collectors robbed the burrows systematically in such a way that a puzzled penguin would lay as many as twenty eggs in the course of five months, instead of the normal clutch of two. It is the second egg that the labourer removes with his long wooden staff, and thus the penguin lays continually to bring the family up to the number demanded by instinct. Some parts of the island are always left untouched, and there the birds hatch out their eggs freely.

For three years, from 1933 to 1935, egg-collecting on Dassen had to be suspended owing to the disappearance of vast numbers of penguins. At this period diamonds were being flown down the coast regularly from the Orange River mouth to Cape Town; and it was suspected that the aircraft had made the birds restless. But the mystery has never been solved. South Africa had to go without penguin eggs again in 1945, although aircraft had been warned to keep away from the island.

In Mary Molesworth's day, the eggs were regarded as suitable food for the slaves of Cape Town. Since then, the penguin egg has acquired a higher status, and epicures in many lands will testify that the huge, rich eggs – with light green jelly and yellow yolk – deserve to rank among the world's delicacies. The taste must be acquired. If you possess it, than a boiled penguin egg chopped up with butter and sprinkled with pepper is a feast indeed. Gourmets say they are as good as plovers' eggs. Others dislike the fishy flavour, and cannot be tempted. Nevertheless, the penguin egg, boiled, curried, scrambled, fried or served cold with salad is a noble dish; fit not only for the shipwrecked sailor, but for the restaurant. Several attempts have been made to find export markets in London and New York. On one memorable night in 1936, penguin eggs appeared on the menus of a hundred restaurants in the West End of London. Once the charm of novelty had worn off, however, the demand ceased. In wartime, perhaps, it might have been a different story.

South Africa remains faithful to this odd delicacy, and cases are railed to every corner of the Union and Rhodesia. In the slave days they fetched a penny each. At the end of last century the price had risen to twopence, and for a number of years between the great wars a penguin egg cost fourpence. Now the Union Government has undertaken the collection, and the last box of two dozen I bought cost ten shillings. No doubt the price will rise again – but I must have my penguin eggs in season. Each egg, by the way, is two-and-a-half times the size of a hen's egg. They contain phosphorus, and are highly prized as a nerve tonic; whether the belief has any foundation I cannot say. One of the penguin egg's peculiarities is that it must be boiled for at least twenty minutes.

The export of penguins has been more successful than the egg ventures. Zoos in many parts of the world have been supplied with Dassen Island penguins. Special arrangements had to be made for each batch, and an attendant, wise in the ways of penguins, travelled with them.

I watched one consignment going on board a mailship in Table Bay Docks between the wars. For days they had been fed on lumps of fish to accustom them to a diet which they obviously found distasteful after catching their own fish alive. A large canvas bath had been rigged for them on the foredeck; and the attendant sat on the edge feeding each bird, almost forcibly, in turn. Nevertheless, the Jackass penguin is a fairly good traveller. Attempts have been made to breed the majestic King Penguins from the Antarctic in captivity; but I believe that Edinburgh was the only Zoo in Europe where chicks were hatched and reared successfully. A King Penguin is probably worth £100 in a European zoo today.

As for the Emperor Penguin, standing four feet in height – that is a noble specimen which never survives a sea voyage. Penguins from Dassen are easy to handle compared with the giants of their species.

Dassen Island has only one man-made track – a rough route which runs from the beach to the lighthouse, through the penguin colonies. I was astonished to see a crazy skeleton of a motor-car using this track, carrying stores from the landing place for a mile across the island. It was a sort of heirloom, passed on down the years from keeper to keeper, and maintained in running order with the aid of lighthouse spares. After a record life it was replaced by a modern motor-lorry.

One of the island headmen occupied his time during the slack season by building a motor-cutter. In six months he had completed a seaworthy craft, thirty-eight feet long, and capable of cruising anywhere along the South African coast. That is as satisfying a way of passing the time on a lonely island as any I can imagine.

One night I followed the keeper into the dark heights of the Dassen light until we reached the lamp room 150 feet from the ground. "The whole tower shivers in a gale," said the keeper. It was bright, but not dazzling, in the lamp room, for the lamp that sends out the long flash is small. The immense lens revolving round the flame gives the brilliance. A weight, running down the centre of the lighthouse, turns the lens on its bath of mercury – simple, reliable clockwork which the keeeper must wind up every two hours.

"You see that a lighthouse man's life is not so easy as it might appear," pointed out the keeper. "We have just finished painting the tower outside – a dizzy job. The lens weighs several tons. That means elbow grease when you have to clean it. There is always paintwork up here to be scrubbed, brass to be polished, lamps to be cleaned, weather records to be kept. We have to think of the airmen, too, nowadays, and note the sky conditions, clouds and wind speeds. There is a wireless station on the island and the keepers are the operators. Nothing new in that; we had wireless telegraph sets in some of our lighthouses in 1914, and seven years later the first wireless telephone sets were installed. Before that, we sent urgent messages from Dassen by pigeon post."

In the daytime I noticed curtains drawn round the glass of the lamp room. Without this precaution the oil of the lamps and clockwork would be set on fire by the intense concentration of the sun's rays inwards through the glass. Curtains are sometimes set alight, and the keepers have always to be on guard against fire. (One man in a French lighthouse was attending to the lamp when the kitchen fire below set the room ablaze. Cut off by the smoke-filled staircase, he descended outside with the aid of a rope and put the fire out).

At all the remote lighthouses, stores sufficient for three months must be kept, for heavy weather has sometimes prevented the tugs from landing fresh supplies on the usual mail days. A large stock of paraffin is necessary – one large cylinder is consumed in two nights at the Dassen light.

Lighthouse men, you find, are often the sons of lighthouse men. They have been brought up in the tradition, and see no hardship in their isolation. Working without supervision, a strong sense of duty carries them through their seven day week. No keeper has ever been found drunk at his post. They are seldom troubled by the fact that they cannot call in the doctor save in a real emergency. Only when their children have to leave them to attend school far away is there a tinge of sadness.

Contrary to popular belief and fiction, the keepers of the

lights live in harmony and do not tire of seeing the same faces every day. This is proved by the fact that there is never a lack of volunteers for lonely lights such as Dassen Island. No "Grand Guignol" drama disturbs the calm routine of the South African coast lights. "At the end of a spell of leave in town I am always glad to go back," a keeper once told me. "When I win the big sweepstake I shall build a lighthouse of my own, and live there, and turn on the light when I feel like it."

A film producer once applied to the Union Government for permission to use Dassen Island as the "location" for an island drama. He failed, for although a lone cameraman can always secure a permit to film the birds, the presence of a whole company might have caused a disturbance. Nothing daunted, the producer borrowed fifty penguins from a zoo, and had thousands of cardboard penguins printed. The picture was made on one of the Canary Islands, with the living penguins giving animation to the beach scene. I believe it looked convincing enough on the screen, but the shrewd penguin could not have been deceived for a moment.

Though Dassen Island is often shrouded in fog, and ships have been lost on the reefs offshore, no fog-horn has been installed. The precious penguins might not like it! The island is usually the first landfall made by steamers bound from England to the Cape; and several have met the same fate as Mary Molesworth's ship. I once met an old sailor who was shipwrecked on Dassen in the S.S. Wallarah in 1891. He was an able seaman named Beamish who preferred sailing ships; but he was persuaded to join the Wallarah on her maiden voyage. Inexplicably the Wallarah struck Dassen Island on a calm clear night.

"We jettisoned tons of cargo – clothing, boots, pianos, rum, whisky and jars of mecury," Beamish told me. "The pianos were in airtight cases, and for weeks afterwards the farmers on the Cape west coast were salvaging pianos. Four tugs came to help us, but in the end we had to abandon the Wallarah, hard and fast on the rocks of Boom Point, the northern arm of the island." I met this old seaman in 1933, just after he had made a sentimental pilgrimage to the scene of the wreck.

The storms of forty-two years had destroyed all traces of the Wallarah.

Dassen Island once saw the most profitable salvage enterprise ever carried out in Cape waters. In 1916 the 7,000-ton freighter Ping Suey was on a voyage from England to the Far East. She was keeping fairly close to the shore to avoid German raiders; and while making for Table Bay she entered a dense fog bank. The Ping Suey fetched up on a sloping ledge of rocks in House Bay, close to d'Almeida's quarters. I saw her there, and she looked like a vessel lying at anchor in the bay. This little anchorage, however, is only safe for fishing boats and small yachts – and then only when the wind is not coming out of the north. Miraculously the Ping Suey had missed all the outlying rocks and reefs, but her position remained extremely dangerous.

Tugs failed to move her. Despairing of salving the ship, the agents concentrated on the cargo. When everything had been discharged into lighters the Ping Suey was still found to be hard and fast. She lay there for eight months, abandoned and becoming a mere rusty roost for the sea-birds. Then a Cape Town firm offered £6,000 for the ship, and this was accepted. The firm engaged two clever salvage engineers who believed they could refloat the Ping Suey. A small fleet assembled while the engineers, using compressed air, pumped the engine room dry. Cables were rigged to an off-lying reef nearly half a mile away. These preparations cost £60,000 and at any moment during the three months of toil a gale from the north-west would have destroyed the ship. In the end, however, the great risks that had been taken were justified; for the Ping Suey came off into deep water with the aid of her own winches.

She was towed to Table Bay Docks, and the salvage men packed a thousand tons of cement into her bilges to strengthen the torn bottom-plates. Thus fortified, the Ping Suey steamed away to the Far East for permanent repairs. She carried a valuable wartime freight of wool and scrap-iron. The Ping Suey was then twenty years old, but ship and cargo were sold for more than £300,000. In 1932 the old Ping Suey, named Attualita and Italian-owned, was sold for £2,500. The salvage men who made a small fortune out of the job never forgot the narrow margin by which they had triumphed. Two days after the Ping Suey had left Dassen Island, a violent gale blew up from the north-west.

One day while the Ping Suey was aground on Dassen, a dead whale was washed ashore. The head was missing. No one thought much about it at the time; but soon afterwards ships were lost off the Cape by striking mines, and the mystery was explained. A pity the obvious clue was not followed up immediately. That was Dassen's only contact with the 1914-18 war. This time, too, a deep peace rested over the island, broken only once when the lighthouse-keepers sighted and reported a three-funnelled ship off their shore. She was a German mine-layer, but this time the minesweepers of the South African Naval Forces cleared the seas.

Dassen Island's population seldom falls below a dozen, and during the egg-collecting season there may be a hundred men hard at work. It has never been difficult to recruit labour for the island. All sorts of people fall under the spell of islands, and the queue waiting for jobs usually holds six men for every vacancy.

At one time the labourers were white men of all nationalities, mainly seamen, but with a sprinkling of odd customers. Many a well-educated Englishman put in months of toil on Dassen last century; sweating out the liquor and saving the meagre reward for the pay-day in Cape Town when all would be squandered all too soon. It was not uncommon to find a broken-down doctor in those old guano gangs – a man who never revealed his skill until some emergency made him remember the Hippocratic oath.

For forty years the egg-gatherers have been Cape coloured men. Perhaps it was inevitable that there should have been tragic incidents among men isolated in this way. From time to time men suffering from monotony or hard treatment have escaped in small boats, and some have been drowned in the breakers on reaching the mainland. The final scandal was exposed in 1932, when deaths occurred on the island as a result of floggings. There were criminal proceedings and the grim affair was debated in Parliament. As a result the whole system was reorganised.

I do not think Dassen Island will again become the scene of sadism.

The fresh penguin eggs are brought to Cape Town almost every other day throughout the season in fishing cutters and other small craft. I knew a tough old seafarer named Charles Broker who secured a contract to carry penguin eggs some years ago. He had bought an aged but seaworthy Admiralty pinnace, which he named Theodora. She was forty-seven feet in length, but very narrow-gutted. Broker installed a cranky motor, fitted up a cabin, and lived on board. In this pinnace he made some of the most remarkable voyages ever attempted along the stormy South African coast. Once he sailed from Table Bay to Angola and back. Again and again he was reported missing. Even when he was on the short Dassen Island run he managed to become six days overdue. But those who knew Broker and the Theodora were never alarmed. If he did not arrive it simply meant that his motor had failed again, and that he was beating back under sail. A double-skin teak pinnace, coppered, is not easily lost.

Until war brought crash boats into Cape waters, the record for the run from Table Bay to Dassen was held by a harbour tug – two and three-quarter hours. Now I suppose the time might be meaured in minutes, but I do not want to race to Dassen that way. The island is always linked in my mind with small yachts and old shipmates. Yachts running free before a fresh sou'-wester, with the log-line trailing out astern and an odour of pea soup coming from the galley. I like to prick off the distance to Dassen on my own chart and read the island names. Waterloo Bay, Boom Point, Spout Rock that throws up the sea like a depth charge, The Triangles and noisy Roaring Sister . . . these are names round the penguin isle, and for me they bring pleasant memories of old cruises. In a changing world I can at least be sure that when I sail to Dassen again the birds and the beaches will be as they were when Spilbergen stepped on shore and gaped at the penguin millions.

He Roamed the Waterfront

THE sea always enthralled Lawrence G. Green. As a schoolboy he roamed the waterfront of Table Bay; this was the realm of adventure he loved as much as he loathed the arenas of organised games. As a boy of 16 he signed on during the school holidays as a deckhand in the coaster *Ingerid* and the hard work made physical demands on him greater than a rugby forward has ever to face! *Eight Bells at Salamander*, written more than a decade ago, is a volume entirely about the sea and ships and the denizens of the deep. He recalls shipwrecks and mysteries that other writers have missed. As a writer Lawrence Green always refused to follow well-blazoned literary trails. To discover something new or bizarre he would toil away in the libraries of London and South Africa. This chapter *Russian Armada Off the Cape* is a brilliant example of Green's industry as a researcher. But for his skill as the reporter superb this dramatic, diverting interlude in the history of South Africa might have been entirely forgotten.

Today with the closure of the Suez Canal Russian ships flying the Red Flag of Soviet Russia round the Cape regularly and efficiently on the long haul from the Baltic or the Black Sea to the East. Reconnaissance aircraft of the South African Air Force watch them from the skies. But at the beginning of this century Signalman Harvey through a telescope from his post on Signal Hill spotted a naval armada on the way to its doom. It was the great, harsh fleet of incompetent Tsarist Russia. The long-awaited sighting of the armada on its way to fight Japan excited all South Africa. "Action Stations" was everywhere the order of the day. Vividly and authoritatively Lawrence G. Green recalls the drama of the Russian fleet off the South African coast and the fate awaiting it.

CHAPTER XI

RUSSIAN ARMADA OFF THE CAPE

SIGNALMAN Harvey called his wife and gave her the telescope. It was the most dramatic scene he had ever known during his years in charge of the look-out station on Signal Hill. "Russians all right – sixteen of 'em," he announced. "No good calling them up, though. They must be thirty miles offshore."

For days everyone from Cape Town to Cape Point had been awaiting news of the Russian fleet. An incident early in the voyage had almost led to war between Britain and Russia; and it seemed possible that the incident might be repeated when the blundering Russians entered South African waters. Night after night the Simonstown batteries had been manned at full strength Even in far away Natal fifty mounted police troopers had been sent to the coast to stand by the obsolete guns on the Bluff and Durban beach.

It was 1904, and Tsarist Russia was at war with little, unknown Japan. The Japanese, who had only recently emerged from medieval ways, had been winning battle after battle on land and sea in the Far East. So the Russians had assembled a great fleet in the Baltic to steam across the world and vanquish their enemies.

It was a mighty fleet on paper. Manned by better seamen, it might have been a powerful fleet. But the Russians were doomed from the moment their Tsar gave his approval.

Russian naval officers of that period sought comfortable shore billets rather than sea experience. They preferred vodka and pink champagne, graft and bribery, to gunnery and manoeuvres. Among them were counts and princes; cruel, self-indulgent and inefficient. They knocked their men down and ordered floggings without allowing the victims to speak in their own defence. They wore uniform arrogantly at all times; on shore and afloat, usually with dirty collars. They smoked their little Russian cigarettes at all times, on and off duty. The ratings, many of them recruited far inland and poorly trained, were stupid mujiks. Sometimes they were mutinous.

Such was the personnel of the fleet which was sent out under the elderly Admiral Rozhestvensky to meet those patriotic fanatics, the Japanese. Rozhestvensky had forty ships and twelve thousand men; but he had to steam eighteen thousand miles and he needed half a million tons of coal for the voyage. Only the Russians could have planned such a fiasco.

Only the nervous Russians could have mistaken trawlers in the North Sea for Japanese torpedo boats. In the confusion that night they sank a British trawler and killed two British fishermen. They also opened fire on each other and killed a Russian priest. Britain sent an ultimatum to Russia.

Although the incident was settled when the Russians paid full compensation, some uneasiness remained. King Edward VII wrote to his Foreign Secretary: "I really think that we see daylight, and what has been a most grave and serious incident may pass away quietly, and perhaps we may be on a better footing with Russia later. They must, however, see that the world cannot tolerate their fleet opening fire on any ship they meet that comes within reasonable distance."

Rozhestvensky had been warned during the voyage that he would encounter fishing vessels in South African waters, and that any repetition of the North Sea incident would be "highly undesirable". He was inclined to be truculent. Russian agents had informed him that a flotilla of schooners, armed with torpedo tubes and disguised as fishing craft, were awaiting him at Durban. It was said that Rear Admiral Sionogu of the Japanese Navy was in charge of this secret mission. So Rozhestvensky replied that any fishing vessel which approached or tried to break through his squadron would be ruthlessly destroyed. Hence the the suspense in Cape Town as the Russians moved southwards.

It was a slow progress. The queerly-assorted Russian fleet was led by the eighteen-knot flagship *Kniaz Suvaroff*, a heavily-armoured battleship of fifteen thousand tons with three sisters, *Borodino*, *Alexander III* and *Oryol*. They were painted black, like most Russian warships, with yellow funnels. They had twelve-inch guns and rams. But other ships were less impressive.

The old battleship *Oslyabya* seemed to be top-heavy. Another ship, *Dimitri Donskoy*, had been a square-rigged frigate; now, with engines that gave her only ten knots, she was on her way to a naval battle.

One vessel named *Kamchatka* was purely a repair shop, and it was not long before the naval ratings and civilian engineers on board came to blows. Another ship was filled by a plant which provided drinking water from the sea. A white hospital ship, the *Oryol* (not to be confused with the battleship) was regarded by the Russian seamen as a floating palace and haven of rest. Thousands of men longed to be taken ill and transferred to her. Morale was low in the doomed fleet of Admiral Rozhestvensky.

Rozhestvensky had many nightmares, but coal loomed even larger in his mind at first than the Japanese enemy. His ships needed ten thousand tons of coal a day. He could not expect help in any British or Portuguese colonial port, but the Germans were friendly and the French were observing a sort of benevolent neutrality. Sixty colliers and storeships of a German line had been chartered. Early in November 1904, Rozhestvensky met them at Tangier, his first African port. There he decided to split up his fleet.

His reasons were obscure, but it is possible that he feared some of his ancient ironclads might capsize off the Cape if they ran into heavy weather. All the ships were overloaded. Many of them carried too great a weight of armour above the waterline. In some the stability had been affected by unnecessary top-hamper in the shape of amenities for officers. It was a Russian naval tradition that officers should live in luxury. Rozhestvensky had ordered the officers to stow coal in every corner, including their own cabins; but the top-hamper remained.

Food was another problem. Strange to say, this grim and inefficient navy fed its men fairly well. Peter the Great had hanged three pursers for serving bad food. Now the men expected liberal rations of tea, meat and vegetable stew, and a quarter of a pint of vodka a day. Every ship was stacked with barrels of salt meat, biscuit and cases of vodka. With all this cargo, the Russian fleet steamed with lower decks almost awash.

So only the most seaworthy ships came by the Cape route. They were the up-to-date flagship and her sister battleships, the older *Oslyabya*, the odd but seaworthy old *Dimitri Donskoy*, the cruisers *Admiral Nakhimoff* and *Aurora*, transports, store ships and colliers and the hospital ship. All the rest went through Suez to meet their admiral at a Madagascar port.

It was slow, as I have said, and the Russians soon felt the heat of the tropics. While they coaled at Dakar an officer dropped dead. Mutiny after mutiny was reported by harassed captains. Rozhestvensky signalled threats all round the suffering fleet, and some he carried out.

He had two nieces among the high-born nursing staff in the hospital ship. One night an unexpected searchlight revealed a boat from the *Dimitri Donskoy* with a lieutenant, two midshipmen and a nurse in it, returning to the hospital ship after a party in the old frigate. According to a French newspaper, the admiral placed the three officers in an open boat with food and water and ordered them to row back to Russia for court-martial. In a circular the admiral referred to the "example of profound depravity" set by these officers, and declared that everyone might reap the consequences.

They coaled again at the French port of Libreville in equatorial Africa. Owing to faulty navigation they crossed the equator more than once trying to find the place. When the admiral landed at this wild spot, French officials told him that cannibals had eaten two white men shortly before his arrival. However, the seamen bought monkeys and parrots, and all hands enjoyed the pineapples, bananas and mangoes. Some of the captains wished the divers to examine the hulls of their ships for defects, but there were too many sharks about.

Great Fish Bay was the next coaling port. This is a huge sandspit harbour in Angola, the last Portuguese desert outpost before South West Africa is reached. Of course the Russians had no right to be there, but they knew the bay was inhabited only by fishermen. However, the Portuguese gunboat *Limpopo* (with one small gun) greeted them and asked them to leave. Rozhestvensky sent an insulting reply. The *Limpopo* steamed away to carry the news to the Governor-General, and Rozhestvensky delivered his final message: "Good-bye, little one. Pleasant passage. By the time you have crawled to the Royal Navy for help, not one of us will be here."

Then came Luderitz, a cheerless, open roadstead but a port where the small German population welcomed the Russians. A gale blew up soon after the fleet arrived. After a delay the coaling started; but warships and colliers were damaged as they rolled heavily side by side. "Men are going out of their minds in the fleet," wrote Chief Engineer Eugene Politovsky to his wife. "It is impossible to sleep as the rats have greatly increased. Some of the ships have lost their anchors. The divers fear sharks, but they have to go down all the same."

At last the coaling was finished. A sub-lieutenant in the battleship *Oryol* had gone mad, racing about the decks shouting: "The Japs are waiting for us. We shall all be sunk." But the hospital ship had gone on to Cape Town (where she was admitted under the Red Cross flag) and the demented officer had to be locked in his cabin.

"Happy voyage and all success in your venture," signalled the German commanding officer at Luderitz as the Russians rolled away to sea again.

Thus the first sight Cape Town had of the Russians was the handsome white hospital ship *Oryol*. There had been incidents, however, before this arrival. Early that year the British freighter *Beckenham* had left London filled with cordite for Japan, and it was thought that the Russians might try to intercept her somewhere in African waters. But the *Beckenham* had kept well away from the ordinary steamer tracks, and had reached Japan after sixty-nine days at sea without calling anywhere or sighting another ship. Two Russian ships prowled along the South African coast after that in the hope of seizing ships laden with contraband. They were the *Smolensk* and the *Peterburg*, armed merchant cruisers. In August the *Smolensk* had stopped the British freighter *Comedian* near East London, but had allowed her to proceed to Durban after a search. British men-o'-war then set out in search of the Russians, finding both of them at Zanzibar.

Now the Russians had become visible to everyone and all Cape Town stood on the South Arm and stared at the *Oryol* with her clipper bow, band of red along the bulwarks and red cross emblems on her funnels. She reminded many people of the Union-Castle mailboat *Scot*, and indeed she had been a British passenger liner before her conversion.

A launch flying the White Ensign paid a courtesy visit to the *Oryol* while she was lying in Table Bay. Soon the ship came alongside the old Loch Jetty for water and fresh food. Privileged visitors were allowed on board. Mr. Knight, a shipping agent who also acted as Russian Consul, arranged with Captain Laklimatoff for reporters to inspect the ship. Everyone was courteous, but few spoke English.

However, the reporters were shown the launches which were intended to dash among sinking ships in battle and pick up the wounded. The operating theatre on the boat deck had four tables. The hospital staff of eighty included a French Red Cross surgeon and twenty Russian sisters. They wore brown or grey uniforms with the red cross on their aprons. Patients lay in hammocks on the upper deck; they were mainly seamen injured in coaling accidents.

Mr. O. Hansen, a shipping clerk on duty while the *Oryol* took on stores, told me that the Russians were extremely worried about Japanese secret agents. One of the Cape coloured labourers had Mongolian features, and he became a marked man as soon as he stepped on board. "A Russian officer, with signs and gestures, made it clear to me that this man would have to be removed," Mr. Hansen said. "I found that the officer spoke German, and explained to him in this language that the labourer was harmless. He accepted my word, but I could see the Russians watching that coloured man's every movement until the ship left the docks."

One day the Russian officers went on shore in a body and sat down to a gay lunch at the Metropole Hotel in Long Street. Then on December 19, the Tsar's "Name Day," there was a party in the hospital ship and she was dressed with flags.

Baron Ostensacken, the officer in charge of supplies, told the reporters that the hospital ship carried enough medical stores and food for a year. She took on additional medical comforts during her stay. But the item which caused wide comment – even in the newspapers – was the amount of alcohol ordered from Cape Town firms. Not only did the ship take on many cases of wines and spirits; the officers, and individual nursing sisters, also placed huge orders. No doubt they needed it before the interminable voyage ended.

Meanwhile the naval and military authorities at the Cape prepared for a Russian "invasion". Ships in Cape waters were advised to show clear lights. It was rumoured that the Russian fleet would call at Simonstown for food and water, though under the rules of war they would not be permitted to remain in harbour for more than twenty-four hours.

The *Cape Times* remarked: "Under the iron rules of neutrality we cannot do much to help the squadron on its way. We will nevertheless regard it with the sentiment which common humanity inspires towards a band of men who have embarked upon a voyage of so much hazard. The adventure is one of which no one can see the end; but if the matter is brought to the issue of battle, it is certain that at least some of the proud ships which are now passing along our coasts will never return."

Some uneasiness was caused by the fact that the British naval force in Simon's Bay consisted of just two ships, the flagship H.M.S. *Crescent* and the small gunboat *Thistle*. Three other gunboats were lying at moorings out of commission. It was announced, however, that a large body of police (about one hundred and fifty men) had been drafted to Simonstown to prevent "disgraceful scenes". The behaviour of Russian seamen on shore was notorious.

But if the Russians lost their heads again at sea and opened fire on innocent fishermen there was no great fleet to deal with them. The people of Simonstown found some comfort in the marching of the Royal Garrison Artillery gunners through the streets every night at eight. They manned the Upper North, Lower North, Noah's Ark and Craig's batteries, returning to their barracks every morning. One unhappy incident was reported. A marine sentry on duty at a magazine shot the sergeant of the guard through the leg. It seemed that the sergeant was creeping up to see if the sentry was asleep and failed to answer when challenged.

Probably the most ludicrous touch was provided by the Table Bay Harbour Board, which posted a notice on the Customs House at the foot of Ebenezer Road: "Owing to the approach of the Russian fleet, the s.s. *William Porter* is to be kept in perfect readiness day and night, with steam up. By order." The *William Porter* was an antiquated little tug with an oversize funnel,

(Some time later she was towed up the west coast but capsized before reaching her destination.) No one ever explained the part which the *William Porter* was supposed to play.

As it happened, there was no need for the British flagship or the tug to intervene. Signalman Harvey and a few others watched the passing of the fleet on December 19 from Signal Hill. The Cape Point lighthouse keepers sighted them and asked the nearest ships to "make their numbers". The request was ignored.

On board the Russian ships the rounding of the Cape was a great event. It coincided with the Tsar's "Name Day", which the hospital ship *Oryol* had celebrated in Table Bay Docks before hastening after the fleet. There were banquets in the wardrooms at sea, and vodka flowed on the messdecks.

Engineer Politovsky wrote to his wife that day: "If we double the Cape in safety, then thanks be to God. We are steaming near the shore. It is hilly, dark and treeless. Table Mountain is distinguished by its height and summit. The swell is tremendous. The ships are rolling. It is fearful to look at *Nakhimoff* and *Donskoy*. Near Cape Town we met an enormous four-masted ship flying the American flag. She was coming towards us. We are expecting to meet three suspicious schooners."

Another officer recorded sighting Table Mountain at eleven in the morning – "a glorious country which reminds one to an astonishing extent of the other end of the Old World, the North Cape". He added that the cruisers were a pitiful sight off the Cape as they were nearly shaken to pieces, while the battleships dived deeply into the swell.

The fleet was running before a gale. It was just as well that wind and sea were astern, as some of the ships might have capsized if they had felt the weather on the beam.

Not long afterwards a sealed bottle was washed ashore on one of the Cape beaches, and the *Cape Argus* published a translation of the letter it contained, written in Russian by one of Rozhestvensky's seamen: "Oh fisherman who may chance to find and read this letter, pray for those who are being sent to their death and pray that this terrible war may soon be brought to an end."

Commenting on the letter, the *Cape Argus* said: "We hope the fleet will be recalled before it is too late. The ships are ill-found and the officers untrained. The whole world may well hope, for the sake of humanity, that this mournful armada may yet turn back ere it be too late."

But the mournful armada did not turn back. A modern Trafalgar was fought in the Sea of Japan when the Russians steamed out of the fog and the Japanese fleet in formidable line ahead joined battle with them. Between the hours of two p.m. on May 27, 1905 and the following midnight, the Russians had lost over thirty ships worth over thirty million pounds, while four thousand of their seamen were killed. The Japanese lost only three torpedo boats. Rozhestvensky, seriously wounded, was taken prisoner, Russia had to sign a peace treaty and Japan became a great power.

Such was the drama Signalman Harvey and his wife glimpsed from Signal Hill that day late in 1904. They watched a turning point, and many of those at sea must have sensed the ultimate disaster.

Lawrence Green Loved the Sea

This anthology, I feel, would lose some of its savour if it did not include one chapter from *Where Men Still Dream*. Written in 1945, *Where Men Still Dream* was the first in Lawrence Green's stirring procession of post-war works. In the years to come connoisseurs of Lawrence Green's literature may well decide that it deserves to keep its place in the vanguard of his amazing output. While on active service in the Middle East in World War II as an administrative officer in the South African Air Force, Lawrence Green planned in rough skeletal outline the autobiography he meant to write when peace came. He decided to write from a personal angle of the ironies and idiocies of war. The canvas of this autobiography would be wide, provocative and international. He would ply his literary trade beyond the South African veld and the mysterious Continent of Africa which wove so strong a spell in him. *Where Men Still Dream*, however, differed vastly from the blueprint in Lawrence Green's retentive mind as he mused on the project in Cairo and in tents in the sands of the Western Desert.

It is a work with a strong autobiographical flavour, yet its scope is mostly South African and African. I do not know why Green changed his mind; it was one of the few personal secrets he did not tell me. Perhaps once back in the settled civilian life of sleepy Cape Town he felt it would be an act of literary suicide to soldier in faraway literary foreign lands! Thus the chapter I have chosen does have a Cape Town background but readers anywhere and particularly yachtsmen anywhere either inland or at the coast can enjoy it fully. Lawrence Green sailed a small yawl in the days when sailing for pleasure was looked upon as a pastime for cranks and slovenly unshaven eccentrics. Today sailing is one of South Africa's major sports and the institution of the Cape to Rio ocean race has widened public interest in it.

Do not fear that this selected chapter is a dull treatise on the mysterious techniques of sailing. On the contrary Lawrence Green, ever the immaculate compère, writes from deep personal knowledge of some immortal characters who liked to go down to the seas in tiny ships – men such as Upington, Pidgeon and others. Upington and Pidgeon have both long since made their last mortal landfalls. Brian Lello whom Green knew well, today edits a yachting magazine and is one of the architects of the Cape to Rio race.

CHAPTER XII

UNDER SAIL

Some of my finest days were spent under sail. They were spread over many years, but because I was young when I started, I think this is the right place to give you another breath of sea air and a glimpse of the men who go sailing and do not call themselves yachtsmen.

A yachtsman is a chap with a blue reefer jacket, often brass-bound, and white flannels, and a paid crew to see that he does not run into trouble. Sailing men dress disreputably and do everything themselves. Any young man living by the sea who finds life futile after the war through lack of a pastime might consider sailing as a means of salvation. Even an owner will agree that it costs less than motoring. Members of a crew do not feel the expense at all. And it is the healthiest and most satistisfactory game on the surface of the globe.

For many years I sailed with the most brilliant criminal lawyer of his day in South Africa. His name was Beauclerk Upington, his cutter was the Innisfallen, built by Dickie in 1910 on the Clyde. We called him "the Skipper." A great man, with a ship to match his own strong character.

The Skipper, as far as I know, had no enemies, but he was openly hostile towards what he called the "smug crowd." Members of his crew soon learnt to recognise these people, for the Skipper often denounced them publicly when he dined hilariously in town after a hard day's sailing. The "smug crowd" included all the pompous people, the hypocrites, those who regarded position as more important than the really human qualities; those who were affected in speech or manner. I shall never forget the consternation at a Royal Cape Yacht Club meeting at which an influential local potentate had been invited to preside. His speech was a remarkably stupid effort and Advocate Upington, K.C., a compelling speaker, of course, was next on the list. He referred to the potentate as "the pompous old swine in the chair."

Young men who sailed with the Skipper learnt more than seamanship. They learnt to make friends in pubs. The Skipper was a penetrating and unfailing judge of character. He had been a Member of Parliament, his fees were large when he chose to work, his reputation at the Bar was unassailable. But he could mix with naval ratings, ship's firemen, fishermen, the humblest of men, gain their respect immediately and show that he understood them. A rare gift, but the Skipper was an unusual man.

In a waterfront pub one day we met a ship's carpenter who told us that he was working on shore as a builder.

"What's your name?" inquired the Skipper.

"If I told you my name, you would not believe me." The carpenter then produced a tattered merchant seaman's discharge book and showed us his name. It was Wildgoose.

"A glass of beer with you, Wildgoose," said the Skipper. "Will you give me a job if I turn up on Monday morning?"

"Aye – I want a tall chap fer carrying planks."

"Now," went on the Skipper, "what would you take us for?"

Wildgoose looked at the tall, lean, grey-headed Skipper, he glanced at the crew, and he summed us up.

"I should say you came orf a ship."

The Skipper was pleased. "What sort of ship?" he asked.

"One of them emigrant ships bound for Orstrylia," replied Wildgoose decisively.

At sea the Skipper was superb. Innisfallen was, in my opinion, a little over canvassed for the fierce winds of Cape waters. (It is easy to start an argument among sailing men, but I think so.) The Skipper always drove her; yet when he took the tiller she became docile, and fewer seas broke over her decks. As he went below he would give his orders in the form of a quotation from a poem he had read somewhere: "Don't you take no sail off her, mister." And under her great mainsail "I.F." would surge on through the night.

Len Crowder, one of my old R.A.F. friends, was at the tiller one day when a heavy squall struck the Innisfallen. Instead of luffing, Len sat as though paralysed with the tiller pulled well in to his stomach. She heeled until three deck planks were covered, and the Skipper came up out of his bunk in a hurry.

"That's the way to capsize a ship, Len," remonstrated the Skipper.

"I thought you said she was foolproof, Skipper."

"Yes, my boy, she is – but not bloody lunatic proof!"

Among the crew just after the First Great War was one Andre Steytler, a man of splendid physique and a great sense of humour. He was a clerk in the pay department of the South African Railways, a position which did not carry a high salary. Andre lived austerely, for a year or two at a time he would not drink or smoke, but he saved for a purpose. At intervals of a few years he would book a first-class passage in the mailboat and make for Paris. While his money lasted he lived royally. Someone who knew him in Cape Town spotted him at the Cafe de la Paix. Andre was wearing a black hat, and he had an aperitif before him.

"What are you doing here, Andre?" asked the visitor.

"Studying art," declared Andre firmly. He made many such trips, and would probably be saving (or spending in Paris) now if the Second Great War had not broken out. Andre, an old soldier, joined up at once. He did not seek a commission, but became a private in the infantry again, carrying his pack through Abyssinia and the Western Desert at the age of forty-five.

Andre Steytler sold me my first boat, the Amitia, a little yawl which had been brought out from Canada by a relative, and which he had acquired cheaply. I used to keep her in Table Bay Docks. One day in 1924 another yawl sailed in and moored in the next berth. She was the Islander of Los Angeles, and her owner was Harry Pidgeon, one man who had solved the secret of life. Pidgeon was then sailing around the world alone for the first time. In 1936 he was back again, and he finished his second circumnavigation successfully at the age of sixty-six. There is a lesson for almost everyone in Pidgeon's way of life. I came to know the man well, and to admire him. His hair seemed no whiter when I met him for the second time, the grey eyes were still keen and steady, the sea-tanned face smiling and healthy as ever.

When our boats lay moored together Pidgeon would come over for supper with me sometimes on Saturdays, and sit yarning until long after midnight. Talking is a luxury when a man has been alone for months on end. It was then that I gathered some of the threads of Skipper Pidgeon's life and I realised that I was listening to a character such as one meets seldom in the twentieth century. For the real Pidgeon is not the Pidgeon of newspaper interviews; not even the Pidgeon who appears so modestly in his own book "Round the World Single-handed." He has been called a hermit, a woman-hater, a lunatic; all descriptions that are very wide of the mark.

Pidgeon, as I came to know him, is a man with a dry sense of humour, keenly interested in his fellow human beings. He sails alone, usually, because it is not easy to find companions able to break away from their work and circumnavigate the globe. On several occasions, however, he has had shipmates. When he left Los Angeles for Hawaii on the second cruise he carried a crew of two girls. "Husky girls, fond of climbing mountains and handling boats," he told me. "My niece, and a friend. Oh, they were all right. And say, I never knew before just how useful it was to have a fair crew aboard. When we made Honolulu the boys used up a whole bale of gasoline showing us over that island."

I looked round the Islander's cabin, wondering how the girls had fared in that strange, masculine place. You have to see Pidgeon's home to believe it. There are no racks or lockers, such as you find in other boats. All Pidgeon's possessions lie in one impressive heap on the deck beneath the coach roof; charts and books in the folds of spare canvas, cameras and tinned provisions mixed up with marlinespikes, water jars and coils of rope. "They can't fall any further," says Pidgeon, "and I know just where to put my hand on what I want."

A hard berth is fitted on each side of the small table. "I always stick to my bunk to starboard, and the girls shared the other bunk," remarked Pidgeon. "One of us was always on watch, so there was plenty of room." Thus the old sailorman solved a problem that might have worried ordinary folk, and having solved it, gave no more thought to the matter. At least the arrangement disposes of any woman-hating tendencies. The man who dislikes feminine company does not shut himself away from the world with "two husky girls" for an ocean passage lasting twenty-eight days.

"They stared at the island peaks when we raised them, and said how green the land seemed after the blue ocean," recalled Pidgeon. "But one of them wanted to sail on round the world. I guess one would have been awkward, so I left the pair of them in Honolulu to go home by steamer."

No doubt it was a wise decision, for Pidgeon is full of sea-wisdom and far more sane than most people on shore. Surely, you may remark, a man must be mad to spend many years of his life enduring hardships, taking great risks, drifting aimlessly from port to port. The answer is that Pidgeon is a completely happy man. He has established a reputation as the greatest small-boat sailor of his day. His lectures have given pleasure to thousands. When he re-visits old ports of call, he finds friends everywhere. All are welcome on board the Islander; he will talk with the same pleasant sincerity to a Governor or a child. There is nothing selfish in Pidgeon's way of life, for no one ever forgets him and all memories of him are happy.

It is wrong, by the way, to imagine that a voyage round the world in a 34-foot boat is a suicidal adventure. Dangerous moments there may be, but if you can handle small craft with the skill of Skipper Pidgeon, the risk is small. Pidgeon built the Islander himself in 1918, and the little ship has been his home ever since. She is not heavily built, as most cruising yachts are. The secret of her survival lies in the care Pidgeon bestowed on her when he planed each plank and drove home each nail. In spite of her light build, she has pounded on coral reefs and distant beaches, emerging from every ordeal unharmed. I saw the Islander stranded in a wicked bay north of Saldanha. She was towed off without a cup of water in her bilge. The building of the Islander was a job of work done well, and it has saved Pidgeon's life many times.

Little ships like this ride over the huge seas that liners plunge through and throw over their bows. The Islander is lively, but she does not founder in a gale. Crossing the ocean in the Islander means much discomfort, but not death. "I am battered and battered and battered in dirty weather until I wonder why I ever left the shore," Pidgeon told me. "But there's no fool like an old fool. When it's over, I forget it."

Many people are puzzled to know what happens to the ship when Pidgeon goes to sleep. Well, the ship sails on. Pidgeon trims the sails and lashes his tiller, and the Islander then follows the course set, anywhere from close-hauled to running dead before a gale. That saves a lot of hard labour. Only when nearing land does he lose sleep. You cannot leave the ship to roar along by herself when land may loom up out of the night. So Skipper Pidgeon is usually a tired man by the time he reaches port – it is the penalty of sailing alone, and he pays it cheerfully.

His physical endurance is astounding. Sixty-six, and he looked no older than men of forty-five. "I had a good breakfast today, and now someone has invited me to dinner tonight – and I don't want to go," he once said to me. "No use overloading the stomach." One meal a day, at sea or on shore, is enough for Skipper Pidgeon. He seldom drinks anything but water. At sea he cooks his meal on a simple wood stove in the cabin, and prefers fresh vegetables and fruit to tinned provisions. He does not smoke. Yet he is no fanatic about diet, drink or tobacco. His own system is the one he enjoys, and it has kept him fit from Alaska to the tropics.

Now you begin to understand why Skipper Pidgeon is able to sail the oceans, visiting the playgrounds of millionaires and islands of lonely exiles, with hardly a cent in his pocket. He pays no rent, performs the work of the ship himself, and needs food costing only a pound or two a month. Little yachts like the Islander are not liable for harbour dues. Friendly yacht clubs are proud to show some hospitality to a man who holds the "Blue Water Medal" of the Cruising Club of North America for his notable deep-sea wanderings.

Nevertheless, if Pidgeon possesses any idiosyncrasy at all, it concerns money. His income depends on a little writing, a lecture here and there, and nowadays an occasional broacast talk. But he does not seek money in these ways, and turns to them only when he finds his pocket empty. They tell a story of his first visit to Cape Town.

"Giving another lecture soon, Skipper?" someone asked him.

"I guess not – I've still got a dollar."

Skipper Pidgeon has a natural gift for lecturing which, if exploited in his own country, might have made him a wealthy man. Yet he would rather talk to a crowd of schoolboys than address a distinguished audience in New York. Money means nothing more to him than a means of fitting out the Islander for her next passage from continent to continent – a few sails, a lick of paint, and some dried fruit in the store-cupboard. He has dispensed with money. Save on rare occasions, then, he has ridded himself of one of the main causes of worry among landsmen. I suppose he hears about depressions, but he must be one of the very few civilised men in the world who have escaped their effects.

One more detail of Pidgeon's sea housekeeping should be mentioned – water. Nearly everyone he meets asks him how he manages to carry enough fresh water. He uses half a gallon a day, and stores 120 gallons in casks and jars; enough for about eight months. His longest passage between ports was 88 days, so that there has never been a shortage of water aboard the Islander. When it rains he has a shower bath. At other times he throws a bucket over the side and bathes in salt water.

Two other men, Slocum and Gerbault, sailed round the world alone, but their boats were substantially larger than the Islander. When Pidgeon was in Table Bay the first time he told me the Islander was really too large for his purpose. He wanted a 25-foot boat. Now he thinks she is just the right size. When he sails up to some romantic anchorage at the age of eighty I expect he will tell the reporters that he is thinking of building a slightly larger craft.

But Skipper Harry Pidgeon will sail on in the Islander. The two have gone together for so long that it is difficult to think of them apart. It has been a wonderful partnership; these two have made strange landfalls. They have raised the peaks of the Pacific, sweltered together off New Guinea, rested in calm lagoons and raced before the trade winds of the world. All this they have done while millions toil and fear to leave their dull routine. That is why I say Pidgeon has solved the secret of life. Healthy, fearless, penniless old vagabond of the oceans, I admire him.

Alain Gerbault, the Frenchman, with his narrow-gutted Firecrest, came to Table Bay too, and I talked to him about his voyage round the world. Pidgeon was a normal man. Gerbault, a great lover of the sea and a brave sailor, was nevertheless a man of a different type, an eccentric hermit. He had endured cruel hardships, and I wondered whether he had always prepared as carefully for his ocean crossings as did Pidgeon.

Pidgeon and Gerbault, and indeed practically all the men I met who had made long voyages in small craft, were experienced seamen. I knew one memorable exception – a powerful Afrikaner from the Northern Transvaal who came to Cape Town on holiday and bought the Amitia from me. His name was Dirk Eloff, and he was a grandson of President Paul Kruger. Heredity does count. This man had something of the physique and the shrewdness of his famous grandfather. I gave him his first lesson in sailing, and he was an intelligent pupil. An idea entered his mind and germinated. He needed money for the enterprise, so he returned to the low veld and speculated in cattle. Six months later he was back in Cape Town with enough money to build a forty-four foot yacht for a voyage round the world.

Eloff's yacht was called Sarie Marais. Her main cabin seemed to me to be furnished with huge jars of wine and a bookcase containing the works of Freud. Soon after the launching Eloff was married on board. He took his wife with him, and three men, who were all novices. They sailed away and reached Panama! I have no doubt that Dirk Eloff would have completed the voyage round the world, but his wife was expecting a baby and the cruise had to be abandoned.

It takes brains and muscle to cross the ocean in a small boat, but I think Dirk Eloff proved that long sea training is not essential. As for the navigation, he studied his text-books as he sailed and made accurate landfalls. There is a fascination about this game which takes a strong hold on the devotees. Years afterwards in the Western Desert I spent many a night discussing rigs, cruises and other nautical points with Brian Lello, a South African war correspondent. We forgot the bombing and all the irritations of war as we talked. Lello had sailed from Durban to the West Indies in a twenty-five foot boat. I was amused at his summing up.

"This war may be the big thing in the lives of the other fellows here, but for me it is only a sideshow," he declared. "I want to see the war finished so that I can get on to something really important."

"What's that?" I inquired.

"I am going to build a small boat and sail her round the world."

Worth the Years of Wondering

DEVOTEES of Lawrence G. Green need no reminder of the spell the oceans of the world held for him. And no reporter responded more vividly to the challenge of the unravelment of a mystery of the sea. In his descriptions of hardy seamen, the queer characters that sail the trade routes and remoter sea-lanes and the awesomeness of the great storm, Green with his stark simplicity of language resembled Conrad in his ability to tell a tale of the sea so dramatically. In his early years as a newspaper reporter Green was never happier nor more fulfilled than when he was in quest of a news story about the sea. A wreck off the coastline of the Cape. A vessel in Table Bay with a queer cargo or even odder passengers. Dark hints of a hell-hole vessel with a mutinous crew. A barque with all sail set due to make a landfall in Table Bay. Lawrence Green would thrill to the siren music of the tantalising sea story. A great and instinctive reporter he would not rest till he could print the truth, and all the truth. Green wrote *Almost Forgotten, Never Told* in his later years after his retirement from *The Argus* in Cape Town. But though much of the book tells of events and adventures long ago, this work shows that Green's youthful zeal for the sea and its abiding mysteries and sublime challenges remained undimmed. Green indeed was a writer whom the years never wearied. I have selected *Epic of the Karatara* because it is in itself a fascinating saga of the sea which can be read with infinite enjoyment even by people whose interest in ships and sailors is slight. Green had to wait 42 years before he could finish this epic of the sea which began in his youth when a South African coaster came back from the sealing islands.

Green believed that the end of the story which he elicited in the Mount Nelson Hotel 42 years later was "worth all the years of wondering". This indeed is a great story of the sea by a great writer.

CHAPTER XIII

EPIC OF THE KARATARA

Perhaps the strangest of all the tales of the "roaring forties" came my way when I was a young reporter. It was an epic, a "Caine mutiny" on board a South African coasting steamer. I wish that I could have sailed to Kerguelen and Marion in the little *Karatara* nearly half a century ago.

I always had a queer, unsatisfied feeling about the *Karatara* affair, but no one could have been more astounded than I was when I heard the truth at last. Some of you will remember the *Karatara*, a fine Thesen coaster of about six hundred tons. She had been away in the south for about two months, and I boarded her hopefully, thinking that a ship which had been through the "roaring forties" would have a story for the newspaper.

The master was a great hulking Scot named Matthew Thomson, a pipe-smoker with a face reddened by the weather, no doubt, and by something more. He seemed none too pleased to have a young waterfront reporter on board. The mate was there, but he remained silent, smiling grimly now and again while Captain Thomson spoke briefly of the voyage. I have before me the paragraph I wrote, stating that the *Karatara* had taken coal to the sealing station at Kerguelen and brought back seal oil. The passage to Kerguelen had taken seventeen days owing to heavy gales. On the way back the *Karatara* had embarked fifteen Norwegian sealers at Prince Edward and Marion, where they had killed seven hundred and eighty-five seals. The men, said Thomson, were glad to see the *Karatara* for they had eaten all their food and had been living on penguins and seal meat.

As an afterthought, Thomson added that he had carried a cinematographer named Ayliffe, who had filmed the birds and seals on the islands. With this meagre statement I had to be content, as Thomson was in no mood for cross-examination. I left the battered coaster wishing that I could have been with them on that voyage to the edge of the Antarctic.

Forty-two years later I received a 'phone call from the best hotel in Cape Town. "You won't remember me," said the voice. "I'm Harold Bayley, and I was mate of the *Karatara* that day when you came on board after our Kerguelen trip. I am now prepared to tell you what really happened . . ."

So my curiosity was satisfied at last through the kindness of Harold Bayley. In the Mount Nelson Hotel that morning I listened to a great sea story, worth all the years of wondering.

Bayley had gone to sea as an apprentice in tramps in 1912, and had taken his mate's ticket during World War I. After years in Atlantic convoys he had strained his eyes and failed the postwar eyesight test. That handicap brought him to South Africa, for there was a shortage of certificated officers, and no medical examination. He was serving in the largest Thesen Line coaster, the *Outeniqua*, as second mate when the marine superintendent offered him promotion to mate in the *Karatara*.

"That means sailing with Captain Thomson – I'd rather stay where I am," replied Bayley. Everyone in the coasters knew Captain Thomson's record – and his failing. He had held senior posts in great Atlantic liners. At one period his captain (in the White Star liner *Adriatic*) was the ill-fated Captain Smith, who went down in the *Titanic*. A fine seaman and navigator, Thomson was also an alcoholic, and his behaviour was unpredictable. Thomson had been dismissed from one ship after another, but he had arrived in South Africa during World War I in command of a troopship bound for Mesopotamia. His conduct during that voyage was such that an official inquiry was held in Durban, and Thomson was relieved of his command. (Bayley was in the same convoy, serving as third officer of the Blue Funnel liner *Nestor*). Thomson's certificate was endorsed, so that he had great difficulty in finding another ship.

For a time Thomson had to be content with a navigator's job on board a whaler operating off the Natal coast. Then he was offered the command of a four-masted barque engaged in a dubious enterprise which involved running a cargo of contraband from the Dutch East Indies to Holland. The barque was intercepted off the West African coast and escorted into Freetown by a British man-o'-war. "I expected to be shot," Thomson once told Bayley. "Luckily I merely landed in Edinburgh gaol."

After the war the Thesen Line gave Thomson command of the *Karatara*, a slow but seaworthy little steamer. She was thirty-seven years old, built in Norway for the Arctic sealing trade. Her plates were thick, to withstand the shock of colliding with floating ice. Her hull design was rather similar to the famous Norwegian "prams" used by fishermen. She was lively, but she gave her men a sense of confidence.

So the *Karatara* lay in Table Bay Docks in the middle of January 1921 while young Bayley argued with the marine superintendent.

"You'll find Captain Thomson a changed man – a complete teetotaler," promised the superintendent. Against his better judgment, Bayley signed on as mate of the *Karatara*. She was to sail direct to Kerguelen, nearly three thousand miles from Cape Town, and the round voyage was expected to last four months. Bayley pointed out that they would need good supplies of food, water and coal. Thomson assured him that it was all on board, and the holds were filled with coal and empty drums for the seal oil.

Just as they were about to sail, Bayley found that he had a dental abscess. The *Karatara* waited while he hurried off to a dentist and had the tooth pulled. "If I had known what was coming I would never have sailed in the *Karatara*," Bayley told me. "It was the toughest job of my whole life at sea."

They had one passenger in the *Karatara* as I mentioned earlier, a short man with a heavy moustache and humorous face. He was H. J. Ayliffe, one of South Africa's pioneer film cameramen. Jack Ayliffe had served in the Royal Navy as a boy and had left the sea to become an actor. Later he started a theatrical agency, and married while on a business visit to Ireland. His wife was not very robust, and he had settled in South Africa for the sake of her health. They had a daughter Beryl,* who was very young when her father sailed in the *Karatara*.

---

*Now Mrs. de Sarigny of Petit, near Benoni. I am most grateful to her for supplying details of her father's career and other information — L.G.G.

They left Table Bay in fine weather, stowing the deck cargo securely while they had the chance. On the second evening the *Karatara* cleared the Agulhas Bank and was heading south-east away from the shipping lanes. She had hand steering-gear, which meant hard work for the man at the wheel in heavy weather. At this period she was steaming at her top speed, between seven and eight knots.

"Have a drink," Thomson invited Bayley. "You'll be drinking alone, as I never touch the stuff – but you're welcome." Bayley was a little surprised by this invitation. He was officer of the watch, but he left the bridge and poured himself a tot of brandy in the master's cabin. Bayley counted sixteen cases of Cape brandy. He understood the brandy was intended for the Norwegian sealers on the small islands.

"This was the beginning of a chapter for which I had never bargained," recalled Bayley thoughtfully. "My skipper did not touch a drop that night, but the following evening he relapsed, and the game was on."

Thomson began to drink his way steadily through the sixteen cases of brandy. Meanwhile the heavy weather set in; and the decks, which had dried out in summer on the South African coast, now leaked seriously. Thomson had given up pretending to keep his watch, and Bayley knew that he was fully responsible for the safety of the ship. There was a second mate. He was a Norwegian, a good seaman, but he had no certificate, no experience in navigation, and was really only the bo'sun. The ship carried three or four deck hands; a Norwegian chief engineer with a Scot as second; Cape coloured men as firemen and a cook and steward.

Every day the seas rose higher, but the little old *Karatara* with her sturdy iron hull was carried along like a duck. Bayley never had any anxiety on that score, but he had other worries. The hand steering gear had to be watched closely, as the rope tackles he had fitted to relieve the strain on the rudder quadrant were snapping every few hours. However, she steered well and was never pooped.

Bayley discovered after leaving Table Bay that there was only one chronometer in the chart room. Few little ships were equipped with wireless back in 1921, and thus Bayley could not pick up a time signal to check his chronometer. Without an accurate time-piece the fixing of longitude in midocean becomes extremely hazardous. Bayley nursed his one chronometer, and fortunately it never let him down.

Overcast skies made navigation difficult, but the ship was still far from land and so this problem was not yet urgent. Bayley's main concern remained the state of Captain Thomson. This did not improve, and Bayley had to consider seriously the possibility of hiding the precious store of brandy. At times he thought of throwing the whole lot overboard. Then he remembered the men on the cold islands. They might need that brandy as medicine.

First of all Bayley moved the cases of brandy into a lifeboat and covered them with canvas. It took some time, and it had to be done while Thomson was out of his cabin; but Ayliffe and the steward helped. Thomson searched the ship frantically. Within twenty-four hours he had recovered the brandy. After that incident Thomson became suspicious and watched Bayley intently.

It became so cold that all hands gathered in the engineroom when they were off duty. That was the only warm spot. Nearly all the bunks were sodden, and the ship had no heating or electricity in the cabins; just oil and candle lamps.

A fortnight passed and the problem of the Kerguelen landfall became acute. Bayley knew from his dead reckoning that he must be closing in with the island, but the sun remained covered and there was plenty of room for error. Should he steer for the northern end of Kerguelen or run past and come up in the lee? Thomson was too drunk to help. The young mate had reason to curse the problems of his first command.

"Twenty-four hours to go, snow and drizzle and not a sight of the sun," Bayley told me. "I knew there was a serious risk of crashing into the uncharted rocks on the unlighted Kerguelen coast at night, and so I altered course to run past the island. This was a sound decision. I covered the required distance, and at five that morning the weather cleared suddenly and I whipped out my sextant and secured a perfect star fix. Then I was able to set a course which brought the *Karatara* to Royal Sound in the south-eastern corner of Kerguelen."

Bayley's navigation was so accurate that he made his landfall at the entrance of the sound within a quarter of a mile of the charted position. This was after steaming more than two thousand seven hundred miles, mainly by dead reckoning. Now he realised that he could rely on his one chronometer.

As the little *Karatara* moved cautiously up Royal Sound she cut through enormous strands of kelp. It was so thick that Bayley said it must have scraped all the barnacles off the hull. Royal Sound, a magnificent sheet of water, led the *Karatara* past a high range of snow-clad mountains, past many isles and islets, past Island Harbour of the old American whalers; and twenty miles from the entrance she drew alongside the whaling station built early this century by Norwegians in the employ of a French company beside the inlet named Port Jeanne D'Arc.

Bossiere, the French concession holder, also started sheep-breeding, and in the beginning he drew on a most unlikely source for labour – Zululand. But the sheep were lost in the bogs of the unmapped interior and the Zulus complained of the cold. "Kerguelen is truly diabolical in its grim ugliness," remarked one French visitor. "It is a savage, naked land of desolation to be shunned by mortals and good angels."

So the French pulled out, and soon after World War I the Cape Town firm of Irvin and Johnson re-opened the factory. I remember the flotilla of adventurous ships they sent there year after year – two wartime mystery ships of strange design, *Kildalkey* and *Kilfenora*, the coaster *Golden Crown*, tiny steam trawlers like the *Galaxy* and *Plough*, the auxiliary barquentine *Sound of Jura*, and modern tankers to bring back the oil.

Seventeen days had passed since the *Karatara* had left Table Bay, and as the coaster made fast to the wooden jetty, Bayley gave thanks for the safe arrival. Had he only known it, the worst ordeals still lay ahead. Bayley's first task was to discharge the cargo of drums and coal on to the jetty without cranes. For a fortnight the ship's overworked winches rattled and the men on the station hauled the coal sacks away, filled the drums with sea-elephant oil and rolled them back to the ship. Port Jeanne D'Arc had a population of one hundred and twenty men at that time. Captain Thomson prowled round the houses and stores, and Bayley knew well enough what he was seeking.

One day, as a relief from the monotonous routine, the Norwegian station manager organised a shooting trip up one of the fjords in a boat with an outboard motor. Bayley, Ayliffe and the young Scottish doctor accompanied him. Kerguelen, the land of desolation, has incredible wealth of bird life, from the soaring albatross to the whale-birds that coo like pigeons; the skua gulls and gentoo penguins, giant petrels and fat cormorants. But the party from the whaling station were out after duck, the teeming hundreds of thousands of wild duck that show no fear of man. Only when the first shot was fired did they rise from their nests, so that their whistling and quacking and beating of wings rose above the endless booming of the wind. "It was murder, but we had to feed the station and the ship," said Bayley. "Our boat was heavily-laden with duck when we stopped firing, and I think we set up a world record for the number of cartridges used."

Captain Thomson was drunk when they returned. He had raided the manager's house and found liquor. There was no gangway, and they had to hoist him on deck in a "bowline on the bight".

Sailing day came and the *Karatara* was ready to cast off when Bayley noticed that the captain was missing. They searched the station and found him in the manager's house, helping himself once more to the liquor. He was carried back to the *Karatara*. The manager asked Bayley: "Can you carry on with the captain in that condition?"

Bayley replied, with inward misgivings, that he would take full responsibility. "However, I think the manager was more worried than I was," declared Bayley.

Soon after sailing Bayley realised that he should have left the captain behind. Thomson applied himself to the remaining brandy with such determination that Bayley had to ignore him and solve all problems himself. Once again Bayley hid the cases of brandy, in the chain-locker this time. Then he joined Ayliffe at supper. Thomson was mad with rage when he discovered his loss. He burst into the saloon and accused Bayley of stealing the liquor. Bayley refused to give his captain any clue to the hiding-place. Thomson then seized a sharp-pointed bread-knife and lunged at Bayley.

"I raced out of the saloon, picked up a belaying-pin and told

Thomson I would knock him out if he attacked me again," Bayley told me. "It was a nasty situation, for I did not wish to be charged with mutiny. However, I had to look after myself and the ship, and there was no other way."

Ayliffe intervened at this stage with a word of sound advice. "Give him back the brandy, or he'll go beserk again," Ayliffe suggested. "Let him finish it, and then he won't be able to blame you."

Off the Kerguelen coast the *Karatara* passed an iceberg so enormous that it ranked as a floating island of ice. Bayley said it rose out of the water like Table Mountain, then vanished in the fog. They had to alter course suddenly to avoid a collision. Ayliffe was in his cabin at the time. When he heard about the berg he wanted Bayley to put back so that he could film it. This was impossible.

Bayley was on watch that night, wearing heavy clothes against the fierce cold, when he was startled to find Ayliffe beside him on the bridge. Ayliffe was in his pyjamas!

"There's something wrong, something dreadful is happening – I don't know what it is, but I can feel it," gasped Ayliffe. "Can it be that we're going to collide with an iceberg, like the *Titanic?* I can feel death very close to me, Bayley."

Bayley urged him to go below to his bunk before the Antarctic cold killed him. He assured Ayliffe that there was not an iceberg in sight and that all would be well; but all was not well and Bayley had good reason to remember the sinister episode off Kerguelen.

Once clear of the land Bayley steered west for Prince Edward and Marion. Now there was no shelter, and the little steamer drove slowly indeed into the strong head winds and seas. During one stretch of twenty-four hours Bayley's sights showed that the *Karatara* had covered only eight miles. All this time the crew were working coal from the for'ard hold to the bunkers. Bayley stood at the winch, sodden rope in his hands, whipping up sack after sack of coal for hours on end. They were fighting the "roaring forties" again, only this time the ship was plunging into the teeth of the wind, not running before. All of them were at grips with the violence of the sea, and inevitably the weaker ones cracked under the strain.

The weaker ones were the Cape firemen. Steam, steam, steam, was the urgent need; and then the bo'sun informed Bayley that the frightened, exhausted firemen were refusing to leave the fo'c'stle and go on watch. "They say the ship is going to sink, and they'll never see Cape Town again," added the bo'sun.

Bayley, cold and tired and worried himself, cursed his luck in sailing with a drunken captain and went grimly to the firemen's quarters. He rigged a hose and played the icy sea-water on them until they overcame their panic and went below. The mutiny was over. Soon afterwards the westerly gale blew itself out and the *Karatara* made good headway.

About this time, and none too soon, Thomson drank the last of the brandy. What now, Bayley wondered – delirium or recovery? Rather to his surprise, Thomson recovered. "What are you going to do about this – report me?" inquired Thomson.

Bayley, the real hero of this drama, replied that he would take no action at all. "From that moment our positons were strictly those of master and mate," Bayley told me. "Now I could appreciate those rare qualities that make a man an outstanding seaman. Trained in sail like most of his generation, he had secured his master's ticket before transferring to steam. Without the drink, Thomson was the finest sailorman I ever met."

It was just as well, for the *Karatara* had a hard battle to reach Prince Edward Island. Her average speed from Kerguelen was four-and-a-half knots, little more than walking-pace. They cruised back and forth in the lee of Prince Edward, but saw nothing of the sealers they had come to embark. Blasts of the siren brought no answering signal. When they visited Marion, however, a boat put off and two sealers boarded the *Karatara*. "Give us a square meal," they asked. "We finished our rations weeks ago, and without seal meat and birds'-eggs we would have died."

Food was running low on board the *Karatara* by this time. Thomson ordered the sealers to collect albatross and penguin eggs to eke out the ship's stores. The coaster steamed from beach to beach, picking up more men and loading six thousand sealskins in the ship's lifeboats. This was a slow and arduous process, for the anchorages were hazardous when it came on to blow.

One night the wind swung round suddenly from north-west to south-west, and the *Karatara* was drifting on to a lee shore. Thomson told Bayley to get the anchor up, but as the chain came in the kelp jammed in the hawsepipe. They had to go over the side in the freezing darkness and chop the kelp away with hatchets. Seas broke heavily over the fo'c'stle-head. The second engineer, who was working the winch in the bows, was picked up by a comber and flung into the well-deck.

Ten days it took them to load those pelts. Now the coal problem worried Thomson and his officers more than the food shortage. Before leaving the islands they had to call at Prince Edward to find the four men who had been sealing there. This time the men were located, and the *Karatara* set off on a great circle course for Durban. She was really bound for Cape Town, but great circle navigation gave her a better chance of reaching South Africa before the coal ran out.

"Hungry days, those were," Bayley recalled. "The weather improved, and our one chronometer worked accurately; but we had fifteen Norwegian sealers to feed besides our own crew, and we lived on rations of bully beef, tea and birds'-eggs. No bread, no biscuit. If we had sighted a ship we would have stopped her and asked for food. But we were on a lonely sea-track, and not a mast appeared on the horizon during that whole passage."

One of the Norwegian sealers was fatter than the others. So they pointed at him every day and remarked: "When the food is finished, he'll be number one." Bayley said the fat man did not enjoy the joke.

Eight tons of coal remained in the bunkers of the *Karatara* when she entered Durban harbour. The watertanks were nearly empty, and there was little food. Someone from a museum boarded the *Karatara* on arrival and offered to pay one hundred pounds for specimens of bird and animal life from the sub-Antarctic. All they could find to give him were two albatross eggs.

"Ayliffe had asked me to have dinner with him on the night we arrived," Bayley told me. "His idea was to find the best meal in Durban to make up for our hardships during the voyage. He came back to the ship soon after landing and told me that he had to leave for Johannesburg at once. He looked very grave, but I asked no questions on parting. However, there was an extraordinary sequel years afterwards, as I shall tell you."

As soon as the *Karatara* had filled her bunkers and storerooms she left for Cape Town, where I met her. Bayley transferred to another ship, but Captain Thomson remained in command of the *Karatara* for a few more voyages. He was drinking heavily with a passenger while entering Knysna harbour; and during an argument he threw the passenger overboard. That was the end of Captain Thomson's career in the Thesen Line and he had to find another ship. Bayley was asked questions about the Kerguelen voyage, and the truth came out.

Why didn't you enter it in the log?" inquired the manager. "I was at sea in another of your ships with a captain who had no deep-water experience and knew no navigation," Bayley replied. "When I reported it, I was told to mind my own business. So I said nothing about the *Karatara* affair."

Thomson returned to Britain. He devised a way of concealing the remarks on his master's certificate, and in spite of his peculiar record he was given command of an ocean-going steamer on the South African run. The end came when the unhappy Thomson committed suicide by jumping overboard in London Docks.

I saw the end of the gallant little *Karatara* myself. She came into Table Bay ablaze from end to end after her cargo of petrol had exploded. Harbour tugs put the fire out, but she was finished. You can still see her rusty hull at one of the Saldanha Bay whaling stations, where she was sunk to make a jetty.

Bayley became a stevedore, a harbour pilot in East Africa, and then a farmer in the Orange Free State. World War II came, and he could have had a naval commission. Bayley refused because he knew that his eyesight was defective. He went to sea again, however, as an able seaman, in a ship commanded by a man he had known as a cadet. Every day the captain called Able Seaman Bayley into his cabin for a drink.

When I met Bayley he had become a successful florist and had just been elected South African president of a world-wide florists' organisation. Quite a contrast, he agreed, with taking a little ship to the sub-Antarctic islands.

Ayliffe set off on another adventurous journey in 1922, when he took the first motion pictures of the Mountains of the Moon and other African peaks. He filmed those early dramas produced in South Africa in the nineteen-twenties – "King Solomon's Mines", the "Voortrekkers" and "Alan Quatermain". I believe he was the first cinematographer in South Africa to film the country from the air. He died in 1949.

Bayley and Ayliffe had their dinner together after all. They met unexpectedly in Johannesburg twelve years after the *Karatara* adventure, and spent the evening discussing those bitter yet memorable weeks on the fringe of the Antarctic. Bayley went home thoughtfully that night because of something Ayliffe had told him.

"When I cancelled our dinner in Durban it was because I had just received a telegram – my wife had died while I was away, and I had to get back to my young daughter as soon as possible," Ayliffe explained. "By the way, you remember that night off Kerguelen when I came up on the bridge in pyjamas and told you that I felt death close to me? Well, that was the night my wife died."

Pageant of the Long Shore

ALL his life Lawrence G. Green regularly took long, brisk and solitary walks along the beaches of the Cape. Blouberg beach was his favourite. As he strode five miles or more in a morning, ideas for a new book or a new chapter would occur to him. I am sure that the theme for *South African Beachcomber*, published in 1958, must have stirred in his mind as he paced one of the beaches of the Cape. This book tells of the lure and fascination of South Africa's coasts and what Green himself describes as "the pageant of the long shore". He writes with infinite knowledge of the men who man the lighthouses, the sea birds, the fishermen and the treasure seekers of South Africa. "Every tide," Green wrote, "washes romance in my path."

Yet though he could capture so admirably the loafing spirit of the true beachcomber and loved to explore the beaches untouched by the tripper it is wrong to assume, as some obituaries did after his death, that Lawrence G. Green was a beachcomber by nature. True, he eschewed the artificial frivolities of aspiring socialites. He did not mind being alone and by some standards he lived simply. Yet he like ordered living, comfort, good food and his philosophy rejected any form of hand-to-mouth living. His penetrative mind, however, gave him understanding of the beachcomber and of impecunious men forever in search of sudden wealth. This chapter, *Every Beachcomber's Dream*, tells of the allure of lost treasure in sunken ships off the South African coast-line. Lawrence Green rediscovers some lost pages of South African history. The result is an exciting chapter on a subject that enchants all people with vivid imaginations from boyhood to old age. When Green wrote this book modern skin-diving and other techniques for discovering the secrets on the sea beds were comparatively in their infancy. Thus the increasing army of South African skin divers, both amateur and professional, are bound to find this chapter exceptionally fascinating.

CHAPTER XIV

EVERY BEACHCOMBER'S DREAM

Every stretch of the South African coast has its legendary treasure, every beachcomber has dreamed of finding wealth. I have had personal experience of such quests. Before you invest in a treasure syndicate, however, I would like you to consider one point which may not have occurred to you, but which you should bear in mind.

Years ago I watched an old diver risking his life in the surf among the rocks of the Cape coast. He brought up nothing that day, but in the hotel bar afterwards he gave me the piece of information which I have never forgotten. "Some divers," he said, "find all sorts of interesting things on the bottom and then come up empty-handed. When all the excitement is over they go quietly back to the spot and do a little profitable diving on their own account."

So you must pick your diver carefully. Newspapers often report the failures, but successful treasure hunts sometimes go unrecorded.

You should also remember that not every sunken treasure chest is worth recovering. On a calm day I could show you the wreck of a Dutch East Indiaman which still gives up a few coins after winter gales; the silver coins known as ducatoons. But seldom is it worth while paying a diver to recover a box of silver. Diamonds and gold are much better, if you can find them. When the treasure has been buried on shore, of course, you can afford to be less particular and set out spade in hand to find the cache.

I like the treasure legend of Vergelegen at Somerset West. It has the ring of truth about it, and the searcher in the Cape archives will find evidence supporting the old tale of the *Schoonberg's* gold and jewels and bars of silver. By sheer chance I discovered further sidelights in long-forgotten newspaper files.

Nearly two and half centuries have passed since the Dutch ship *Schoonberg* ran ashore near Cape Agulhas in fine, clear, summer weather. Some reports said this was due to the negligence of her officers. It was suspected, however, that Captain Albertus van Soest had wrecked his ship deliberately so that he and other conspirators might steal valuable items of cargo. The ship took the sand gently in Struys Bay and all hands waded on shore safely.

She was loaded mainly with tea from Batavia, and she also carried pepper, eastern timber, bales of silk – and exquisitely transportable boxes of gold and precious stones, silver and ornaments. A strong south-easter raged the day after the wreck, and the *Schoonberg* began to pound and break up.

Some of the ship's company marched along the shore until they came to the Bot River mouth. There they met a farmer who had just shot a hippo, and the castaways were glad to join him in a feast. Captain van Soest remained on the spot until word of the wreck brought his fellow conspirators to Agulhas with ox-wagons. Then the cavalcade left for Cape Town loaded with selected cargo from the wreck.

Van Soest's accomplices were Jacob van der Heyden of Vergelegen, Hendrik Klopper and Jacob Malan. (Van der Heyden and Klopper had bought the famous Vergelegen farm after Willem Adriaan van der Stel had been recalled to Holland.) It seems that the conspirators buried most of the valuables at Vergelegen, handing over the rest to Governor de Chavonnes to allay suspicion.

Nevertheless, the Governor was suspicious. He did not understand how an experienced master could have thrown away his ship in calm weather. He regarded it as something more than a coincidence that the ox-wagons from Vergelegen should have made straight for the wreck. His inquiries proved that Captain van Soest had visited Vergelegen on several previous occasions, and that the captain had smuggled tobacco and rum with the aid of the farmers. Finally the Governor learnt that seamen from the lost ship had been spending gold and silver in the taverns of Cape Town.

Governor de Chavonnes sent Valk, the harbour master, and Jan de la Fonteine, senior merchant, to the wreck to see whether anything more could be salved. They found only the bones of the *Schoonberg*, for she had been set on fire and burnt down to the waterline. So the Governor ordered the arrest of Captain van Soest and his accomplices. According to one authority, the crime preyed on the mind of Hendrik Klopper, who committed suicide. Captain van Soest was sentenced to death and broken on the wheel. Van der Heyden and Malan were deported in chains to Batavia. They declared that only Klopper knew where the treasure had been buried. As they remained unshaken in this statement after being tortured, the Governor reluctantly accepted their word and ordered them to be deported to Batavia in chains. And the missing treasure of the *Schoonberg* remained in its hiding place on Vergelegen.

No doubt the farm was searched again and again. I found details of one search, reported in the *Cape Argus* of October, 1859. The writer stated that a ship's bell and copper kettle had been found near the homestead by labourers digging up roots of old trees. The bell, engraved with the name *Schoonberg*, was to be seen on the farm of Mr. P. van der Byl at Eerste River. According to the reporter, the farmer who buried the treasure had been assisted by a servant named Nicolaas Niemaan and a slave boy. The slave boy had been shot. Niemaan had run away, crossed the colonial frontier and lived among the kaffirs for many years. Before he died Niemaan had met a white man named Verley and told him that the treasure had been buried in the orchard behind the Vergelegen homestead.

Thus the search in 1859 recorded in the *Cape Argus* was based on Verley's information. The reporter saw a hole fifteen feet deep, but nothing had been found. Perhaps the boxes of gold and precious stones, silver and ornaments are still there after nearly two and a half centuries. But if you remember the words of my friend the diver you will realise that people who find sunken or buried treasure do not always shout about it.

All along the Agulhas coast you hear tales of lost treasure, most of it sunken treasure, some of it buried in the sand. One party after another has searched the dunes round about Gansbaai for an iron chest which a Boer commando captured from the British. It was filled with money for paying the troops, and the men of the commando hid it in the dunes when they heard that strong British forces were approaching. Some children were supposed to have seen the chest during World War I, but the sand blew over it again and the money has never been recovered. A milkwood tree on which a cross was carved is said to be a clue to the treasure.

Farmers in the Bredasdorp district will show you with pride some of the furniture of the British troopship *Arniston*, lost in 1815 at Waenhuiskrans. Local fishermen claim to have located two of the ship's treasure chests in a deep cleft in the reef where the ship went down. They may be right, but the tables of Burma teak, the chairs and settees which have been polished for generations; these are the only treasures the *Arniston* has yielded to the people of the shore. Her anchor and cable still lie rusting on a lonely beach. And there is a tablet at the scene of the wreck in memory of four young boys who were drowned. It is said that their mother made the long voyage from England to the Cape under sail, and then travelled by ox-wagon to Waenhuiskrans, to see the place where her children perished. Only six men survived the *Arniston* wreck, and nearly four hundred people, including fourteen women and twenty-five children, were drowned. Long afterwards a human finger bone was found, still encircled by an engagement ring.

Mossel Bay is the home of many treasure tales, and a poor man with a spade was rewarded there not long ago. It was in May, 1951, that old Dail Vaaltyn, a coloured man, was digging a trench in the park when he found a large coin. Vaaltyn then turned up the earth at a faster pace than ever before. He dug up coin after coin until it became clear that nothing more remained in that area. Vaaltyn then handed the whole collection over to the police, and the official list revealed thirteen gold coins of British, Prussian, Dutch and Belgian origin, and dozens of silver, copper and bronze pieces. Someone had stolen a collection of coins from the Mossel Bay library four years previously, but this collection did not tally with the missing coins. Vaaltyn's coins went back to the year 1700, and the most recent bore the year 1877. Some of the coins were scorched, as though they had been in a fire. Burnt scraps of paper money were found with the coins, but these could not be identified. No one claimed the hoard, and so after six months, the collection was handed over to Dail Vaaltyn.

An old-fashioned dagger, found in a dune just outside Mossel Bay, formed the origin of a pirate's treasure tale. Another legend (which Dr. H. E. S. Fremantle, M.L.A., investigated) was based on the visit of an eighteenth-century treasure ship. While the captain and officers were on shore hunting buck, the crew seized the chests filled with money and jewels, buried the loot on shore and then ran the ship on the rocks. The guilty seamen dispersed and escaped detection. Years afterwards one of them returned to Mossel Bay, and very soon he was spending money liberally. This man was said to have told a minister of religion the whole story. The man died. Some time later the minister went out with a spade to find the two treasure chests described by the dying man. One iron chest was unearthed, but it was empty. Mossel Bay treasure hunters are still seeking the other chest.

Valuable flotsam came to Mossel Bay in 1824, when the English ship *Mary* was wrecked there. A beachcomber known as "Mossel Bay Jack", a former British sailor, was living there at the time, gathering oysters and selling shells for lime-burning to the farmers at three rix-dollars a wagon load. "Mossel Bay Jack" roamed the beaches every day after the loss of the *Mary;* and aided by bands of Hottentots he gathered many chests of indigo dye stuffs. These he exchanged at Captain Hallett's store for groceries and spirits, especially spirits.

Sail on eastwards to Ballot's Bay, on the coast six miles from George, and you may survey the scene of the Von Mollendorf treasure legend. This is so persistent, and it has come down through the years with so much detail, that one can hardly escape the feeling that a treasure of some value was indeed lost when Von Mollendorf floated to the shore on a raft.

Joseph Wilhelm von Mollendorf, son of a Prussian fieldmarshal, came to South Africa towards the end of the eighteenth century. He transhipped at Cape Town, but the vessel which carried him round the coast has not been identified with certainty. She may have been the Dutch East India ship *Maria*, which put into Plettenberg Bay in 1788 with her crew suffering from scurvy. A south-east gale drove her away from the anchorage, and she was wrecked farther along the coast.

About the man Von Mollendorf there is no doubt at all. His treasure may have become exaggerated with the years, but his descendants believe that he had the equivalent of many thousands of pounds in gold coin and jewels in his iron strong-box. When the ship went down he made a raft, placed his strong-box on it and drifted hopefully towards the entrance of the bay now known as Ballot's Bay.

Ballot's Bay is a rocky cove with a narrow entrance partly barred by a submerged reef. The sea breaks heavily on the reef at times, but there are calm days when fishing boats can use the entrance in safety. According to legend, Von Mollendorf lost his box on the reef. He was able to save his life, but his arm was shattered and had to be amputated.

For weeks after his recovery Von Mollendorf haunted the little bay, mourning over his lost wealth. Local farmers heard his tale and tried to help him. In calm weather they could see the iron box wedged between two boulders about fifteen feet below the surface; but they were unable to raise it.

Von Mollendorf never became resigned to his loss. He married an Afrikaner girl on the farm Kommandokraal in the Oudtshoorn district; and often he took his children to the little bay and told them of the wealth that would be theirs if only he could reach the box. But every attempt failed.

Van der Westhuizen, a farmer who married one of Von Mollendorf's descendants towards the end of last century, carried on the quest. He also made inquiries in Germany, secured a portrait of Field-Marshal Wichard Heinrich von Mollendorf, and collected a number of documents. Van der Westhuizen was also said to have traced a fortune owned by Joseph Wilhelm von Mollendorf, a fortune untouched and awaiting claimants in a German bank. But this determined man seems to have disappeared while the South African War was being fought. The last of the Von Mollendorfs in South Africa died about half a century ago.

Many people declare that they have seen Von Mollendorf's box. Mr. Edward Robertson of Sandkraal farm, in the neighbourhood, has stated that one salvage party rigged a cable across the entrance to Ballot's Bay and sent a diver down. The diver hoped to steady himself with the aid of a rope and pulley running on the cable, but the current was too stong and the attempt was abandoned.

Ballot's Bay supported a fishing settlement years ago. It is a great place for geelbek, but the graves and the ruined cottages tell a grim tale of boats that capsized in the surf and families who decided that the risk was not worth while.

Some of those fishermen will tell you that Von Mollendorf's box is still there, and that Ballot's Bay will never give up its treasure. I am not so sure about that. There is another story of two Ballot's Bay fishing-boat owners who became suddenly rich and retired from the hard life of the coast. The sea is not always in turmoil. Wait long enough, and there comes a day and a tide when the most treacherous reefs may be approached without fear.

Stand on the scrub-covered heights of Robberg (the Cape Seal of the charts) and look down into the bay which the Portuguese called Formosa and the Dutch named Plettenberg. Here it was that the galleon *Sao Goncalo* anchored more than three centuries ago on a voyage from India to Lisbon. She was leaking badly, and her master landed part of the cargo of rice so that the carpenters could reach the strained planking.

For two months the *Sao Goncalo* lay off the river mouth. Then a gale drove her on shore, and one hundred and thirty-three of her company perished. Her captain, a feeble old man, was on shore that day with five priests and about one hundred seamen. The narrative of the settlement they formed, and the boats they built, is part of the history of South Africa. But you will not find the story of the *Sao Goncalo's* treasure chest in the history books. The late Miss Sanni Metelerkamp, a member of the Rex family of Knysna, gathered this legend from old Plettenberg Bay farmers and gave me the results of her inquiries.

It seems that Bushmen living in the Robberg caves discovered the iron-bound chest long afterwards on a lonely beach. It was embedded in sand and far too heavy to move. They told a white man about their find, but when they returned to the spot some time later the sand had covered the chest again. Years later a farmer located the chest and went off for a team of oxen to haul it away. Once again sea and sand combined to hide the chest. After strong south-east winds, relics which are believed to have belonged to the *Sao Goncalo* are washed on to the Robberg beaches – semi-precious beads, old blue china and little tear bottles.

A man who deserves to find a chest of gold is Mr. H. G. Harraway of Port Elizabeth, a most determined treasure hunter. He has preserved many records and relics of the 1820 settlers, and this taste for history led him naturally into the field of wrecks and their stories.

First he secured a licence from the Commissioner of Customs to salvage four wrecks along the coast near Port Elizabeth. Then he searched the archives and other sources of information. Among his helpers were "Bunny" Hodges and other ex-soldiers, keen fishermen who knew the coast well; and they reported a strange object in a deep pool at Sardinia Bay near Cape Recife. They were puzzled because, unlike most submerged objects, this one was not encrusted with shellfish.

Harraway formed a theory that it must be of brass or bronze. Divers were sure it was a cannon. It was a most difficult salvage operation, for the sea was rough; but in the end the cannon weighing six thousand pounds was hauled up the beach and hidden in the dunes. Unfortunately the effort had been watched, and rumours of a treasure-chest went round the district. Vandals attempted to cut up the cannon with hack-saws for scrap metal, and the valuable old piece was mutilated.

Mr. Vernon S. Forbes, senior lecturer in geography at Rhodes University, Grahamstown, identified the cannon as one mentioned by Colonel J. R. Gordon, the Dutch explorer, while returning in 1778 from his famous Orange River journey. Gordon drew a panorama of the coast, and noted on it that he had found traces of a wreck at the very spot where the cannon was found. The survivors had built huts in the dunes, but had evidently died of hunger and thirst, for Gordon and his Hottentot servant buried a number of skeletons. "Two rusty anchors and a cannon lay in the sea, which I could not identify because of the waves," Gordon wrote. Not far away Gordon discovered a beautiful carved ivory box which appeared to be a Roman Catholic symbol.

Harraway sent all the available information to the curator of the artillery museum at Woolwich. Experts who examined the photographs described the cannon as a Dutch brass naval gun about three hundred years old. It is a rare specimen, possibly the only existing relic of the work of that fine craftsman, Conraet Wegt Woert. This historic cannon has been presented to the Port Elizabeth municipality. Harraway still hopes to recover further objects from the wreck.

A relic of Portuguese explorers came to light at Port Alfred in 1908, when a boarding-house was being rebuilt. It was an iron-bound box, and the hearts of the discoverers must have beat faster as they forced the lid. Bundles of paper which had been soaked in water were thrown away before any scientist could examine them. There remained a number of plaster of Paris fragments. When these were restored, they formed an image of the Virgin.

Professor E. H. L. Schwarz (of "Kalahari redemption" fame) took charge of the investigation, consulted the Portuguese records, and came to the conclusion that the box might have been left there by Bartholomew Diaz. He put forward an alternative theory that the Portuguese used the Kowie river as a stronghold during their slaving expeditions, with Bushmen as their victims. The real treasure of that box was the paper which was destroyed before Professor Schwarz came on the scene.

One of those tantalising treasure stories published without names of people or exact details of places, yet bearing the obvious stamp of truth, appeared in the *Cape Argus* many years ago. While the Eighth Kaffir War was being fought there was a large garrison stationed in a village on or near the coast in the Eastern Province. The military pay office was an old building with a strong-room, always guarded by a sentry.

One day the sentry noticed that the pay clerk was in the habit of hanging the strong-room keys on a peg near the door. The sentry plotted with several friends; they waited their chance, and at last the absent-minded clerk left the key on the peg and went home.

Feverishly the soldiers worked to remove nearly forty thousand pounds in gold coin from the strong-room. They filled the wooden boxes with sand, leaving a top layer of coins, then screwed up the boxes again.

That day a child had been buried in the little graveyard near the powder magazine. The thieves opened the grave, and above the coffin they buried bucket after bucket of golden sovereigns. Before daybreak the grave had been closed, the strong-room swept, keys replaced on the peg.

It seemed to be a perfect crime. Even when the theft was discovered soon afterwards (owing to an unexpected request for money from an outlying fort) the men on guard duty could not be shaken in their story that they knew nothing of the missing gold. At the court martial, however, the sentries were convicted of failure to carry out their duties while on active service, and every man was sentenced to transportation to Tasmania.

Twenty years later a map reached the Eastern Province from one of the convicts, showing where the money had been buried. A syndicate was formed, the graveyard (no longer in use) was located. They opened every grave in search of the treasure, but not one coin was found. Someone had been there before them.

If beads were really valuable, the people of the coast beyond East London would be wealthy. Many of the beads are cornelians, brown and transparent, cut by hand and drilled laboriously by hand; some elongated, some round, some shaped like diamonds. All beads washed up by the sea are known on this coast as "*Grosvenor* beads", though they come from many old, forgotten wrecks.

One of the most respectable beachcombers I know makes a hobby of searching this coast whenever his firm releases him for a month. Always at low spring tides he finds natives scooping up the shale in flat tins, spreading it on the rocks, throwing sea water over it to wash off the light grit and sandstone. Then the beads are revealed.

Samples of the cornelian beads were sent to the British Museum authorities in London for examination. The report described them as beads of Indian origin at least two thousand years old. Some historians believe that the beads were carried by Phoenicians who sailed down the East African coast centuries before Christ and traded with the Pondoland tribes. It is significant that the Pondos have inherited memories of "great white birds" that came by sea bringing strange men. It is possible, however, that the visitors were Arab slave-traders. Pondo women wear necklaces of cornelian and other ancient, foreign beads to this day.

More exciting finds have been made in recent years at Haga Haga, thirty miles from East London, by Mrs. M. W. Dunlop-Ainslie – nothing less than a collection of cut gems. One flawless diamond, nine rubies, and emerald and many cornelians have been picked up by Mrs. Dunlop-Ainslie, all inside sea shells and covered with sand. Miss Courtenay-Latimer, director of the East London Museum, has made a number of expeditions to Haga Haga and has recovered several beautiful cut amethysts. Here again there is a legend of a chest wedged in the rocks and slowly giving up its treasure. The ship which carried the chest may have been the *San Diego*.

My friend the beachcomber found a quantity of blue Chinese porcelain bearing the maker's name in Chinese characters. This was in perfect condition. He heard of silver doubloons being washed up, and natives showed him a beach which they called "the place where the money comes out of the sea".

One great riddle of the coast near East London is the inscribed rock at Kayser's Beach. Is this a clue to buried treasure? Many investigators hold that view, though no one has been able to give a satisfactory interpretation.

The rock stands midway between high and low water marks. Within a circle are various letters and figures. They must have been cut into the hard sandstone to a depth of six inches with a hammer and cold chisel, but weathering has reduced the depth to an inch. The inscription consists of a Portuguese cross and the letters N, NE, JN, L/L/LL (or 77/7/7) and a snake-like line.

Sir George Cory, the historian, studied the inscription about seventy years ago and sent photographs to the British Museum some time later. Experts there reported that it was a genuine old Portuguese inscription resembling others found on the South African coast. They were unwilling to commit themselves further. Miss Courtenay-Latimer put the riddle before some of the leading American archaeologists, and they declared that two of the letters formed a sign indicating a spring of fresh water. Another authority suggested that the letters JN might be the initials of the old Portuguese explorer Juan da Nova, discoverer of Mossel Bay and certain islands in African waters.

Cory discovered three old graves in the neighbourhood. He also noted a native legend of shipwreck. Three ships known to have been lost on this stretch of coast were the *San Joao Baptista* in 1622, the *Nossa Senhora do Atalaya* and the *Sacramento,* both in 1647. Several attempts have been made to locate treasure. One seeker, a farmer named Gower, employed a witchdoctor, and dug a pit thirty feet deep at the spot selected three miles from the rock. He found nothing. It is possible that the inscription merely indicates a landing place with fresh water, but the old Portuguese went to a great deal of trouble when they made that mysterious carving.

Now here is the last of those iron-bound boxes which appear so prominently in these treasure legends. Durban people speak of "Treasure Beach" at the Bluff, and there is reason to believe that this beach has indeed yielded a fortune.

Eighty or ninety years ago a wreck was battered to pieces in the surf below the Bluff. A stumpy mast appeared at low spring tides for some years, and then a large iron-bound box was seen. Mr. O. E. Bjorseth, an amateur fisherman, noticed the box in eight feet of water, prodded it, and in 1909 he decided to employ a diver. Unfortunately the diver was defeated by the surf. Years afterwards, however, the Durban newspapers reported that an Indian named Patel had picked up a copper cylinder full of diamonds, rubies and emeralds near the site of Bjorseth's box. The origin of this hoard was never settled, but the stones fetched twenty thousand pounds. Patel received half that amount and the rest went to the government.

Finally, a word about the much-discussed *Grosvenor* treasure. I would not invest in any *Grosvenor* syndicate now because I believe that the main treasure was recovered years ago. A man at Port St. Johns collected so many silver coins from the wreck that he was able to melt them down and have them made into a large and handsome cup. He was one of many successful treasure hunters of the early days.

The men who started lifting the riches of the *Grosvénor* were Captain Sidney Turner and Lieutenant Beddoes of the Natal

Pioneers. Turn up the files of the *Natal Mercury* for May, 1880, and you will find the story of their efforts. They had a team of natives, they blasted the wreck with dynamite, and they found gold coins, silver and jewellery. Others followed, but not all of them talked to the newspapers. Remember my friend the diver? You should think of him before joining a treasure expedition. Some treasure tales *were* true, and many an empty iron-bound chest lies on the ocean floor.

What happens if you do find treasure trove? Roman-Dutch law in South Africa is clear enough. If you find anything valuable yourself on your own farm, you will probably be allowed to retain the lot. "Treasure trove", of course, means treasure hidden so long ago that there can be no claimant. If someone else finds the hoard accidentally on your land the law requires you to split fifty-fifty with him.

Before starting an organised treasure hunt on someone else's property, see that a simple legal agreement is drawn up. In the absence of such an agreement, the whole amount will belong to the owner of the property.

The late Lieut.-Colonel H. F. Trew of the South African Police was an authority on the treasure seeking which followed the South African War. One party after another set out to find the "Kruger millions" and other hoards, and Trew issued the permits. The conditions in those days were that anything discovered had to be handed over to the government, who would pay one-third of the amount to the finder. A policeman accompanied each party. Many farmers had buried their capital when the British troops invaded the Transvaal, and some had died before they could dig it up again. Naturally, the heirs were entitled to many of these hoards. Trew watched the recovery of large amounts of money and jewellery.

Escape from the Rat-Race

SALDANHA BAY, the Langebaan lagoon and the lonely Cape beaches are recurring themes in the many works of Lawrence G. Green. Their beauty, their moods and the messages the pounding surf or the rippling waters of the lagoon whispered to him helped to mould the philosophy of a solitary man who yet loved the company of close friends and convivial eccentrics. This chosen chapter is the first from *A Decent Fellow Doesn't Work*, an intriguing title which Green would quote with impish relish years after he coined it. This title and the book itself, written a decade before his death, reflect a significant stage in the life and outlook of a superb literary impresario who normally kept his own personality and philosophy modestly in the background. Twice in his lifetime, once during World War II (as I have told you earlier in this book) and again in the last two years of his life Lawrence G. Green decided to write his autobiography. On each occasion he methodically sketched the general structure of a book destined to be forever denied South African literature. In *A Decent Fellow Doesn't Work* Green, however, abandoned much of his personal reticence and wrote about himself, his private beliefs and his inner thoughts far more freely than he had ever done before. In the first chapter of this book, which I have chosen for reproduction, he does not mention Saldanha Bay or the Langebaan lagoon across the bay by name, a strange omission for one so meticulous. I think Green meant this chapter with its memorable prose to be the expressed articles of his inner faiths. To him Saldanha and Langebaan symbolised sanctuaries of escape from the rat-race and the soulless marketplaces of greedy competition, which he loathed. Some passages from this chapter are majestic.

Yet it is reflective of the ambivalence of Green's character – and perhaps his philosophy too – that he should by implication so warmly applaud the maxim of Brooke the Langebaan beachcomber – *A decent fellow doesn't work*. All his adult life Green seemed to envy men who spurned the claims of modern living and became hermits with a care only for today. Yet the irony is that Lawrence Green himself was the epitome of unslothful journalistic industry.

CHAPTER XV

WOODSMOKE AND WINE

LONG ago, on a hot and mellow evening beside a quiet lagoon, I breathed the mingled fragrance of woodsmoke and wine. Aromas carry a magic that no man of science can explain. Those two powerful old ghosts, woodsmoke and wine, entered my life that evening, and they still open the mysterious doors of memory for me and roll back the years.

Blue wisps drifted from a dying fire on the beach, where someone had been grilling meat. In the waterfront tavern the barrels gave out their sweet, fruity wine, shot through with the fumes of Cape brandy. Such was the atmosphere that comes back to me so often; the little country tavern near the southern tip of Africa; the faces of the drinkers, not only Afrikaners but a chance gathering of nations; the sounds and the talk and the trivial episode that influenced my outlook on life.

I had rowed across two miles of salt water from a very different scene, a coasting steamer loading noisy drums of oil at a whaling station ablaze with furnaces and reeking of mighty flesh. When the meat is newly-harpooned the boilers give off a beefy odour, not at all unpleasant.

That afternoon the oceanic beef had overcome the old-fashioned marine smells of the little ship. Scrubbed decks, polished brasswork, new paint and shining teak could not stand up to the belching factory close at hand. Even the happy little whiffs from the coaster's galley were swamped by the melting whale meat.

I remember the small rosy cloud of flamingoes on the lagoon as we rowed; the spreading of darkness, the moon on the water and the splendour of the stars. We passed two bird islands, redolent of ammonia where the guano whitened the rocks, varied by the wet seaweed odour from the beaches.

It was so peaceful in the lagoon. Outside there was the war

that was just touching South Africa; a solitary German raider laying a minefield that claimed a few unsuspecting victims. My coaster was the *Ingerid,* and she had steamed close inshore as usual, and missed the mines. She had crept alongside an old wooden hulk at the whaling station, her iron plates splintering some of the timber. No sooner had the main engines ceased their steady pounding and booming than the winches came into action, clattering all day as the drums went thudding into the holds.

But now, away from the ship and the whales, there was the hush of peace. I could hear the surf pounding the coastline on the far side of the narrow peninsula, beyond the whaling station. Farms near the village, with their cows and sheep, contributed soft noises of the night. Then the keel of our dinghy rubbed the sand and my thirsty shipmates hauled it up and made for the bar.

All I knew of the village at that moment, late in 1916, was the row of lamplit or candle-lit cottages and the long, broad beach. I came to know it well as the years passed, and I wish that I could tell you that it has remained unchanged. Certainly it has not been entirely transformed, though jet aircraft rush and whistle over the roads once used by Cape cart and rumbling ox-wagon. But time has been kind to the lagoon. When the aircraft are in their hangars; when the black cormorants sweep in from the sea in long skeins; when the white gannets dive into the bay like thunderbolts; on such days I am back in the old village of woodsmoke and wine.

On that first night I would rather have roamed the beach than entered the bar. I hardly knew the taste of wine at sixteen. But no, I was hustled inside by my friendly companions, and there I stood blinking while the smoke drifted in through the window and the taps gave out their rich amber, their golden and purple wines. Insects rang on metal paraffin lamps. Faces became clearer against the whitewashed walls. Some of the drinkers were there only for a night; others belonged to the village, and I came to know them later.

In a dimpled whisky-bottle on a bar shelf was a tall Cape Horner. They had a larger, framed ship-model, too, in those days. At sixteen I was more interested in ship-models than in wine-casks. I gazed at those little ships, every halyard, sheet and ratline in the right position. "Aye, stare at 'em, sonny," came a deep voice at my elbow. "They're vanishing from the oceans now – we shall not see their like again." That was something I had not realised, for there were always masts and yards in Table Bay Docks at that period. I had failed to observe the passing of an era.

Among the crowd in the bar were a number of Italian seamen from a steamer in the bay, and an Italian who owned a general store in the village was entertaining them. Flushed with wine, the host told them something of his life story. "I was a sailor, see. Came to Table Bay in a barque. One night I got fighting with a Spaniard. Over a girl we were fighting, of course, and that bloody Spaniard got his knife in me. When I come out of hospital my ship was gone, so I sailed up here in an Italian fishing boat, and worked bloody hard and made a little money. Now I've got my own shop. Ha, the big feller is going to sing for us. He's good, that big feller."

The big feller was a seafaring Hercules with a face I could not forget. He had close-trimmed curly hair and dark, good-natured eyes. A great chest swelled under his jersey. He wore seaboots, in contrast with the *velskoene* of the wondering, genial local farmers. The big feller ordered another beer and drank. Then he put down his glass and cigarette and sang.

I thought it was the most wonderful singing in the world. He had no piano accompaniment and seemed not to need it. In a rich baritone he gave snatches of opera and lilting comic songs with puckered face and humorous gestures. Never did he tire. A pause while he turned to his beer, then another song. True melody there was in the hushed bar that night. He stood in a ring of light under one of the lamps, and made me see Rome under the stars. He was exalted. He never missed a note.

As he ended I could hear everyone drawing breath in admiration. Then came the burst of applause. "Go on!" we urged. He set down his glass and sang again, so that the great volume of his voice poured through the listening crowd and touched the waters of the lagoon:

> *Venite il agile barchetta mia*
> *Santa Lucia! Santa Lucia!*

When it was over a shipmate of the singer told us in broken English that the man's name was Guiseppe, and that he had sung in half the ports of the world. "That scar on his forehead – that was in Valparaiso," remarked the seaman reminiscently. "Si, a Chilean girl fall in love with his voice, and she 'ad a 'usband . . ."

Always the same story with seafaring men. "Over a girl we were fighting, of course, and that bloody Spaniard got his knife in me . . ."

Norwegians from the whalers were in the bar, those fine, blue-eyed men with reefer jackets and striped shirts. The barman had a stone jar of *aquavit* for them, the fiery potato spirit of the fjords with its taste of caraway seeds. "*Skal!*" one of them would say. "*Skal da!*" sounded the deep voices as all raised their glasses I have listened to much drinking ritual in my time, but that Norwegian toast is the most adventurous of all.

"*Skal!*" I am offshore with the Vikings again, the skipper at his harpoon gun. A flash and a crack, the line streaks out, and I can smell the acrid powder as the great blue whale leaps almost clear of the ocean, spouting blood and dying against the orange band of sunset. My friend Captain Olsen, veteran of the Antarctic, comes back slowly along the catwalk to the bridge. "*Skal!*"

The village had an Irish doctor in those days, red-faced, merry, one of the hardest drinkers of the lot. Elsewhere in the district most doctors had motor-cars. This village was not easily reached by car, however, not even by the Ford Model-T, and so the doctor used boats and horses. He rode about the countryside with his instruments, morphia and cough mixture, laudanum and bismuth in his saddlebags. Great tales were told of his kitchen-table surgery, but I think the patients were as brave as the surgeon.

When I visited the village again after the first war I missed the doctor. It seems that he had been careless about his fees and never charged the poor, with the inevitable result that he could not pay his own debts. The lawyers were pressing him. One day they received a cheerful message of farewell by wireless from the outgoing mail steamer. Now only the older people remember him, but his red and beaming face still appears before me in the aroma of woodsmoke and wine.

Fishing skippers always gathered in that tavern when they had landed their catches. Many of them relied entirely on sail, though the silence of the lagoon was disturbed occasionally by the "put-put-put" of unreliable marine engines. Sun-dried fish hung then, as they hang now, outside almost every cottage on the beach. And there is another familiar aroma which cannot be mistaken. *Bokkoms!*

Fishermen work hard when they are at sea. Farmers have their seasons when no day is long enough. Yet I cannot say that the old village impressed me as one of those places where the gray-faced coronary thrombosis patient, the stomach ulcer sufferer and other victims of worry and pressure formed a large part of the population. There were days when the fishermen could only sit on their stoeps and wait for better weather. Farmers ploughed their land after the heavy May rains, when the world smelt of moist earth; and they sowed their wheat and rested comfortably until the poppies grew among the high green stalks.

I always thought of the village as a leisurely place after my own heart. No doubt the idea arose in the bar on that memorable first night, for I heard an argument which puzzled me at the time. When I understood the meaning of it I knew a little more about this world of ours. At sixteen I passed a turning point that some never reach.

Among the seafarers and the farmers in the bar that night was a middle-aged man who was conspicuous in city garb. He was too smart for his surroundings, too loud in his opinions, and certainly the worse for his whiskies. I learnt afterwards that he was a commercial traveller. As he drank he became more aggressive. Suddenly he turned on a serene, slow-drinking young man who was leaning on the counter. "Got a job yet Brooke?" he demanded.

"I'm not looking for one at the moment," the man called Brooke replied pleasantly, looking up from his beer. Dreamy, sun-tanned and lean; that was my first impression of him. Perhaps there was a pallor under the tan. He did not look strong at that moment. Later on, when I knew him better, I found that the dreamer had a brain and a philosophy of life, and muscles like whipcord.

"You're a beachcomber," declared the traveller with an edge on his voice. "You sit outside your shack in the sun all day, and now and again you condescend to go sailing or swimming, or you may drop a line into the water and catch a fish. Why don't you do some work?"

"A decent fellow doesn't work," replied Brooke the beachcomber with a sort of humorous pride.

This shattering phrase was greeted with a roar of approval by all who caught the meaning. Glasses were refilled, the words were repeated joyfully in various accents, and finally the idea became a toast. "A decent fellow doesn't work. *Skal ! Gesondheid ! Viva !*"

By this time generous measures of wine and *aquavit*, brandy and beer had been consumed. The quiet tavern beside the lagoon had become riotous. Someone put forward the idea of teaching the village police constable a lesson. For some reason the whalermen hated him and he was unpopular among the farmers. When the lights went out in the bar there was a move towards the police station.

Though not unduly timid, I have never been in favour of attacking police stations. Apparently the men who had brought me to the village held the same law-abiding views, and so we launched our boat and rowed away across a bay like a lake. I heard afterwards that the constable had barricaded himself in his house, while the Norwegians threw stones on the iron roof, opened the stable-doors and drove the horse on to the veld. Then they, too, discreetly vanished into the night.

Presumably the beachcomber had sauntered back to his cottage before the attack started. There he would be secure against trouble and the evils of work. I thought of him that night, and for many a day afterwards, and soon I began to envy him. I knew, too, that I would have to return one day to the calm lagoon, the woodsmoke and wine, and learn Brooke's secret. A decent fellow doesn't work!

When the day came, they told me in the village that Brooke had left the shack on the beach and moved up the lagoon. He had a small place there where he grew vegetables and lay in the sun.

"So he's farming now?" I suggested, wondering how I could approach him.

"Not farming exactly," replied my informant. "He owns an irrigated garden plot and some bees. If you feel like a walk, go along the edge of the lagoon and buy some of his honey. You'll find it has a marvellous flavour at this time of year."

I set out into the wonderland of spring. Deep snow lay on the Cape mountains that week, but here the sun had created a warm, perfumed world of arum lilies and purple vygies, golden bushes and sheets of white chincherinchees. Drab plovers ran from me on the beaches, kicking the sand cleverly over their eggs. When I deviated inland a little way, past the wheatfields, I heard the "*kwotkwot, kwotkwot*" of quail feeding on the grain.

Brooke's place was about thirty minutes from the village. I walked happily through the blaze of babiana, the creamy marigolds and other purple flowers that seemed to have a drop of red wine in their centres.

This shore of the lagoon impressed me as the finest part of the whole isolated landscape. The bay is everywhere magnificent, running fifteen miles from north to south if you include the lagoon; a fine deep curve in the north, eight miles wide, and the green lagoon with its tides and sandbanks in the south. When the sandflats and mud of the lagoon are bared at low-tide you see the feeding-ground of flamingo, curlew and sand-piper. Here in the sea-grass, with eager beaks, are migrants and rare waders filling themselves in a rich marine pantry.

Scattered over a sandhill I saw the hives, and there was Brooke's cottage near the lagoon. Just a little thatched place with the blue, heart-shaped morning glory climbing over the roof. He had a board on the gate: "Morning Glory – Charles Brooke".

Charles Brooke was lying in a hammock strung from the tough branches of a manitoka tree. He looked better, deeply tanned, eyes clear and untroubled in his good-natured, rather lop-sided face. He wore only a shirt and shorts. I could see that he had put on no weight. By this time, I thought, he must have been nearing thirty. The war had ended. I had started work as a reporter a few years before this visit; and here was Brooke who lived as he pleased and let the bees work for him.

Brooke did not remember me, and indeed there was no reason why he should. "It was one night in the bar, five years ago, when a rather objectionable customer was asking you why you didn't find a job," I reminded him.

Brooke laughed and repeated the words that had aroused my interest. "A decent fellow doesn't work," he declared again, with a glance at the hammock.

"I quite agree, but how is it done?"

"When I made that remark in the bar I was recovering from war service in German East Africa," explained Brooke. "I did not feel called upon to make excuses, but I was trying to shake off the malaria, and I was as weak as a mouse. Malaria was the curse of that campaign. I was seldom under fire, but the malaria nearly killed me. So when I was invalided out of the army I hired a shack on the beach and lay in the sun, and gradually I recovered. But there are some people who can't bear to see others leading a decent life – hence the argument in the bar. I still say that a decent fellow doesn't work."

"You've done some work here," I pointed out as I admired the flaming garden and prosperous vegetable patch, the ripening figs, the blossoms on the apricot trees.

"This is not work – this is what I like doing," Brooke replied. "What I really meant that night was that an intelligent man avoids any work which does not give him pleasure. Work that you like doing is a hobby. It does not shorten your life with sheer fatigue or worry."

I bought a jar of honey, and the sun fell on the incomparable golden liquid. Brooke quoted a poem I had not read at that time:

Stands the Church clock at ten to three?
And is there honey still for tea?

"That was written by another Brooke – died in the war while this Brooke was loafing beside the lagoon," he mused. "No relation, but I happen to know the church at Grantchester. You see, I was born not far from there. I wish that I could have written that poem."

My first visit to "Morning Glory" was short, for I did not

wish to outstay my welcome. Brooke informed me that it was time his bread came out of the oven. The cottage was filled with the hot, reassuring aroma; it flooded out like an answer to hunger when he opened the door. Sweet as a walnut, it was, and I breathed it with enchantment.

"Whole-meal bread," Brooke said. "I don't usually do this, but I just wanted to see whether I could bake my own. I put the wheat through the coffee-grinder, and it seems to be turning out all right. Well, so long, and come again soon!"

Six pelicans were flying in formation as I walked back, with a whole squadron of small gulls above them. I saw herons, too, and pheasant, and brilliant yellow and blue bee-eaters darting out of holes in sandy ridges. The lagoon panorama lingered in my mind; the triumphant fields of wild flowers, painted acres more miraculous than any formal garden; the tranquil cottage and Brooke himself.

Whenever I ate the honey I saw the easy-going, lop-sided face of the man who allowed the bees to work for him. This was honey which brought all the charm and romance and sweetness of unspoilt veld to the tongue. No other honey flavour can approach the blended nectars of the southern August flowers. I had bought for a few shillings the very essence of the spring. My breakfast cannot end without honey, and I enjoy red honey from the bluegum trees, the darker prickly pear honey, the orange blossom and willow honey. Brooke's honey, as I always call it, had the flavour of paradise.

Summer was not far off when I found my way down the lagoon again, and soon the land would be drying up under the south winds. Yellow *vygies* and huge masses of blue haze remained as relics of spring.

Brooke asked me inside the cottage this time. I was impressed by the good taste and comfort he had achieved. Built-in cupboards of polished hardwood adorned the recesses. He had deep chairs. Every colour was exactly right. A scent of thatch mingled with the garden odours, the fresh herbs and flowers.

He had built himself a little dinghy, and sometimes he rowed across the lagoon and walked over the long peninsula to the ocean beach. I knew that beach, with the surf bursting on the gleaming sand. He loved walking there; and always there was driftwood to be picked up, fine planks of oak and teak. "Most of my furniture came from the timber I found on that beach," said Brooke. "A rich beach it is, the richest in Africa – and you can take your troubles there, and all bitterness and worry, and lose them in the sand."

Only now and then did he reveal his philosophy of life in this way. But I recall another phrase he used that afternoon.

"I find peace here," Brooke declared. "Why should I waste my best years in the city saving up for freedom in old-age? I've got freedom now."

There were questions I would have liked to ask him, the problem of income especially; but it was too soon. He showed me his garden and pantry and I could see that his comfort was costing him far less than others paid. The smoker at the back, an oil drum and bricks, was a fair example of his ingenuity.

"You have to discover the sort of wood that gives the right flavour," Brooke explained. "These lagoon waters are full of *harders* and *marsbankers*, that the people of this coast catch in nets and salt and dry in the sun. I smoke mine, and exchange them with the farmers for something I want, like wheat or a side of bacon or a stone jar of wine."

So I began to see the shining lagoon and its shores as a vast larder. Across the entrance were the isles of the gulls where the fishermen gathered pale green eggs, rich as any laid by plovers. On the floor of the lagoon were beds of *perlemoen*, the South African abalone, queen of shellfish. Deep in the reeds fringing the lagoon lived the descendants of pigs that ran wild long ago. Among the scrub and bush round the lagoon were the small antelope called *duiker* and *steenbok;* and a man with a shotgun would also bring home pheasant and partridge and guinea fowl. I could see that Brooke's meals were neither expensive nor monotonous.

That evening I watched the flamingoes feeding on the sandbanks, loveliest of all birds, the pink flushing the whiteness of the plumage. On the shore were the bluegum trees with their colonies of finches, and the twisted manitokas where the weaverbirds nested.

Reluctantly I left Brooke and strolled back with bare feet to the village. It was soft on the seaweed, with the high tide almost reaching the bushes. Once I rested in the shade of a pillar surrounded by water, a portion of a cliff which had become detached by wind erosion. It stood up from the shallows like an exclamation mark. Wild pigeons and herons nested in its crevices, secure from wild cats. On the summit of the pillar grew white daisies with fawn tints, a tiny patch where the wind had blown the seeds into a crumb of earth.

I walked on in the shallows, where the jelly fish floated and hermit crabs scuttled over the mud in their borrowed dwellings. Once I observed the cormorants driving a shoal of fish ashore while a gang of ravenous seals hung on the outskirts and joined at last in the massacre.

Yet the lagoon always dominated the picture. The lagoon, a living thing, quivering and golden under the sun, shimmering with silver under the moon, the great hush guarding its waters like a benediction.

Full summer when I drove to the village again, and nearly all the wild flowers had withered. The lagoon wore its green summer face, light and brilliant as a tourmaline, deep water showing up plainly in darker green channels.

I had been able to do a small service for Brooke in the city, and he received me as a friend. My limbs had been smothered by city clothes and I swam in the lagoon again and again. Brooke, of course, was lean and brown, "I wear shorts most of the time – just shorts," he said. "But I put on a shirt for dinner in honour of my daily flask of wine."

"How have you spent your time since I was here last?" I inquired gently.

"Time?" repeated Brooke. "This lagoon is timeless. You may find a year here passing quickly or slowly, but in the life of the lagoon a year is no more than the tick of a clock. I have no achievements to report, for I am without ambition. And yet I have done something with my time."

I sat enthralled while Brooke told his tale. Once when the moon was full the night held so much magic that it would have been a shame to let it pass in sleep. Brooke took his dinghy and rowed out of the lagoon into the bay, and then headed for open sea. The ocean was a lake that night, all the way from South Africa to South America. When he turned at last he saw the false dawn, the light in the eastern sky which is followed by darkness. True dawn found him between the north and south heads of the great bay. As he came back to the cottage the sun was hot. He drank his morning tea, rolled on to his bed and slept till afternoon.

"You can do that sort of thing up here," went on Brooke. "What does it matter? The lagoon is timeless."

Then he spoke of the days he had spent among the low, flat islands near the head of the lagoon. Hidden in the reeds he had watched the sandpipers, and the terns wading and crying "tchu-tchu" after their long migration from the Arctic.

Brooke knew all the birds of land and sea. Once he pointed out a penguin swimming in the transparent shallows. The flightless bird appeared to be flying at last in the only medium where the short flippers would give it speed and grace. "The poetry of motion," muttered Brooke.

I was drawn again to "Morning Glory" before that summer ended. There was no game on the lonely farm tracks, but once I swerved to avoid a little tortoise. Close to the lagoon a lynx went loping brazenly in daylight across the track, a red African caracal, hated by all farmers.

Brooke knew all about the lynx. "A whole family of them live among the rocks at the top of that hill," he said. "I could smell them before ever I saw them. They'll tackle me one of these days, and tear me to pieces." He was smiling.

"I can hear the summer voice of the lagoon today," remarked Brooke, changing the subject. "When the south-easter blows, the water laps against the beach all the time. If you lived here you would pray for the gentle sou'-west wind. The south-easter is a curse. You can't go out in the dinghy without getting soaked. The south-easter blows day after day. I tell you, my friend, the summer is not the finest time on this lagoon. Everything on shore dries right out. It's a cruel place in summer, and when you walk over it you can see what it has done to human beings for thousands of years. They were killed by sun and wind, sun and wind, and their bones are under those dunes."

It was the first time I had heard a note of complaint about the lagoon from Brooke, and I wondered what lay behind it. But I asked him whether he had found signs of primitive man.

Yes, he had picked up stone chips and flakes used by the people of the dawn world as they feasted on shellfish. Wherever he went there were still beaches untouched by progress, and little bays where civilised man had left no marks, unless you counted an occasional sailing yacht lying at anchor, or an empty bottle washed up on the sand. Once the district had been covered with trees and ferns, and the fossil patterns could still be traced along the shores of the lagoon. Then it became a dune world, and the sand buried many strange little people, Bushmen and Strandlopers, who had known better times.

Autumn seemed endless that year and no harsh winds disturbed the lagoon. Each week, Brooke told me, he expected the first winter gale to drive him into his cottage. Yet week after week he lay naked under the sun without a shiver.

I arrived one day in my city clothes and cast them off on the warm beach sheltered by the sand cliffs. The autumn glow held me spellbound. I was more reluctant than ever to leave the lagoon.

But that year the autumn ended suddenly. One day, said Brooke, he was lazing in his garden stripped to the waist and reading one of his books over again. In the evening the clouds were massing, and at midnight the sky was filled with thunderclouds and forked lightning. He lay in bed listening to peals of thunder. It was an unusual experience, like the hail that rattled on the rainwater tanks outside the kitchen.

Dawn, too, was a new spectacle, a red and menacing dawn with the sun rising amid clouds aflame. The rain that followed pinned him down to the cottage. He had expected a dry winter on the lagoon, away from Table Mountain where every cloud turned into rain; yet for days he was a captive in his room.

By sheer luck I arrived on a bright and serene morning. One of those still days when thatched and whitewashed cottages far away stood out in marvellous clarity. I told Brooke how fortunate he was, and he was inclined to agree with me. But he made one queer remark that puzzled me for years. "I honestly don't know whether I love this place or hate it," Brooke declared vehemently. "Perhaps that it the secret of its charm."

Such was Brooke, such was the lagoon, in those faraway years between the wars. I came to know the seasons there, and the pattern of Brooke's life in solitude. I learnt that it was possible to support life comfortably on a very few pounds a month. I could almost have made out a list of Brooke's bookshelf from memory – Rupert Brooke's collected poems, Roger Fry's "Vision and Design", Frazer's "Golden Bough", books on bees and birds and fish, novels by Somerset Maugham, and not surprisingly Thoreau's "Walden".

Yes, I knew the books but I did not know the man. I had entered the sanctuary of the lagoon and felt the great silence. Often in the city I thought with longing of the peace of Brooke's cottage. Yet not even for the sake of leisure and peace would I have spent year after unbroken year of my life there alone, alone, alone. Brooke had a secret. I went out into the world to the cities and the solitudes, knowing that I would return to the lagoon. I would listen to Brooke again, and I would hear the voice of the lagoon. But would I ever know Brooke's secret? Perhaps he had already revealed it, when he said to me one day: "The only lonely places are the cities. Here I can lose myself in my surroundings."

Vanishing Men of the Axe

LAWRENCE G. GREEN started to gather material for *There's A Secret Hid Away* shortly after he retired in 1954 at the age of 54 from active newspaper work. In the opening chapter he declared: "Now that I have all the time in the world I am picking up old threads. Sometimes I discover the truth about unusual experiences and odd characters who touched me lightly and left me wondering. Memories of strange encounters and forgotten dreams, unexplained mysteries and elusive rarities have been filling my mind." The book he wrote in this mood of unhurried reflection contains many chapters rich in human and historical interest. Again choice of a chapter was difficult. *The People and the Trees* has been selected because it reveals Lawrence Green in an unusual setting for him. As he confessed in this chapter, normally the lonely desert and open spaces inspired him. Here, however, he moves into the dark dankness of the Knysna forests and goes on to discuss vividly the human interest behind the trees of South Africa. He tells too the full story of the famous Wonderboom near Pretoria. This chapter opens with some facinating nostalgic tales of the hardy woodcutters in the Knysna forest. He saw them as men of a race apart, "probably the most isolated white people in South Africa". These men of the axe are a vanishing breed. Luckily Lawrence Green with a rare human understanding told their story so graphically before they could become the people that time forgot.

CHAPTER XVI

THE PEOPLE AND THE TREES

Every town, almost every village in South Africa has a tree with a story, often trees with traditions. Almost everyone has memories of remarkable trees and forests, and the people of the forests.

It would be hard to find many of the old type of bearded woodcutter in the Knysna forests today. They are dying out, and a way of life which was not altogether desirable is vanishing, too. Backward the old men were; yet they could perform feats with the axe which the younger generation would not dare to attempt. One thirsty, barefooted *takhaar*, I remember, would hold a match between his toes and bring his axe down with such precision and restraint that he would split the match without touching his own flesh. He gave this memorable show outside the bars of Knysna village in the certainty that appreciative on-lookers would slake his thirst. I am glad to say that he never raised his axe after raising his glass.

Those old woodcutters lived so deep in the green silence that they formed a race apart, probably the most isolated white people in South Africa. I was assured that some of the grown men and women had never seen a village, while there were children who knew only the faces of their parents and their too numerous brothers and sisters.

Last century these strange folk dressed in skins and lived in *skerms* with only three walls. The old men I met, with their long beards, were like Rip Van Winkles in a modern world. Progress had hardly touched these isolated characters. I thought of them as a tragic race apart; people living so far from civilisation that they had no chance of rising above their environment. A friendly, generous people struggling for their mere food in one of the hardest trades in the world. But so primitive that it was found almost impossible to help them.

Of English, Scottish and Afrikaner descent were these men of the axe. For more than a century they brought the enormous stinkwood and yellowwood trees crashing down; felling, squaring, sawing in those hot, moist, sunless backwoods. They were paid by results, and they showed themselves no mercy as they hacked out their livelihood from the ancient trees. Seldom were they well-nourished; yet they were capable of enormous labour.

For them the call of the woods was irresistible. They went out first as little boys, carrying water for the working parties, robbing wild hives, shooting bush-doves, making fires for the coffee. Small wonder that they could not be kept at school for long. As soon as they had reached their 'teens they were ready to sweat over the huge, felled tree-trunks with axe and saw. The woodcutter could see no farther than the dense wall of his forests, no other future for his children. Year after year the number of trees allotted to woodcutters in the government reserve was reduced. But in the mind of the woodcutter there was no threat to his existence, no plain warning.

The foreman on a private forest estate told me that he once took a middle-aged woodcutter with him on a hunting expedition to the open veld near George, fifty miles away. They travelled by motor-car, and the woodcutter was astounded. "I never thought Africa was so large," he exclaimed.

There is a pathetic story, too, of a woodcutter who went mad, ran amuck with his axe, and killed a coloured boy. He was sent to an asylum in Cape Town. At the end of three years, during a period of sanity, he escaped and trudged back towards his beloved forests. He had no map, no knowledge of the road, nothing but a strong, sure instinct, like a homing pigeon. Fearing detection, he marched at night, avoiding villages, taking a route that lay along mountain slopes. For more than three hundred miles he stumbled on, coming at last to the lonely shack where dwelt his wife and children. One night he spent with them; then he was found and taken back. "Sentence me to years of imprisonment if you like," he pleaded, "but let me know that one day I can come home."

Such is the spell of the forests. Men bred in cities feel as though they were facing a sinister and mysterious presence when they step out of the sunlight into that mass of creepers, ferns and trees. They would lose themselves in five minutes after leaving a path. The woodcutters find their way by sun and stars, and never lose their keen sense of direction. But early this century a woodcutter's child disappeared in the forests. There was a great search, and undoubtedly the child would have been found but for the sudden rain that washed away all track and trace of the poor, frightened thing. All trace obliterated for ever – except a hat, which they took back to the mother . . .

The talk when woodcutters gathered was usually of accidents. There was the man whose legs were pinned down by the tree he had just felled, the only miscalculation of that kind on record. When found, he had worn his fingers almost to the bone in his effort to dig away the earth beneath him.

Planks arrived at the Knysna factories looking as though they had been planed by machinery; twenty-feet long, without a deviation of one thirty-second of an inch, all done by axe and saw. Yet most of these old craftsmen were earning from two to five pounds a month. When I visited the woodcutters a quarter of a century ago it was possible for a woodcutter in a private forest, with the help of two young sons, to make eighteen shillings a day clear profit. But such earnings could not be maintained for long. Rain and illness, usually through over-exertion, brought the average income down to a small figure.

The little body of men licensed to fell trees in the government forests numbered about three hundred at that time. No new names had been added to the roll of registered woodcutters for many years, so that one old type has died out.

Each year the trees to be sold were numbered by Forest Department officials, the woodcutters inspected them, drew lots for the trees, and gathered at different forest stations for the allotment. They had to pay for the trees, of course, and there was an element of chance in the business which appealed mightily to the old men. If all their trees were perfect they secured good prices. But there was always the risk of rot, bad heart and poor colour, and sometimes it was difficult to persuade the forester that a tree was defective enough to justify a refund of the purchase price.

Old woodcutters, however, claimed that they could look at a stinkwood tree and tell at once whether the wood possessed that typical dark colour which was so desirable. The demand for stinkwood furniture, of course, is comparatively recent. Thousands of tons of it went in wagons.

Many of the woodcutters could not read, write or count; but they knew to the nearest penny how much was due to them for their work. Like the alluvial diamond diggers, their output was often pledged far in advance to their storekeepers. They were improvident, but they disliked being in debt. It was a tribute to their honesty, as a class, that they were allowed to buy necessities for months on end when, through illness, they were unable to pay. One man owed a hundred pounds at the end of a long illness. He paid back every penny within a year, and had something over; but prodigious amounts of sawdust and sweat went towards the repayment of that debt.

They could have improved their standard of living by growing some of their own food; but they were never content to till the soil for long. During slack times some of them worked as farm labourers. Then, just at a time when they were most needed, they would hurry back to the forest life.

There were far too many boy and girl marriages in the forests. Youths of twenty, who had saved enough money to buy axes, considered that they were set up for life. Another crazy shack of poles, boards and galvanized iron appeared on someone else's land. The young man took a girl of fourteen or fifteen as a wife. And another huge family was raised.

With all their faults and follies, the woodcutters were, in the main, sober and law-abiding. The police often had to stop the brewing of bee wine, a devastating spirit made from wild honey and yeast. At New Year, the chief festival of the forests, the woodcutters sent for barrels of wine and played their guitars and concertinas. For the rest of the year they worked. Meat was a luxury to be enjoyed, at most, once a week. I visited one of their stores in the main forest and saw displayed the simple things they bought. Meal, coffee, sugar and tobacco; those were the most important items in the woodcutter's daily life. Sardines and bully beef were not bought every day. Old Dutch medicines were there, of course, for emergencies. And rows of field boots and blankets and tools, expensive articles to be stared at wistfully and purchased only after deep thought.

It is estimated that the Knysna yellowwood tree takes two thousand years to grow. And the old woodcutters were men of earlier centuries, like the trees.

Once there was a fire in these forests that terrified man and beast. It was the fire that swept from Swellendam to Uitenhage in 1869, the greatest fire in South Africa since the white man came. If there is anyone still living who remembers that fire clearly, then he must be almost a centenarian. But I met several old people in Knysna years ago who talked about the great fire as the most vivid event of their lives.

That fire raged along a course of four hundred miles, and spread out in some places over a front of more than a hundred miles. It is hard to say where or how it started, and one newspaper reported: "From Uitenhage to Riversdale the country appears to have burst simultaneously into a blaze. The glorious forest of Knysna is destroyed." After a careful study of the records, however, I think that Uitenhage saw the opening of this catastrophe.

It was on February 9, 1869, that the people of Uitenhage awoke to a misty dawn. This was followed by the hottest wind they had ever known, a north-east wind like a flame, a wind that put a stop to every sort of work and drove the bewildered people indoors. At noon the shade temperatures was one hundred and twelve degrees. It was difficult to breathe. Late that afternoon the wind was blowing from the south-west at hurricane force.

They had seen a mass of smoke in the distance earlier in the afternoon. Now the sun was covered and it was difficult to find a way through the blinding smoke in the village.

News reached Uitenhage that the farm of Captain Boys, the showplace of the district, had been destroyed with all the household treasures and a fine collection of old Dutch masters. Mrs. Boys and her four daughters had saved their lives by wrapping themselves in blankets and taking refuge in the river. Ashes smothered the Cape road for miles. Wagons and freight were burnt out. Many sheep were lost, while some escaped with the wool scorched close to their skins. This was a cruel day for the wild creatures of the forest, too, and buck were so tamed by fear that they crouched on stoeps in Uitenhage. The village itself escaped.

Humansdorp appeared to be in great danger, and the church bell rang the alarm. The whole Tsitsikama forest as far as Cape St. Francis was ablaze, while the hills to the north of Humansdorp were also in flames. "It was like a prairie fire in America," wrote a Humansdorp resident. "Resinous odours filled the air and a hurricane carried smoke, fire and sparks. High overhead flew great sheets of flame. The sun was as red as fire, and more than one person thought that the final day of God's just retribution had arrived. The fire was two miles from the village when the wind veered to the north-west. We were surrounded by fire, yet not a house in Humansdorp was touched."

There were forty-one deaths in the Humansdorp district, some people being burnt to death while others were killed by the heat. Grain crops which had been reaped and the ripening mealies and beans were lost.

Knysna saw the frightening drama of the fire on the following day, which happened to be Ash Wednesday. Mr. B. H. Darnell, owner of the fine Westford property, recorded his experiences: "At dawn the berg wind, the sirocco of South Africa, was blowing steadily from the north. The temperature was a hundred degrees before eight in the morning, and at nine we saw a great fire raging in the flats above us. I knew it was all up with Westford. As the sole guardian of thirteen women and children I was distracted. Denser and denser grew the smoke and brighter the glare of the fire, while the thermometer rose higher and higher and the wind increased in violence. At first I could only hear the noise of the fire. Presently, above the smoke, I saw liquid fire pouring over cliffs, and below them, on the opposite bank of the river, great streams of fire."

As the fire roared on, Darnell and the women and children found themselves literally at the mouth of a blow-pipe. They ran for the river and joined people who had found safety on the pontoon. There they were safe, but the fire had made a clean sweep of Westford. Houses, trees, gardens, orchards and forest had gone. "The labour and pleasure of sixteen years has been swept away in a few minutes," Darnell reported.

When the main fire had passed, Darnell walked along the

river bank surveying the devastation. Not only buck, but elephants, had been roasted alive. He could find hardly a sign of life except a cunning old baboon which had avoided the fire and now crouched in the desolation. Mighty trees were still crashing in every direction, some hissing as they fell into the river. By a benevolent freak of the fire, all the villages in its path, including Knysna, escaped destruction. So close did the flames pass, however, that the heat in Knysna was intense. The toll in the districts was indeed heavy.

In the Knysna area the Duthies of Belvidere had been burning the veld for grazing. This made a fire-path, and so the great blaze left their famous estate untouched. But the fine Portland farm owned by the Barringtons was almost entirely destroyed. Cottages and forest on Eastford (a glebe of the English church where the bishop lived) were burnt out. The Newdigates of Forest Hall lost two thousand acres of forest, but the house was saved by its iron roof. Dozens of small farmers lost their homes, stock and crops. The poor woodcutters, who had the least to lose, probably felt the effects of the fire more than anyone else, for they could not afford to replace their small possessions.

Mr. Barnard of Buffels Vermaak, a neighbour of Darnell, made for the river when the fire became intense. He took a chest containing thousands of sovereigns and the family silver with him on a small cart. The fire came so close to where he had sought refuge that he and his family had to stand up to their necks in water to avoid catching alight. They saved their lives and their money, though the gold and silver melted in the chest.

A schoolmaster on the flats above Phantom Pass, between Westford and Portland, was giving a Bible lesson when he noticed the fire in the distance. Suddenly a whirlwind appeared, black with smoke. The wind rose to a roar and whined its menace in the roof, shaking the whole building so that all knew it would collapse at any moment. The door had jammed, but the children and master scrambled through the window just in time. They could see the flames leaping from hilltop to hilltop, missing the homes and trees in the valleys. It was so dark at two in the afternoon that survivors had to light their lamps.

One family stacked their furniture in the open and prepared to load it on to a wagon. The flames came before they could move off, taking the furniture and sparing the house.

Snakes were observed writhing madly, with mouths open, in the effort to escape. Frightened birds flew into houses, and thousands of birds were smothered by the smoke. A man saw eight buck standing together and cooling their burnt feet in the river.

A conversation between Newdigate and Barrington after the fire was recorded many years ago, and provides a valuable sidelight on the disaster and the philosophy of the victims.

"You are a marvel to be so cheerful after what you have gone through," remarked Newdigate.

Barrington replied: "I have much to thank God for. My dear wife and all my children are safe. We are pioneers in a new country, and I fear that I for one was selfish in wishing for earthly comfort. My children escaped by a miracle. A native boy helped to take the little children, one a baby in arms, to a piece of bare rock well above the forests. My home has gone, above all my valuable library is in ashes. I still have a few bottles of wine and a sack of meal, but my stores for the year have gone. I have already started to build again. After all, I have the land, the cattle, servants, wagons and sawmill – and my wife and children."

People in Cape Town, with their traditional kindness, held a public meeting to raise money for the needy victims of the fire. Bread, clothes, bedding and food were rushed to the afflicted districts. Knysna held a day of thanksgiving and special church services on March 14.

In the forests the fire still smouldered. The ashes were still warm in pits and caves six months after the inferno. And the origin of it all? Veld burning, the hand of man, the old curse of South Africa.

In the Knysna forests, impressive though they are, I always feel that there is too much to see. No doubt that is why I prefer deserts to the lush country. The isolated tree makes a landmark.

I was flying round the Pretoria countryside with Major "Duke" Meintjes in an old DH 9 long ago when Meintjes pointed out the Wonderboom. This is a tree to remember, a tree that became a forest. Very soon I drove out for eight miles, through the narrow break in the Magaliesberg called Voortrekker Nek, to explore this marvel at ground level.

The Wonderboom is an evergreen wild fig tree which owes its world-wide fame among botanists to the extraordinary manner of its growth. It is about seventy-five feet high, a hemispherical mass with thirteen individual trunks which have sprung from the original central trunk. Many years ago the branches became too heavy and took root like strawberry plants or climbing shrubs. This process is all the more unusual when you consider that this particular fig tree (*Ficus Pretoriae Burtt Davy*) is more of a tropical growth, and Pretoria is almost its extreme southern limit.

Dr. I. B. Pole Evans, the botanist, described the Wonderboom as "the most remarkable example of its species in Africa and a national monument". Its age has been estimated at three centuries. The central mass of stem has a circumference of eighty-one feet, and the whole tree forms a canopy over an area large enough to shelter hundreds of people.

Bushmen lived in a cave overlooking the Wonderboom centuries ago. There is a legend that when natives attacked the cave, the Bushmen escaped through a secret tunnel which penetrates the mountain. However, no trace of this old sanctuary has been found.

Charles Zeyher the botanical collector seems to have missed the Wonderboom during his visit to the neighbourhood with Burke in the eighteen-forties. The first mention of the tree was made by a Swiss missionary named Creux in 1862, and his measurements show that the tree has grown little since then.

A Natal trader named Menne was camping under the Wonderboom with his servants and cattle in the early days. Fires were blazing and the evening meal was being prepared. Into this pleasant scene rushed a black rhino. It stampeded the cattle, charged the servants, scattered the cooking pots and fires. Then, after staring at the disconcerted humans it broke out of the tree circle and departed. White and black rhino rubbed their hides against the Wonderboom in those days, but they will not be seen there again.

In the wagon days the Wonderboom was a favourite outspan.

Transport riders halted there. Close by is an old fort, built to protect the road to Pretoria from warlike natives. During one native campaign a whole commando with sixty wagons made its headquarters under the tree. Many a Dingaan's Day celebration has been held there.

Dr. W. G. Atherstone, the geologist, who identified the first South African diamond, examined the Wonderboom in 1873 and carried away a twig. Since then almost every herbarium in the world has been supplied with branches.

Lady Florence Dixie rode out to the Wonderboom a few years after Atherstone, accompanied by Sir Evelyn Wood, General Ballairs and Colonel Gildea. She commented in a book she wrote on the natural defensive strength of the position. "One of the principal sights which we were bent on seeing that day was the great Wonderboom, or wonderful tree. When we had threaded the Pass and skirted a reedy lake from which the cry of the wild duck arose, the tree, with its heavy mass of foliage, hove in sight, looking like some huge giant amidst the dwarf vegetation that surrounded it. Putting spurs to our horses, several of us raced to reach the spot first, which foolish exploit under a hot sun made both ourselves and our horses very hot, and rendered the dark, cool shade of the great tree doubly acceptable and refreshing. Examination proved it to be of an ambitious and progressive nature, the larger branches, as soon as they became developed, drooping earthwards until, taking root, fresh life springs forth from the younger scions of the old stem."

An interesting water-colour of the Wonderboom in 1879 by Mrs. Archdeacon Roberts shows the loop connections from the main stem by which the tree propagated itself. These were chopped off by vandals this century, while the interior of the main trunk was burnt out.

Further damage was caused as the result of the dreams of a woman prophet in Pretoria. She declared that a great hoard of gold lay buried near the roots, or in the huge trunk itself. The story became linked with the legend of the "Kruger millions", the boxes of gold which the President was supposed to have hidden when he was forced to leave the Transvaal. Dr. Leyds, who accompanied Kruger on that journey, made it absolutely clear that no republican gold was buried during that period. Treasure legends never die, in spite of contradictions. Many holes, some seven feet deep, were dug round the main stem, and the last remaining connections between the main trunk and the second and third outer circles of trunks were severed.

Across the Aapies River, but not far away, is the Klein Wonderboom of the same species. This is the home of many birds which enjoy the wild figs and other fruits of the area. There you may see starlings plum-coloured and green, sunbirds seeking their nectar, warblers and crested barbets, woodpeckers and doves. Dr. Austin Roberts identified two hundred distinct species in this neighbourhood. The whole area is now a nature reserve and bird sanctuary, a strong contrast indeed with the wild days of the *oudstryders* and hunters.

Another tree of adventure is the baobab. When I sleep under a baobab far from the cities I think of the creatures that roamed beneath that grotesque tree thousands of years ago. For the weird baobab is probably the oldest living tree, reaching five thousand years under favourable conditions.

It belongs to the tropics, of course, and you find them all the way down Africa from Egypt to the Transvaal, always within sound of the "ping-ing-ing-zzz" of the mosquito. I camped under an enormous baobab in the far Kaokoveld once, and drank the acid, lemon-tasting beverage made from the seed capsules. As a remedy for malaria, however, I would prefer paludrine. The old explorers had to use what they could find. Natives make an alcoholic drink from these seeds, the "Laughing Spirits" of many a night of revelry. Monkeys also love the fruit, and in many parts of Africa the baobab is known as the monkey bread tree. David Livingstone called the baobabs "those upturned carrots". He slept in a hollow baobab and declared there was room for thirty men inside the trunk.

An eccentric official at Katima Molilo in the Caprivi Strip found a new use for the old baobab; he installed a flush lavatory, probably the only one on the African continent. However, he moved all the equipment out again after encountering a mamba there. Baobabs growing in Northern Transvaal villages are sometimes used as garages. More than one farmer has discovered that the interior of the tree has a preservative atmosphere; you can keep meat fresh there, and it is a good, cool place for a dairy. Towards the end of last century there was a bar in a fat baobab outside Leydsdorp, a famous haunt of the goldseekers.

Native chiefs in Abyssinia and farther south have been buried in the trunks of baobabs. Their bodies have become mummified owing to the preservative action. No doubt that is the reason why certain baobabs are reputed to be the homes of devils. After dark the devils lie in wait among the twisted branches for victims. Place your ear to the trunk and you will hear the devils inside chuckling. Even the boldest native sings as he passes a baobab at night, never pausing to listen to the evil voices.

Perhaps the bees are responsible for the legend. Wild bees often perforate the soft trunk of a baobab and lodge their honey in the recesses. This is regarded by many native epicures as the finest honey in Africa.

In dry areas the top of the baobab trunk acts as a reservoir, catching rainwater and dew. When you see pegs driven into the trunk you may be sure there is a natural reservoir above. Early travellers recorded their gratitude for this wise custom, saying that the water saved their lives. However, the tree reservoir is not without its perils. I heard of a lone Bushman who climbed in search of moisture, fell into the deep, hollow trunk and perished. But in lion country the baobab may be a lifesaver indeed. The foot traveller who has to sleep beside the road feels much more comfortable in the branches.

The baobab, cream of tartar tree, received its botanical name *Adansonia digitata* from the French traveller Adanson. He examined fine specimens in Senegal two hundred years ago. (Cape Verde, where Adanson landed, gained its name when the early Portuguese sighted the green leaves of the baobabs in the desert.) Scientists have calculated from the rings in the cross-section of the main trunk that the baobab may live twice as long as the Sacred Bo-Tree of Ceylon, the fig tree planted nearly three centuries before the birth of Christ and worshipped ever since. Humboldt, the explorer, spoke of the baobab as "the oldest organic monument of our planet".

The bottle-shaped trunk of the baobab swells out in the course of the centuries to a diameter of thirty or forty feet. Some specimens have a girth greater than their height. The maximum height is about seventy feet. Then the soft, spongy trunk branches out into huge, nightmarish branches carrying little golden lamps of flowers.

Probably the best-known baobab in Africa is "The Tree" close to the Victoria Falls, and seen by every tourist. (This should not be confused with the tree on Livingstone Island at the very brink of the Falls, on which Livingstone carved his initials.) Many baobabs have been declared "historical monuments" to save them from destruction. Many fine specimens have been protected in the streets and gardens of Messina. Between the wars a large baobab was worth about a hundred pounds, and a firm cut them down and pulped them for paper. Since 1942, however, it has been illegal to fell a baobab anywhere in the Union.

One remote baobab in the Zambesi valley records stirring and tragic pages of African adventure. Old hunters chose that tree as a monument to friends who would hunt no more. The inscriptions read as follows:

Rider, died fever Lake Ngami 1850.
Maher, killed by Baralongs 1852.
Wahlberg, killed by wounded elephant 1857.
Dolman, died of thirst in Kalahari desert in 1851.
Robinson, taken by crocodile Botetli river 1851.
Pretorius, died fever near Victoria Falls 1862.
Bonfield, killed by crocodile Ovamboland 1861.
Burgess, blown up, gunpowder accident 1860.

If a baobab tree is cut down, say the natives, lions will surely visit the spot. A hunter once told me that there was some ground for the belief; the water stored in the trunk would attract the animals in a dry season.

Truly the baobab marks the path of African adventures. And surely it is the most fantastic of South Africa's five hundred varieties of native trees. Always their vast trunks and mushroom branches give the landscape an impression of their size, coupled with a grey breath of old age. I think the early Dutch explorer's description remains the most fitting: "*Eenen boom die, niet minder dan de Olyphant onder de Beesten, een monster is onder het geboomte.*" (A tree that, no less than the elephant among the animals, is a monster among the trees.)

The Seamy Past of Salisbury

IN his Southern Africa roamings Lawrence Green mostly chose remote places in the Cape Province to explore. *Full Many a Glorious Morning* was written during the last five years of his life. He decided to visit by rail and road four countries in Southern Africa and the result was an unusual yet absorbing work. His visit to Rhodesia was a sentimental journey. Years before, just after World War I, Green made a bizarre journey in "a cantankerous motor car" on a commercial stunt to prove the value of a fuel made from prickly pears. His companion, the driver, set out to drive this weirdly-fuelled car from Cape Town to Bulawayo. With memories of that strange adventure to spur his imagination, Green revisited Rhodesia decades afterwards. As usual he kindles into vivid flame the embers of the past rugged pioneering days in Bulawayo and Salisbury, devoting separate chapters to both cities. It was difficult to decide which chapter to include in this anthology. The selection of Salisbury was impelled by whimsy rather than logic and I trust that the parochial patriotism of Bulawayo will not feel flouted. Lawrence Green's revelations about Salisbury's lurid past and his observations on the spacious sophisticated city Rhodesia's capital is today will enthral all readers.

In the closing words of this remarkable chapter Green allows himself a rare personal meditation, revealing once again his love of the sea and his inner psychological compulsion to live within sight and sound of the oceans which inspired some of his finest passages. "I have carried my claustrophobia with me," he wrote, "Salisbury's largest sheet of water, Lake McIlwane with its creeks and islands, is not large enough for me. I must have the ocean at my door." Those light, final words I think are the key of real understanding of the nature of this shy, retiring yet entirely gifted man. And he died with the ocean at his door.

CHAPTER XVII

SALISBURY CAMEO

THEY call it the Kopje and the old spelling seems appropriate here as it does in Franschhoek and Stellenbosch. This koppie overlooks Salisbury, Rhodesia, one of twenty-seven places of that name in the world as post-office men know to their cost. I have come up here to get my bearings and I am not at all surprised to find a ghost beside me.

He is a handsome young man, tall and lean, with curly hair and a full moustache. I recognise him easily though I knew him only as an elderly man – William Ernest Fairbridge, first mayor of Salisbury, editor and owner of the first Salisbury newspaper. When Fairbridge retired he had an office in the newspaper building in Cape Town where I worked for years. He had collected an enormous library of Africana and Rhodesiana and the history of Southern Africa (which was his lifelong hobby) was literally at his finger-tips. I consulted him often. I still study the cards, the thousands of indexed cards on which Fairbridge entered the sort of information which is not to be found in orthodox history books.

So the soft and cultured voice of the scholar comes back to me as I stare at the high Salisbury buildings, the blue-flowering jacarandas sent here from Durban, the lake resort and the gardens and all those signs of settlement that are established only after many years. As I listen to the voice, modern Salisbury fades out and I hear the curfew in Market Square below the koppie; the noon gun that was sometimes fifteen minutes late. I can see the red lamps in Pioneer Street down below and the gallows within the walls of the old Fort.

Salisbury is one of those cities (like Nairobi) which have grown up by accident on the wrong site. When the Pioneer Column approached this spot three horsemen were sent ahead to find the place selected for the fort. They reached the bush-covered hill at the eastern end of the present city and thought it was Mount Hampden. Selous often camped at Mount Hampden; he loved the place and recommended it as the Fort Salisbury site. In fact, Mount Hampden lies a few miles to the north. The weary Pioneers pitched their tents thankfully at the foot of the hill and the position of Salisbury was fixed for all time.

While I was in Salisbury the newspaper reported that someone had watched a civet cat hunting in a patch of grass on the outskirts of the city. A black mamba had been seen in the same area. *Eheu! fugaces.* Fairbridge often spoke of the wild life in Salisbury during the early years (and long afterwards) and he would not have thought much of a civet cat. A lioness was shot on the outspan a year after the occupation; two years later a lioness was killed on the Kopje and about the same time an Avondale housewife shot a lion from her kitchen window. Residents often put up buck in their gardens and very welcome they were in those days of food shortages. Fairbridge told me that in the middle eighteen-nineties a Salisbury coat-of-arms was proposed and designs were invited. Lord Bryce, a visitor, suggested the last lion retreating before the first lamp-post. Rats were more dangerous than lions at that time for they bit people while they were asleep and one man had his false teeth stolen by a rat. Cats were sold at five pounds apiece. Zebras ran through the settlement. Dr. Rutherford Harris, an unpopular official, was bathing in a river on the Salisbury outskirts when a crocodile seized his buttocks. He freed himself but spent weeks in hospital; and the crocodile was found dead in the pool next day. Pioneers said the mere taste of the unspeakable Harris had killed the crocodile. Harris left Rhodesia after this adventure and became a Cape member of parliament.

Fairbridge told me that the first building in Salisbury was a bakery, though the arrival of the first billiard table caused more excitement. A lottery with eight hundred pounds in prizes was organised two years after the occupation, so that the metal cages in the modern hall in Kingsway are merely carrying on a tradition. Women were not allowed into Mashonaland for some time after the Pioneers arrived, but one slipped in disguised as a boy. After the ban was lifted a Miss Hlawazak reached Salisbury and announced that she was walking to Cairo. She went on alone and died of fever in the wilds.

Two murders were the talk of early Salisbury. First there was the trial of Louis Andries, a Jewish sailor from Holland who had trekked inland to make a fortune. Andries was accused of shooting one of his companions, a watchmaker named Beeley near Tuli. The trial was held in Salisbury with Dr. Leander Starr Jameson, the administrator, on the bench. There was no apparent motive and Andries claimed that Beeley had committed suicide. Later in the trial Andries stated that he had seen someone near the wagon, an unknown person who was responsible for the shooting. Dr. Jameson and his four assessors found Andries guilty. "Prisoner at the bar, you have been found guilty of murder," Dr. Jameson announced in a faltering nervous voice. "As a doctor it has always been my study and purpose to save life and now I am bound to take it away."

Fairbridge protested against the death sentence on the grounds that the evidence was unsatisfactory. Nevertheless a gallows twenty feet high was built in the courtyard of the Fort. Sir Henry Loch, high commissioner at the Cape, confirmed the sentence. Then the authorities had to find a hangman. A volunteer named Morton was appointed and an official letter was sent to Cape Town asking for technical advice on the procedure at an execution. Fairbridge told me that the reply was preserved in the archives of the Chartered Company. Every detail of rope and drop was supplied and the Cape Town hangman ended his letter with these words: "If these instructions are faithfully observed I guarantee that satisfaction will be given to all parties." Jameson published the hour of execution as eight in the morning but at daybreak Andries was led to the gallows accompanied by a Mr. Hyman who read the Hebrew service. There was no crowd at that hour. It was reported that death was instantaneous. Morton was shunned. The people who had thoroughly approved of the death sentence would have no dealings with the hangman.

Soon after this grim episode a native known as Zulu Jim murdered four white people including a woman and child. "I shall have to keep the scaffold standing as a permanent institution if this goes on," wrote Jameson. There was talk of lynching and an excited mob headed for the gaol. The mob halted outside the small thatched building where Zulu Jim had been held but the gaoler had smuggled the murderer out and hidden him elsewhere. Jameson arrived on horseback and addressed the angry crowd. One man was swinging an axe, another had a coil of rope which he had taken from the verandah at Meikle's store. Jameson addressed them, appealing not only to their sense of justice but also to other instincts. "We are on the eve of a boom," he declared. "This act will prevent you from reaping your reward. Let the law take its course. If we don't hang Zulu Jim you can hang me."

Jameson was again the judge and Zulu Jim was sentenced to death. With the confirmation of sentence from the Cape there came a reprimand from the high commissioner; Jameson had gone too far in promising the death sentence before the trial. Zulu Jim was hanged in public as a warning to the native population. Banks of earth thrown up by the Pioneers in Cecil Square for the Fort were used by those who wanted a clear view. The gallows were set up in the open. Morton the hangman waited on the platform with Dr. Edgelow. The condemned man arrived with a Roman Catholic priest, surrounded by police, and was given a cup of brandy. Then his arms were strapped, the white cover was placed over his head. Morton tightened the noose and pulled the lever. It was his last execution. No one would drink with him and he left Rhodesia. In later years a prison warder acted as executioner but he made it clear that he would perform this task only when natives were to be hanged; it was laid down in his contract that he would not be called upon to hang a white person. Decades passed before another white murderer was sentenced to death, a woman. She was reprieved. However, there was an embarrassing incident in Dr. Jameson's time when a white man was sentenced to death for murdering a native. A petition was drawn up setting out extenuating circumstances and in the end the death sentence was reduced to a fine of two hundred and fifty pounds. The man went to Jameson and pleaded that he would need time to pay off such a large fine. "Give me an I.O.U. then," Jameson demanded. The I.O.U. is probably still filed in Salisbury.

Salisbury of the eighteen-nineties had a gaol which was noteworthy for escapes rather than security. Law and order were in the hands of amateurs. A despicable character who was serving a long sentence for stealing Lobengula's "peace offering" of one thousand sovereigns was among those who got away. Another convict devised a method of escape that made Salisbury laugh. He was a hold-up man named Edwards, famous for his smart appearance and expensive clothes. A plumber by trade, he was put to work on plumbing jobs in gaol. Edwards used his tools, shears and soldering irons to make a lifelike effigy of himself, a full-size dummy complete with auburn hair, reddish-tinted beard and moustache, boots curving upwards at the toes. It was so realistic that the warder going on his rounds at night was completely deceived. Edwards, hidden in a workshop, slipped out of a window, climbed over the garden fence and disappeared into the night. However, he was recognised in Beira by a detective on leave; the old debonair Edwards, one of the smartest men in the seaport. Edwards shot at the detective but the detective brought him down. Edwards then returned to Rhodesia to serve a sentence of eight years.

Hotels of a sort arose in Salisbury in the very early days. Fairbridge remembered the first piano ever seen in Mashonaland being carried into the Masonic. Another hotel had pole and reed walls and a bucksail roof. When the proprietor put on a St. Patrick's Day dinner the menu consisted of local fowls, roan antelope, sable cutlets, pumpkin, sweet potatoes and green mealies. He charged a guinea a guest, but this included whisky and gin. Slater's Hotel was a burnt-brick place thatched with grass. Tommy's Rest (or the Salisbury Hotel) was a weather-worn marquee. The proprietor advertised "cleanliness and civility a speciality". Meals cost half-a-crown, served on tin plates with iron forks. Salt came in a tobacco tin. There was a mud floor. When the first club was opened someone asked Dr. Jameson to suggest qualifications for membership. "Anyone who has been out of gaol for three months should be eligible," replied Jameson firmly. Tom Meikle and others opened the first brewery. Meikle and his brother James were of Scottish descent. They came to Rhodesia from Natal and started various enterprises (including the famous hotel in Salisbury) which still flourish. Towards the end of the century the first Cecil Hotel was built and part of this hotel remains as the core of the Legislative Assembly. The dining-room became the debating chamber. Old serving-hatches may still be seen. Between the wars there were many attempts to build a new parliament but the old hotel building survived. An unusual feature of the place was that although it was two-storied the upper floor could only be reached by a shaky outside staircase. It was a dingy and dilapidated parliament at that period, flanked by attractive lawns. On sunny days the whole Assembly moved out on to the lawns at the tea interval. Benches in the debating chamber are of Rhodesian *mukwa* timber with flame lily carvings by an African craftsman. Among the busts in the public corridor are Smuts and Selous. Huge elephants' tusks are used as lamp standards in the entrance lobby. A painting of the Victoria Falls by Thomas Baines, more than a century old, gives a brilliant impression of the great scene, thanks to skilful cleaning.

Other relatively historic buildings in Salisbury are the first government house with its wide verandah in Montague Avenue; the red brick market hall which displayed the first clock, built four years after the Pioneers arrived; and the police bandstand on Cecil Square. Here and there a Victorian cast-iron balcony reminds the Capetonian of Long Street. Hitching-posts have almost disappeared but a *msasa* tree in North Avenue which Selous used as a target is still there.

Barmaids arrived in Salisbury when the ban on women was lifted. Pioneer Street, the first street in Salisbury, became a street of bars and little shacks known as "tearooms". A police officer's wife wrote at this period: "The entrance to the town from the south is Pioneer Street, a street of cottages and shops. All the cottages appear to be occupied by women. It is quite sad to pass along at dusk seeing these houses wide open and lit up with lamps with red shades. The windows of all rooms are open because of the heat and one catches a glimpse of the tawdry-looking bedrooms hung with scarlet turkey twill and garish mirrors. The women sit in chairs in front of the houses in various stages of undress waiting for their prey. Most of them are foreigners, French or German, but there appear to be quite a number of English and Colonial women, too. They are easily spotted in the street, their dress and their way of walking with a defiant air. Poor things, what will be their end?"

Most notorious of all the women of Pioneer Street was the character nicknamed French Marie. She was French by birth and she transferred her activities from San Francisco to Salisbury (with a troop of girls) when she heard of the opportunities in that new country. French Marie was a tall, well-built women who often wore riding-breeches or shorts and a slouch hat. She was so powerful that she could change a heavy wagon wheel. If there was any trouble in her establishment she used a stockwhip or her fists; even tough customers avoided falling out with her. She visited the Victoria Falls very early this century with a wagonload of girls. Then she became respectable and worked as a prospector, miner, trader and butcher. Natives called her Mfazi Kaputula, the "woman in shorts". She would go into bars (where women were not allowed) and drink and play dice or cards with the customers. After a few drinks she tried to cheat; then she became unpopular because no one dared to denounce her. French Marie had a pretty daughter and when the girl grew up her mother watched her closely. At a dance one man showed the girl a great deal of attention. French Marie took the man aside and warned him: "Mac, if you get up to any funny business I'll put a bullet in you." Marie was a fine horsewoman. One night she galloped up to a farm-house with two lions after her; but she borrowed a rifle, shot both lions, and returned to horsewhip the farmer because he had been afraid to go out with her. Marie left Rhodesia for Brazzaville in her old age.

Few people in Salisbury were able to put glass in their windows in the early period. Fairbridge said that even Dr. Jameson had to be content with coarse cotton material known in pioneer slang as "limbo". Ugly, bare walls were the rule, but some housewives used the cheap and gorgeous fabrics sold by the Portuguese to the natives as a substitute for tapestry. The absence of glass was felt keenly during the purgatorial dust storms that swept the new settlement. But there were even more serious shortages and Salisbury was often a hungry settlement before the railway line came up from Beira. Fairbridge said that the first bunch of grapes sold there fetched twenty shillings. Whisky was sold at forty pounds a case at one period, while even a bottle of Cape brandy went for twenty-five shillings. A cabbage was worth eighteen shillings. Men with cartridges went out after duck and snipe in the vlei between the Kopje and the Causeway; and one hunter shot a ten-foot python in Pioneer Street. Hen's eggs were five shillings each during the worst period of the famine. Chinese and Indian market gardeners had small-holdings on the Makabusi river banks but they were unable to grow enough food. Many white people lived mainly on kaffir corn and millet seeds ground between stones.

They talk of the "suicide season" in Salisbury, the sweltering period during September and October when temperatures rise to the maximum. Mr. G. H. Tanser, educationist and historian, tells me that this sinister phrase originated during the summer of seventy years ago when Salisbury was short of water, prices were high, many men were out of work, locusts ravaged the countryside, and the few doctors could not cope with the numbers suffering from dysentery and malaria. A bridegroom shot himself just after the wedding; seven other desperate Salisbury citizens followed his example within a few weeks. Salisbury breathes again when moist air is drawn in from the Congo and the temperature drops as the cloud cover increases. Then the thunder and the rain mark the end of the "suicide season".

Salisbury's public gardens cover forty-four acres. When the first money was voted for this purpose just before the end of last century the first curator had to kill off lions among the rocks and swamps. He planted two thousand trees in a year and laid out an orchard of plums and apricots to relieve the food shortage. Mealies were grown for the same reason. Mangoes and pawpaws had priority over roses. The time came when it was possible to concentrate on decorative trees and flowers; and these gardens supplied the streets of Salisbury with the distinctive Rhodesian bauhinia with pink and white flowers. The gardens are also famous for roses, African flame trees with red flowers and scarlet flamboyants.

Cash was scarce in Salisbury soon after the occupation and an undesirable credit system grew up, with barter as the alternative. Fairbridge used to ride about the town signing up subscribers to his *Mashonaland Herald* and accepting candles and marmalade in payment. British South Africa Company cheques were also used in place of money, endorsed and passed from hand to hand like banknotes. Fairbridge was able to organise the printing of fairly good banknotes in Salisbury during the Rebellion; one pound, five pound and ten pound notes on paper of good quality but without a watermark. Gold was found in the township at this period but not enough of it to serve as currency. During the rush part of Causeway was pegged. A reef was found in Cecil Square but this was not worked. Gold was the money that every one wanted, sovereigns and half-sovereigns.

Rickshaws and prospectors with donkeys were prominent in the streets of early Salisbury; bicycles were seen everywhere between the wars. Old-timers still think wistfully of the police band that played in Cecil Square after church on Sundays. Here, too, interesting auction sales were held on Saturday mornings. You could pick up bargains in everything from guns to books, for civil servants went on leave to Britain every three years and some sold their possessions to pay expenses.

Among the popular bars in Salisbury early this century were the Posada in Manica Road with a counter thirty-six feet long, advertised as "the most luxurious bar in Rhodesia". Characters with strange nicknames, Mazoe Bill and Scorpion Jim, slaked their thirsts in this tiled basement. A famous sponger of those days made a point of never accepting more than sixpence from any one benefactor. He earned a steady living in that way for years and never went thirsty. Another personality of a different sort, Strachan of the Pirate Bottle Store, was a champion walker. He arrived on foot from Kimberley soon after the Pioneers, walked for thousands of miles in Rhodesia, and nearly died of thirst during a walk to Beira. He went for fifty-four hours without water and was saved by natives.

What do you look for when you reach a city that is new to you? In this streamlined world of painful similarities I try to find something different and often this is a hard task. Not in Venice or Amsterdam, perhaps, but many cities are just petrol filling stations, rows of shop-windows, flats and villas. I found the blessed touch of individuality in a Salisbury suburb where some inspired resident decided to build a house on the huge boulders that covered his property. He was an engineer and he planned each portion of the house separately. First he built one room on a tremendous rock, obtaining access by a narrow, winding flight of steps between two other rocks. When the rock surfaces were found to be too small for further rooms the engineer extended them by means of iron girders and cement built up to make a base level with the topmost curve of the rock. This suburban castle must be seen to be understood. Rooms are connected by passages, some of which are outside the rooms and curve upwards to the next level. Others follow tortuous paths between impressive boulders. Rooms conform to the areas available on the rocks and have irregular shapes. From outside a room may seem to have very high windows, but this is because the floor has had to be raised round the crown of a rock to make it level. As the rocks resemble a cottage loaf (with many upper portions) there is always an overhang below each room. This would make a burglar's task difficult. Battlemented gateway and walls complete a residence which only a most ambitious neighbour would try to copy.

What else is there to give Salisbury its own personality? The bells, of course. I shall remember the bells of the cathedral of St. Mary and All Saints as the sound of Salisbury. This is the largest "ring" of bells in Africa south of Khartoum; ten bells of copper and tin, each with its name and its flame lily and rose, cast by the firm in Whitechapel that made Big Ben.

There are the hotels where men in Saville Row clothes mingle with bush shorts and tropical suits. The hour of the sundowner gives you the essential Rhodesian scene, good-humoured and noisy. You will also notice the young coloured women serving as usherettes in the cinemas; the African troops and African constables. When I was in Salisbury not long ago the followers of the French Marie tradition were still in business but there was a movement to drive the old Pioneer Street entertainments underground.

Salisbury may have an international look now and again but at heart it is still a farmer's market town. From the Kopje I gaze out over a district where the forests have been cut down so that eight hundred farmers may grow their food crops and raise their cattle. Tobacco grows up to the edge of the airport. Two miles from Cecil Square are the auction floors of the world's largest individual tobacco market.

Many parts of Salisbury made me think of the place as a small Johannesburg. Smart as paint, scented with syringa and frangipani, it is a worthy capital no doubt. However, it is not the sort of atmosphere that makes me wish to linger. I have carried my claustrophobia with me. Salisbury's largest sheet of water, Lake McIlwaine with its creeks and islands, is not large enough for me. I must have the ocean at my door.

Riddles of the Universe

SENTIMENT alone could force me, if there were no other justification, to end this anthology with a chapter from *Thunder on the Blaauwberg*, one of Lawrence Green's later works published in 1966. Firstly note the spelling of "Blaauwberg". With a fierce derision of the pundits of the Place Names Commission who changed to Blouberg the spelling of the village which held him in willing bondage for so long, Lawrence Green declined to observe this nomenclature ukase. To Lawrence Green, Blaauwberg would be forever Blaauwberg as long as he lived. In earlier annotations I mentioned how Green striding along the beach at Blaauwberg would ponder on new ideas for future books and chapters. The sound of the surf was the music that gave him inspiration. Yet those lonely walks along the sands of Blaauwberg had a deeper meaning in the life of this splendid man who was my friend.

That beach was his spiritual cathedral where he wondered about the universe and puny man's brief passage through this world of ours. Lawrence Green was not religious in the sense that he was not a church attender and that inter-denominational dogma or dispute did not interest him. Yet he thought often with a discerning philosophical detachment on the mysteries of eternity and after-life. In the opening chapter of *Thunder on the Blaauwberg* Lawrence Green writes in detail about memorable walks and the contentments and happinesses these excursions gave him. Listen to these wistful words: "Here in all weathers is the gift of health; yet on many days of the year I am alone in this life-giving air. Why is it that so few have discovered the vision of eternity? I want nothing better than this, the lovely sands of Blaauwberg with the seas breaking gently and the seabirds calling". When in the last months of his life illness assailed his strong physique and forbade his striding for five miles along this beach an emptiness entered his daily life.

I have chosen *A Visionary Rides By*, the second chapter in this work, *Thunder on the Blaauwberg*, strictly on its merits but also because I sense somehow that Lawrence Green would approve this selection of a valedictory chapter in this anthology. John William Dunne, famous author of *An Experiment with Time*, mathematician and mystic too, sat for hours on the rocks at Blaauwberg, meditating as Green so often did. Green writes compellingly of Dunne's early life in the Cape and I am sure posterity will be glad that Green has preserved much incident that might otherwise have been lost in the life story of the remarkable, fascinating John William Dunne.

CHAPTER XVIII

A VISIONARY RIDES BY

Though earth and man were gone,
And suns and universes ceased to be,
And Thou wert left alone,
Every existence would exist in Thee.
                                EMILY BRONTË

OF all the rare, strange and curious personalities who have passed through Blaauwberg village I am inclined to place John William Dunne at the head of the list. One of the old men of Blaauwberg told me that Dunne used to ride across from Stellenbosch during the 'nineties of last century. Dunne was a dreamy, rather sad Irish lad, fond of sitting alone on the rocks for hours with a fishing rod. He stayed with the Dales at Highclere in the village. Sir Langham Dale, a man of great attainments as educationist, writer and archaeologist, was vice-chancellor of the South African College. Dunne was the eldest son of General Sir John Hart Dunne. He was educated privately, for this restless genius would not have fitted comfortably into the public-school system. No doubt his parents were worried about his unusual outlook on life when they sent him from Ireland at the age of seventeen to learn farming in the Stellenbosch district.

They need not have worried. The moody son became a brilliant thinker. He made a deep impression in two entirely different branches of research – aeronautics and immortality. When he died in 1949 at the age of seventy-three, John William Dunne was regarded by a number of leading thinkers as the philosopher who had produced genuine scientific proof of life after death. Be that as it may, there is no doubt that Dunne's accounts of dreams that came true and his theories of time and the mystery of existence had a profound influence in academic, religious and other circles. Dunne is still widely quoted. His works have been re-published again and again. And all this started in a most peculiar way while he was approaching manhood at the Cape. I imagine that some of his sensational visions took shape while he sat rod in hand on the Blaauwberg rocks waiting for the white stumpnose to bite.

Dunne became far too introspective during his farming interlude. Hopefully he sent a short story to a Cape Town magazine. When there was no reply he fell into a savage mood and lost all belief in God. He decided that two different characters were in possession of his body. While obsessed with this idea he rode into Stellenbosch in search of reading matter, and by chance he borrowed from the library Robert Louis Stevenson's novel "The Strange Case of Dr. Jekyll and Mr. Hyde". This appeared to confirm his views about himself and he regarded the experience as a direct intervention by God. Soon afterwards Dunne attended seances of the Cape Town Spiritualistic Society. This was the circle organised by a leading dentist of last century, Dr. Berks T. Hutchinson of Queen Victoria Street. Hutchinson's nephew, the great C. W. H. Kohler of wine fame, learnt dentistry there and also attended the seances for a time. I do not know whether Hutchinson and Kohler had any influence on young Dunne; but Dunne stated that members used the planchette and played the "willing game". The "ouija board" was then in vogue for automatic writing. Table-tilting formed part of the proceedings. Dunne saw through the tricks, however, and left the society disgusted. He found more satisfaction at the weekly sessions of the Cape Town chess club. Spiritualism, he decided, was dangerous, for it led to the growth of credulity and weakening of the critical faculties. However, he was invited by "another sceptic" to attend a different sort of seance in the board room at the Mowbray town hall. This was a gathering of Afrikaners, with an Afrikaans-speaking woman of fifty as the medium. Dunne could not understand a word of it, but when the medium referred to him, someone translated her words: "She says there is a young man here tonight who will be the greatest medium the world has ever seen." The medium also advised Dunne to give up smoking. Dunne never attended another seance, but he recalled the medium's words in later years, when he became aware of "psychic intrusions".

Dunne joined the Imperial Yeomanry as a trooper in 1900 and went on active service in the Orange Free State. He claimed "a great spiritual experience" while riding over the veld under a full moon. It was a revelation. He became aware, without hearing a voice, of "the friendliness of God". He was invalided out of the army after a short period in the field. On his return to the Cape he started the aircraft experiments which placed him among the pioneers. He studied the sea birds, probably on Blaauwberg beach, and made paper aeroplane models. Even in those days he was concentrating on the "swept-back wing" design, gaining special inspiration from the albatross. Above all he wished to achieve automatic stability. That must have seemed an ambitious dream indeed at a time when gliders were so flimsy and unpredictable that few dared to venture into the air with them. Dunne was still feeling the strain of war, and in January 1901 he travelled to Alassio on the Italian Riviera to recuperate. There he recorded the first of a long series of prophetic dreams, those celebrated precognitive dreams which were to form the basis of his theories.

In his first dream he was on the Nile near Khartoum when three white men in ragged khaki marched up from the south. Under the dusty sun-helmets their faces had been burned almost black. "We have come right through from the Cape," said one. "I've had an awful time. I nearly died of yellow fever," said another. On the morning after the dream Dunne opened the latest London *Daily Telegraph* and saw large headlines announcing the arrival at Khartoum from the Cape of an expedition organised by the newspaper.

As soon as he was fit enough Dunne rejoined the army, this time as an officer in the Wiltshire Regiment. He returned to South Africa, and he was in the Orange Free State again, in the spring of 1902, when he noted the most vivid and remarkable dream of his life. I will give it in his own words:

"In my dream I recognised the place as an island of which I had dreamed before – an island which was in imminent peril from a volcano. And when I saw the vapour spouting from the ground I gasped: 'It's the island! Good Lord, the whole thing is going to *blow up!*' For I had memories of reading about Krakatoa, where the sea, making its way into the heart of a volcano, flashed into steam and blew the whole mountain to pieces ... There followed a most distressing nightmare in which I was at a neighbouring island trying to get the incredulous French authorities to despatch ships of every description to remove the inhabitants of the threatened island ... All through the dream the number of people in danger obsessed my mind. I repeated it to everyone I met and at the moment of waking I was shouting: 'Listen! Four thousand people will be killed unless –"

When the newspaper arrived some time after the dream, these were the headlines that met his startled eyes:

> Volcano Disaster in Martinique
> Town Swept Away
> An Avalanche of Flame
> Probable Loss of Over
> 40,000 Lives.

Dunne spent years pondering over those two dreams. He was worried about the Martinique casualties, for the London *Daily Telegraph* figure was ten times the number which had entered his head during the dream. How could such a discrepancy occur if he was really clairvoyant? It occurred to him that he might have imagined both dreams after reading the newspaper reports. In other words, these were cases of what the psychologists call "identifying paramnesia". A person feels that he has been to a place before though he knows that he has not. Dunne was not satisfied with this plausible explanation, however, and when he saw the future in later dreams he made sure that the dreams had occurred before the arrival of the newspapers. His later dreams were no more accurate than the Martinique casualties; but while details might differ the resemblances to the truth were so strong that he refused to allow the possiblity of coincidence. He took care to record all that he had dreamt before opening the newspapers and satisfied himself that the dreams came before the printed reports. A nightmare vision of a factory fire was followed by news of the event. Then there was an encounter with a frenzied horse. Dunne dreamt it. Next day he and his brother had to run for their lives when a maddened horse came thundering down the path. Dunne then began to think of dreams as

A VISIONARY RIDES BY

images not only of past experiences but of the future. Sometimes the images were blended together. Dunne's dreams were like other nightmares, only he was living through them on the wrong nights. They were *displaced in time.* Finally the mind of Dunne conceived the idea of time which still causes so much discussion. Dunne the aircraft designer was a fine mathematician, and in his cautious and humble book entitled "An Experiment with Time" he set out to prove his theory with the aid of mathematics. It appeared in 1929, and I do not know how many thousands have been sold since that dramatic first edition. J. B. Priestley described it as follows: "One of the most fascinating, the most curious, and perhaps the most important books of this age. Everybody who has the slightest intellectual curiosity should become acquainted with it." Comparatively few readers could follow Dunne's advanced mathematics, but the ordinary reader was enthralled by the dreams and the sequels. In his early experiments Dunne relied on sleep to give him these views of the future. Later on he claimed that he could pick up a brand new book which he had never opened and see images of the contents. But the waking experiments were never so intense or informative as the dreams, though they were disturbing.

Let us examine another of Dunne's visions, this time bound up with his life as a flying pioneer. Dunne was taking part in a military aeroplane contest on Salisbury Plain in 1912, piloting one of his stable aircraft. In those days the Royal Flying Corps was such a tiny unit that it was a rare experience to see a new face. Dunne, however, met one officer for the first time. All the rest were old friends. Dunne left Salisbury Plain after the contest as he was not especially interested in the army manoeuvres which followed. He was in Paris when he dreamt that a monoplane crashed in a meadow. The new officer he had met on the Plain walked towards Dunne from the wreckage and remarked: "It's all that beastly engine, but I've got the hang of it now." The officer had, in fact, been killed in a crash at about the time of Dunne's dream. Once again inaccuracies should be noted. The main part of the dream was entirely wrong, for the officer did not walk out of the wreck. Dunne also established the fact that the crash was due, not to engine failure but the collapse of a wing. Finally, the officer had not been the pilot but the passenger when the crash occurred. Dunne did not attach great importance to this dream as he often dreamt of aeroplane crashes in those early and perilous days.

Far more awe-inspiring was his dream of a train disaster in the autumn of 1913, at a scene which he recognised clearly as a stretch of open country north of the Firth of Forth bridge in Scotland. He saw a train which had just fallen over the embankment, with several coaches lying at the bottom of a slope. Next morning Dunne discussed the dream with his sister, and told her of his impression that the accident would occur during the spring of the following year. And on April 14, 1914, the "Flying Scotsman" jumped the parapet fifteen miles north of the Forth Bridge and landed on the golf course below.

Looking back on this series of dreams, Dunne noted that although World War I was about to open, only one of his dreams gave him an idea of what was to come. He saw Lowestoft being bombarded by a foreign fleet, but when he awoke he could not identify the nationality of the warships.

Years passed before Dunne was able to work out a theory to explain his prophetic dreams. He had proved that the dreams were not false memories. He rejected "astral wandering". He did not regard himself as a medium and he was dubious about telepathy. Moreover he knew that he was not a freak; what he could do, others could do. At last Dunne decided that while he was asleep his mind and soul wandered about through the past, present and future. He built up a theory of the spiritual universe in the same way that Einstein worked out a new idea of the material universe. Human experience, according to Dunne, was not a railway track with a terminus at each end, but a roundabout, on which each individual passed the same point many times. The present is merely an episode in a continuous experience. Dunne called his theory "serialism". Man must have a spirit, he declared, in order to roam about time in this way. Dunne never pretended that he could predict the future. Only certain episodes which he had seen in dreams could be predicted, and even then such episodes were subject to the distortion which occurred in many of his famous dreams. He declared that the "future" was best observed when the mind was freed by sleep from the normal waking images.

Dunne's theory started a vogue. Many thousands of people all over the world tried to write down their dreams each morning. Dunne advised people to have a notebook and pencil handy. Often the dreamer can recall only a single incident. Dunne said that if a person concentrated on that incident, the rest of the dream would return. Details were important. Everything should be written down. Psychologists have improved on Dunne's method since his death. They, too, know that the pictures of the night are soon overwhelmed by the things seen in the real world. So on waking the dream-recorder is advised to remain with his eyes shut for a few moments, giving himself time to piece together the shreds of memory. The mind may seem blank, yet most people dream five times a night, each dream lasting from ten to twenty minutes. The final dream before waking is usually the longest, and this is the one which is easiest to remember. Dreams are not always pleasant, of course, but the part the dreamer plays in them is of no more personal significance than the actions of a character on the stage. Dunne suggested that those who wished to experience prophetic dreams should provide the mind with a "link idea" leading into the immediate future. Interpretations of some dreams are still highly controversial; yet it does appear that the dream, when better understood, may prove to be not only the authentic voice of the subconscious but also a revelation of the unseen world. Dreams are not to be ignored because we cannot explain them.

Have you grasped the elements of Dunne's reasoning? Some of his later theories evaded the keenest minds, and it is only by finding a number of analogies that his serialism becomes clearer. We know that the present exists; past events have existed but future events do not exist. You can imagine the future, but there are no memories of the future. Dunne said that our field of perception of events moves through time and therefore its time-speed must be measured with reference to another time of a different dimension – serialism. Our conscious perception of events, perceiving ourselves as observers, involves the existence of a sequence of observers (ourselves) with the conscious observer at the head of the sequence. This is another form of serialism. Dr. Brian Inglis, the medical writer and distinguished journalist, put Dunne's theory like this: "Dreams, he thought, contained images of both past and future experience, blended together. We go through our lives (to use the standard simile) like a railway passenger sitting with his back to the engine: we see what we have passed and are passing, not what lies ahead. But the conscious 'I' is not the whole 'I' – or else how could we be aware of our existence in relation to the world? And the 'I' in the background, apparently, is not compelled to sit with his back to the engine; he can see at least a little way ahead. While I am awake my own self-consciousness normally prevents me from seeing everything this background 'I' can see; but in sleep this barrier between us is down, so that in dreams I may see through his eyes as well – future as well as past." Dr. Inglis was highly critical of the theory, but he pointed out that Dunne had issued a fascinating challenge, and that recent research had tentatively established prevision.

Dunne's serialism amounted to a new attempt to solve some of the mysteries brought to light by modern science, notably in physics. He stated his belief that nothing ever died in the dimension of serialism. "A rose which has bloomed once, blooms for ever," Dunne wrote. "As for Man, he is not accorded distinctive treatment; he merely remains with the rest." Here is another example. You drive through a beautiful stretch of scenery and then enter an ugly town. The beauty is not merely a memory; you can return to it at will. Look down at the whole landscape from a mountain; there is the beauty and the ugliness, all in one frame, and that greater field of vision is the view serialism provides. Time one is a fixed sequence. Time two is the dimension which enables you to study at leisure any part of the route. Time one is like a piano keyboard. Time two enables you to strike the notes in any order and recover the experiences of a lifetime. A well-known scientist interpreted Dunne in this way: "An event which I regard as happening now will be regarded as having happened in the past by an observer on another star . . . or as about to happen in the future."

Dunne was not, apparently, a member of any particular church. He looked upon his work as of theological importance, however, and used it to combat the growth of materialistic thinking. In his philosophy all things are immortal. Time is not flowing "like an ever-rolling stream", because in his view all states of existence are eternally present. Everything which exists does so for ever because there is no special reality about any particular moment. Raymond Chapman, a devout churchman, came to this conclusion: "Dunne was a great man, and a humble one, whose thinking took him into spiritual realms that he had not expected."

Dunne became friendly with H. G. Wells early this century, for they were interested in the same things. It is probable that the novel by Wells called "The Time Machine" influenced Dunne's thinking; though Wells declared that he wrote this phantasy "as a lark". Wells described Dunne's time theory as "fantastically interesting". (One reviewer said that Dunne had achieved something akin to Darwin's "Origin of Species" in its effect on mankind.) Wells also admired Dunne's aircraft designs, and was so impressed with the "Dunne type" wing that he secured the co-operation of Lord Rayleigh, president of the Royal Society, and himself an authority on the mechanics of flight. Dunne flew some of his models in Wells's garden; and Wells made use of Dunne's strange ways in his novel "Bealby". As the years passed, however, Wells said that he watched Dunne with "deepening consternation". Towards the end of their long friendship Wells thought that Dunne had adopted the role of "something between a cosmic Sherlock Holmes and an Eastern sage". He described one of Dunne's later books, "The New Immortality" as "incomprehensible and unreadable". Discussing the Dunne theories shortly before World War II, the shrewd H. G. Wells wrote: "Most people, I think, find this world in space and time so full of interesting things that they do not think very much about death and the hereafter. What we common people want, when the question of immortality is put to us fairly, is more of the same queer mixture, and to be able to go on doing things – particularly to be able to go on doing things." Wells complained that Dunne's immortality was a "vast museum of experiences".

It all began with a dream, and so we return to the starting-point of Dunne's theory. If prevision be admitted – not just a shrewd forecast here and there, but the accurate prediction of the "unpredictable" – then the basis of our past opinions of the universe are destroyed. The cumulative evidence produced by

Dunne is certainly remarkable. Was it sufficient to prove his claim that we may habitually observe events before they occur?

Here comes the great divergence. Dunne himself was fully aware of the classical objection to the idea of prophecy; that if we are aware of future events we can sometimes prevent them. In other words, if you see yourself going down in some *Waratah*, you stay on shore as a Mr. Sawyer did when the ship left Durban. No doubt there were prophets among the earliest human clans, but during thousands of years there has been no proper study of prophecy. Certainly there have been innumerable failures. Vague language is the hallmark of the cunning prophet, and if he is vague enough it is almost impossible to denounce him as a false prophet. Modern scientists, I think, are mainly in favour of coincidence as the answer to successful prophecies. No fiction writer would dare to make use of the coincidences which occur in everyday life. Where does coincidence end and true prophecy begin? Many well-informed people have been doubtful about Dunne's prophecies on the ground that the details of his dreams were often falsified in the events that followed. Science demands accurate, confirmatory details. But no critic has been able to destroy Dunne's theories. Research organised since Dunne described his dreams has been in favour of precognition. (I am referring now to the work of Professor J. B. Rhine in America and Professor S. G. Soal in London.) There have also been authentic yet almost incredible examples of dreams coming true. If you dream the winner of one horserace correctly it may mean nothing more than a profitable incident. But a certain John Godley (now Lord Kilbracken) dreamt a whole series of winners in the late nineteen-forties; he recorded his dreams and secured the signatures of witnesses. I believe the scientific explanation of this feat was that Lord Kilbracken was merely a clever student of form, and his sub-conscious mind summed up the probabilities while he was asleep. It is possible to predict a volcanic eruption, too, and there are many kinds of human behaviour which can be assessed in advance. All too frequently (or all too seldom) we shape the future ourselves; what happens today is the cause of the events of tomorrow, and only a fool is taken by surprise. Yet I have lingering fragments of faith in Dunne's visions, and complete faith in his honesty.

A VISIONARY RIDES BY

So far Dunne the dreamer and serialist has over-shadowed Dunne the aircraft designer and pilot, and I must add a word about his brilliant work in aviation. It was the South African War that made him aware of the need for something more useful than balloons. I have mentioned his models. Backed by the War Office, he built a full scale aircraft at Farnborough in 1905, a biplane with his beloved backswept wings and upswept tips. This machine was taken secretly to the Duke of Atholl's estate in Scotland; and the Duke's private army, the Atholl Highlanders, surrounded the aerodrome and turned strangers away. Dunne flew the biplane himself, first as a glider and later with two engines giving a total of fifteen horse-power. This episode has been officially credited as the first flight of a military aircraft anywhere in the world. Dunne then built another machine at the Farnborough factory. So little money was available that when he asked for enough linen to cover both sides of the wings he was refused on grounds of economy. Dunne and Cody were working together on tailless aircraft in 1909, but the experiments were stopped after £2,500 had been spent. Dunne then formed a syndicate and built a number of pioneer aircraft. One formidable biplane had a stupendous undercart and there were so many struts and bracing-wires that the speed was reduced considerably. It is noteworthy, however, that Dunne's designs really were stable, and no one was ever killed in one of his aircraft. Dunne gave a wonderful demonstration in the Dunne-V biplane in 1910, for he only touched the controls on take-off and landing. He flew a monoplane across the Channel in 1913 and sold the design to a French syndicate. This aircraft proved to be so reliable that a Captain Felix was able to give the first display of wing-walking. Dunne served in both world wars. He helped to design the first "Pterodactyl" machine in 1920, and he was still being consulted during World War II as an authority on tailless aircraft. Perhaps the two interests in Dunne's life were not so far apart after all. The man who soared away from earth in one of the first aeroplanes made great flights of imagination. This versatile genius was also a crack revolver shot, a boxer, a skilful fly fisherman and author of books for children. Those who knew him agreed that he was a charming person with the manner of a soldier. He looked more intellectual than most soldiers, with a broad forehead and military moustache. Shy with strangers, he talked well on his own subjects. Dunne married a daughter of Baron Say and Sele, and they had a son and a daughter.

"We have always more knowledge than we suspect ourselves of having," wrote Dunne in one of his books. "I do not believe that Man has reached his zenith. There is adventure in eternal life. There is none in eternal death. And I am all for adventure." Truly the thoughtful youth from the Stellenbosch farm travelled a long way after riding over the dunes to Blaauwberg all those years ago.

INDEX

Ahmet, Cairo dragoman, on meaning of firewalking, 50-51
Ais-Ais, weird health resort, 108
Afrikaner Koffiehuis, history and meeting-place, 131
Alexander, Sir James, saw "Great Snake", 106
Amitia, Green's first yacht, 177
Andries, Louis, murderer, execution 245
Arend, Hadji Amor, vouched for Wallagie's great thirst, 60
Arniston, wrecked troopship 202
Atherstone, Dr W. G., examined Wonderboom in 1872, 238
Atholl, Duke of, 265
Atholl Highlanders, 265
Ayliffe, H. J., pioneer film cameraman, career, part in Karatara epic, death premonition, strange reunion, 185-196

Baines, Thomas, artist, 248
Baird, Sir David, 65
Ballot's Bay, treasure legend, 204-205
Baobab, "the tree of adventure", 239-241
Barry, Dr James, visits "tronk", 80
Bayley, Harold, mate of the *Karatara*, telephones Green after 42 years, ordeals on epic voyage, sails *Karatara* home etc, etc, 186-196
Beamish, able seaman, survived wreckage of *Wallarah*, 159-160
Beddoes, Lieutenant, found *Grosvenor* treasure, 210-211
Biccard, Dr F.L.C., medical author, 116
Biccard, Dr Louis, country doctor on horseback, simple remedies in saddle-bags, describes life of country doctor and operations on farms, dentistry, 116-118
Biltong, sixpence a pound, 22
Billingham, Thomas, search for Richtersveld gold, 103
Bjorseth, O.E., 210
Bleek, Miss Dorothea, on Bushman languages, 29, on "White Lady of the Brandberg", 36
Boys, Captain, historic home destroyed, 233
Brandberg, "museum" of Bushman art, 34
Breakwater prison, history and hardships, IDB offenders, iron discipline, cat-o'-nine-tails, famous escapes, the treadmill etc, 73-80
Breuil, Abbé, on age of Bushman paintings, 33, 35, named "Girls' School", 36, mentioned, 37
Broker, Charles, 162
Brooke Charles ("a decent fellow doesn't work"), first meeting with Green, life at lagoon, cottage and way of life, philosophy, library etc, 217-226

Brooke, Rupert, poet, 220, 226
Brownlee, Major Frank, first magistrate of Grootfontein, 41
Bucton, Mrs Jessie, tells story of Piketberg's mountain farms, 119-122
Bushmen, romantic survival in Africa, habits, hardiness, world's most miniature people, knowledge of nature, simple wisdom, easy childbirth, huge appetites, Bushmen paintings, mythology, cunning prisoners, knowledge of medical remedies, massacred, devoted to truth etc, etc, 27-46
Büttner, Prof, C.G., discovered Bushman paintings, 33
Bux, Kuda, demonstrates fire-walking, 53
Buxton, Lord, Governor-General, reprieves murderer, 82

Carstens, William, prospector, 102-103
Chapman, explorer, on Bushman poisons, 38
Cochran, Trooper, recalls springbok migrations, 15-16
Coe, Mayne Reid, discovers secret of firewalking, 54-55
Cole, Sir Lowry, 154
Cookery, traditional South African, 125 onwards
Collingwood, Percy, notorious safe-breaker and escaper, 76
Collyer, L.J., storekeeper and recorder of Onseepkans, 87-88
Cornell, Fred, his "Great Snake" account, 104-105
Cory, Sir George, theory on rock inscriptions, 209-210
Courtenay – Latimer, Miss, expert on beads, 209
Cronwright-Schreiner, S.C., baffled by springbok mystery, 21, saw countless springbok, 24
Crowder, Len, 176-177
Cumming, Gordon, picturesque hunter on slaughter of buck, 22-23

Dale, Sir Langham, 225
D'Almeida, Antonio, of Dassen Island dynasty, penguin expert, 148, on dassie mystery, 154
D'Almeida's Island, see Dassen Island
Darnell, B.H., 234
Dart, Prof. Raymond, anatomist, on Bushman characteristics, 29-30
Dassen Island, history, unique penguin colony, bird life, shipwrecks, lighthouse dramas, early inhabitants, salving the Ping Suey, 147-162
Davie, T.B., of Prieska, 23-24
De Chavonnes, Governor, suspicions in *Schoonberg* swindle, 200-201
De Lima, Joseph Suasso, 59
De Sarigny, Mrs Beryl, 187
De Villiers, John, wine prize-winner, 127
Dijkman, Mrs, celebrated recipe book, 127-129, 134, 135
Dix, Lady Florence, describes Wonderboom, 238
Drury, James, taxidermist, 41
Duckitt, Charles, 114
Duckitt, Miss Charlotte, 115
Duckitt, Frederick, 114
Duckitt, Hildagonda, of "Where Is It?" fame, 114, 127, 135, 143

INDEX

Duckitt, William, acquired famous farm, wine-maker and pioneer of Darling District, 113-114
Duckitt, William, Junior, 114
Duke of Edinburgh (Prince Alfred), opens breakwater prison, 73
Dunlop-Ainslie, Mrs M.W., 209
Dunne, Gen. Sir John Hart, 255
Dunne, James William, author, aeronaut, philosopher, prophetic dreamer author of "An Experiment With Time", early life in Cape Town, Free State, association with Blouberg etc, etc, 254-266
Duthies, of Belvidere, 235

Elizabeth Island, see Dassen Island, 151
Elliot, Lt-Col R.H., surgeon, on firewalking fatalities, 52
Eloff, Dirk, owner of *Sarie Marais*, married on board, sails to Panama, 182
Escoffier Auguste, mentor of Leipoldt, 138

Fairbridge, William Ernest, editor, historian, Rhodesian pioneer, 243-246, 247, 249, 250
Ferroli, "Frenchie", desperado, 77
Firewalkers of Africa, 49-56
Firewalking, description of Durban ceremony, 49
Firewalking, diet and preparation, 53
Forbes, Vernon S., 206
Forest fires, from Swellendam to Uitenhage, tales of eye-witnesses, 233-236
Fraser, Sir John, on springbok invasion of Beaufort West, 18-19
Fremantle H.E.S., investigates treasure legend, 203
French Marie, tough woman of Pioneer Street, 249

Gallows Hill, public executions, terrible scenes, 82-83
Gerbault, Alain, hermit of the seas, 181-182
Gladstone, W.E., 73
Goodhouse, place of shimmering heat, 87-96
Goodman, Gwelo, artist, 66
Gordon, Col. J.R., explorer, 206
Goske, Isbrand, 119
"Great Snake" Legend, 103-106
Green, Lawrence G. captures spirit of Karoo, reporting genius, 10, fascination of South West Africa, deep research on Bushman habits, 26, interest in magic, voodoo and supernatural, mystery of firewalkings etc, 48, love of Cape Town, city's "own author", trilogy on Mother City, strange characters, 58, pioneer of South African home-spun literature, crime and punishment, man of compassion, 72, discovered dramas of Orange River, meets great characters, travels on dusty roads, 84, spell of Western Province, hunting in Swartland, interviews old-fashioned country doctor, 110, delight over food and wine, praise of Cape cookery, 124, unrepentant preoccupation over food and wine, 136, Dassen Island visits, interest in natural history, 146, spell of the sea, deckhand, forgotten drama of Russian armada, 164, plans autobiography, sailing days, famous

lone sailors, 174, in Conrad tradition, solves mystery of 42 years, 184, beach walks inspired him, interest in treasure-hunters, 198, break from reticence, sanctuaries from rat-race, his philosophy, private beliefs, 212, moves into world of trees, saga of Knysna axe-men, story of Wonderboom, 228, sentimental journey to Rhodesia, ocean at his door, 242, spiritual cathedral, mysteries of eternity and after-life, 254

Groote Post, famous Darling farm, 114
Guerin, Eddie, 79

Hahn, Dr Theophilus, trader, on Bushman paintings, 33
Ham Charles, street violinist, 62
Hansen, 0, 170
Harraway, H.G., seeks chest of gold, 206-207
Harris, Dr Rutherford, unpopular pioneer, 244
Harris, Major Cornwallis, 18
Harvey, Signalman, sighted doomed armada, 165, 172-173
Hertzog, General J.B.M., Swartland boyhood, 116
Heyes, Ernest, prospector, famous journeys on foot, explores "Wondergat", 100-102, 105
Hicks, Sir Seymour, 61
Hiddingh, Dr Jonas Michiel, rich medical doctor, owner of Newlands House and uncle of famous eccentric, 64-67
Hiddingh, Michiel, wealthy eccentric, 64-70
Hodges, Bunny, 206
Hoffman, Alfred, companion of Reinhard Maack, 34-35
Hollern, Lawrence Arthur, Cape Town's Charlie Chaplain, career and misfortunes, quayside antics, accident, 61-62
Holman, Lieut. James RN, blind traveller, 113
Hopefield, history, 118
Hugo, Jacobus Francois, wine king, 126
Hutchinson, Dr Berks T., Cape Town spiritualist, 256
Huysing, Henning, 112

Ingerid, coaster in which Green served, 214
Inglis, Dr Brian, theory on dreams, 261
Innisfallen, famous yacht, 175-177
Islander, Pidgeon's craft, 177-182

Jackson, Albert, Kalahari trader, experience of massed springbok, 25
Jackson, "Cuban", criminal, 79
Jameson, Dr. Leander Starr, passes death sentences, 245-246, mentioned 247, 249
Jochmann's Cave, 34

Karas, white firewalker, Sea Point performance, 51-52
Karatara, coasting steamer, epic voyage of danger, drama and menace of drunken captain, 185-196

INDEX

Kerguelen Island, history, Zulu interlude, whaling, 190
King Edward VII, 166
King, James, Cape hangman, 82
Kilbracken, Lord, dreamt of Turf winners, 264
Kinnear, G.A., sees "Giant Snake", 104
Klaver Vlei, Swartland farm, Green's hunting memories 112-115
Klopper, Hendrik, a *Schoonberg* conspirator, 200-201
Kok, Adam, cooking won him freedom, 123
Kok, Adam III, trek leader, 123
Krapohl, H.J.C., botanist, 88
Kruger, Johannes, German murders of Bushmen, 40
Kruger, President, affection for biltong, 132

Lake McIlwaine, 253
Leibbrandt, Rev. H.C.V., 104
Leipoldt, Dr C. Louis, epicure, 128-129, on crawfish, 129, on value of biltong, 133, secrets of cookery, exotic dishes, ideal christmas menu etc, etc, 137-144
Leutwein, German governor of South West Africa, 40
Lello, Brian, 174, desert yearning, 182
Lewis, A.D., irrigation expert, 85-86, Orange River (1912), 97-98
Livingstone, David, saw springbok migation (1875), theory, 19, on baobabs, 239
Loch, Sir Henry, 245
Lotziero, Carlo, pavement harpist, 62
Lutz, Japie, 86

Maack, Reinhard, surveyor, explored famous Brandberg caves, copied Bushman paintings, 34-35
Malan, Dr D.F., 116
Malan, Jacob, *Schoonberg* conspirator, 200-201
Mamre, mission village, home of good servants, 115-116
Marcus Island, 155
Martinique disaster, Dunne's dream, 257-258
Masson, Francis, English gardener on springbok habits, 17
McLoughlin, Jimmy, 133
May, "Chicago", 79
Mazoe Bill, 251
Meikle, James, Rhodesian pioneer, 247
Meikle, Tom, Rhodesian pioneer, 247
Meintjes, Major "Duke", 236
Metcalf, Miss Elizabeth, 120
Metropole Hotel, Russian officers celebrate, 170
Michelburne, Gen. Sir Edward, 151
Millais, John, 16, life of Selous, 24
Molesworth, Major-General Arthur, 153
Molesworth, Mary, shipwreck ordeal on Dassen Island, 153-154, 156, 159
"Morning Glory", home of beachcomber Brooke, 219 onwards
Morton, Rhodesian hangman, 246

Mossel Bay, many treasure tales, 202-205
Munnik, Senator, saw public executions, 83

Newlands House, history and ownership 64, 65, 66
Nortier, Dr Peter Le Fras, researcher, secrets of *rooibos* tea, honoured by Clanwilliam, 136 and 137 onwards, on freshwater fish, 139

Orange River, history, dramas, famous prospectors etc, etc, 85-109
Osborn, Dr T.W.B., study of firewalking, 53-54
Ostensacken, Baron, huge liquor order, 170

Petersen brothers, in remote Aussenkehr, 98
Pidgeon, Harry, lone round-the-world sailor, way of life, humour, philosophy, lecturer, etc, etc, 177-182
Piketberg, origin of name, mountain farms, ancestral home of Griquas etc etc, 119-123
Ping Suey, Dassen Island wreck, salved, 159-161
Phillips Cave, 33
Plettenberg Bay, treasure legend, 205-206
Pole Evans, Dr I.B,, on Wonderboom, 237
Politovsky, Engineer, 169, 172
Priestley, J.B., on "An Experiment With Time", 259
Pringle, Thomas, on springbok migrations, 17
Purves-Stewart, Sir James, theory on firewalking, 54
Pyper, C.R., trained Bushman farm workers 43

Rabinowitz, S.C. ("King Solomon of the Richtersveld"), pioneer and prospector, search for legendary copper, diamond discovery etc, 98-100
Red House, home of noted eccentric, 66-70
Reitz, Col. Deneys, biltong addict, 132
Roberts, Dr Austin, 239
Roberts, Mrs, 238
Roeland Street gaol, history, escapes, executions, last hanging, condemned cell etc, 80-82
Rooibos tea, 136, 137
Rowley, Arthur Edward Patrick, street singer and vagabond, wit and erudition, free meals, 62-63
Rozhestvensky, Admiral, commander of doomed Russian armada, 166-173
Ruperti, Martin, 113

Salisbury, yesterday and today, pioneers, seamy side of life etc, etc, 243-253
Schertz, Dr Ernst, Bushman expert, 31, 32, 35, 37
Schinz, Dr Hans, poisons' experiment, 38
Schoeman, Dr P.J., discovers new Bushman clan, 29, 30, 31, 32
Schwarz, Prof. E.H.L., Port Alfred mystery, 207
Scorpion Jim, 251
Scotland, Alexander, secret agent, 90-91

INDEX

Scully, William Charles, author, poet, sensational springbok migration, 20, shot koubok, 21, on springbok multitudes, 23
Sionogu, Rear-Admiral, 166
Slade, Mrs H.M., see Jeanette van Duyn
Smuts, General J.C., Bushman art, 35, Malmesbury accent, 111, 116
Somerset, Lord Charles, 65
Springbok migrations, 1-25
Steytler, Andre, yachtsman and traveller, 177
Stockenstroom, Sir Andries, on migration mysteries, 17-18
Suicide season, Rhodesia, 250
Swartland, history, legendary characters, Piketberg etc, etc, 111-123

Tanser, G.H, 250
Timmins, Howard B., partnership with Lawrence Green, 72
Thomson, Matthew, drunken master of *Karatara*, behaviour on epic voyage, decline and death 185-196
"Treasure Beach", on Durban Bluff, 210
Trew, Lt-Col. H.F., on treasure trove law, 211
T'samma, Bushman's staple diet 45-46
Turner, Capt. Sidney, found *Grosvenor* treasure 210-211

Upington, Beauclerk (Skipper), advocate and brilliant helmsman, contempt for pomposity, etc, etc, 175-177

Vaaltyn, Dail, 202-203
Van der Byl, Major Piet, 126
Van der Heyden Jacob, a *Schoonberg* conspirator, 200-201
Van der Merwe, Gert, dramatic springbok migrations, 11-15, philosophy, 15
Van der Spuy, Cecil, magistrate, on physical fortitude of Bushmen, 31
Van der Stel, William Adriaan, laid out Newlands House estate, 65, 112
Van Duyn, Jeanette (Mrs H.M. Slade), authority on Cape cookery, 128
Van Riebeeck, Jan, 17, imported patat, 129, praised dassie dish, 140, 152
Van Spilbergen, Joris, early Dassen Island visitor, 151
Van Soest, Capt. Albertus, master of the *Schoonberg*, fate, 200-201
Von Zastrow, 40-41
Van Zyl, Sergeant J.W., 30
Vedder, ex-Senator, on Bushman farm labour, 42
Vergelegen, treasure legend, 199-201
Versfeld, Hildagonda, 114
Versfeld, J.P.E., builds mountain paradise and famous pass, encounters with leopards, grows tobacco, etc, etc, 119-122
Vioolsdrift, brave settlement attempt, 96-97
Von Mollendorf, Joseph Wilhelm, search for lost wealth, 203-204
Vredenburg, once litigious village, 118-119

Wallagie, champion eater, 59-61
Wallarah, Dassen Island wreck, 159-160

Waterston, Prof. David, 54
Weidner, Carl, of Goodhouse, strong character, visionary of the deserts, career, love of Goodhouse, created oasis, built pont, derision of politicians etc, etc, 87-96
Wells, H.G., friendship with J.W. Dunne, 263
Westford, famous Knysna property, 234-235
Wilson, Harry, maniac, escape from gaol, 77-78
Wines, Cape, 125-127
Wolf, Father, missionary, 105
Wonderboom, famous tree, 236-239
Woodcutters, of Knysna, hardy men forgotten by time, 229-233
Woollends, George, famous Cape Town bootblack, hammock in Adderley Street, 63-64
Woutersen, Jan, Dassen Island pioneer, 152

Yzerfontein, salt pan, majesty of flamingoes, 112

Zeyher, Charles, 237